THE AGE
OF ARTHUR

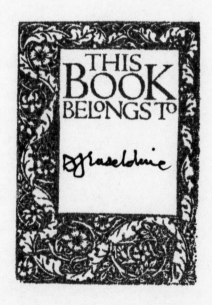

THE AGE
OF ARTHUR

A History of
the British Isles from 350 to 650

JOHN MORRIS

Senior Lecturer in History
University College London

Volume Three : Church, Society and Economy

PHILLIMORE

1977

Published by

PHILLIMORE & CO. LTD.

London and Chichester

Head Office: Shopwyke Hall,
Chichester, Sussex, England

*First published by Weidenfeld and Nicolson
1973*

© John Morris, 1973, *revised* 1977

ISBN 0 85033 291 5

*Printed in Great Britain by
Unwin Brothers Limited,
Old Woking, Surrey*

To

C. E. STEVENS

who inspired

CONTENTS

MAPS

INTRODUCTION

This book surveys the history of the British Isles between the end of Roman Britain and the birth of England and Wales. Its aim is to make that history manageable, like the history of other periods. *(sic – the Roman govt & forces left in 410)*

In the 420s, the government of Roman Britain enlisted Saxon, or English barbarians from Germany to strengthen their defences; but in the 440s the English rebelled. Half a century of bitter fighting destroyed the Roman economy and technology of Britain, but the British won the war, under the leadership of Arthur, who restored the forms of Roman imperial government. The empire of Arthur lasted for some twenty years and on his death fragmented into a large number of small independent successor states. The English were contained within substantial defined reservations until they rebelled for a second time, at the end of the sixth century. In a generation they subdued most of what is now England; thenceforth the independent native British were confined to the west, and were called Welsh, a word that in old English meant 'foreigners'.

The personality of Arthur is unknown and unknowable. But he was as real as Alfred the Great or William the Conqueror; and his impact upon future ages mattered as much, or more so. Enough evidence survives from the hundred years after his death to show that reality was remembered for three generations, before legend engulfed his memory. More is known of his achievement, of the causes of his sovereignty and of its consequences than of the man himself. His triumph was the last victory of western Rome; his short lived empire created the future nations of the English and the Welsh; and it was during his reign and under his authority that the Scots first came to Scotland. His victory and his defeat turned Roman Britain into Great Britain. His name overshadows his age.

Two centuries of war and of separate co-existence moulded a political society unlike that of Europe, where Roman and barbarian experience merged more easily. These centuries are a historical period in their own right, more than a transition or interlude between Rome and the Middle Ages. To be understood, a well-defined period needs a name, as clear in meaning as Roman, Norman or

Tudor. The fifth and sixth centuries in Britain are properly termed the Age of Arthur, for modern historical convention normally labels periods according to their principal rulers. In early medieval Europe it distinguishes Merovingian and Carolingian periods, so called after dynasties who took their names from individuals. The Carolingian age extends from the grandfather of Charles the Great to his grandchildren's time; but the substance of history does not turn upon the personal ancestry of rulers. Though he had no royal father and founded no dynasty, Arthur was the heir of the emperors before him, and the kings who followed knew themselves to be 'heirs of great Arthur'. He straddles two centuries, and names them as fitly as Charles the Great names the eighth and ninth centuries in Europe.

The Arthurian age is the starting point of future British history. Thereafter, Britain has comprised England, Wales and Scotland; previously, these three countries did not exist. Their later history is harder to understand if their formative years are overlooked; for nations, like people, tend to form habits in infancy that their adult years harden and modify. But the early history must be seen in its own context; if its evidence is superficially raked over in a search for the origins of later institutions, then it is as uninformative as an archaeological site plundered by treasure hunters.

These centuries have often been termed the 'Dark Ages'. They are not dark for lack of evidence. The quantity of evidence is immense and unusually complex, hard to understand. Therefore it has been neglected, abandoned to a small number of specialists, who have often been obliged to limit their studies to their own particular patch. The specialist in pagan English pottery or brooches is rarely conversant with the literature of early Ireland, with late Roman administration, with Welsh or Germanic law, with Italian theology or old Welsh poems, with the techniques of the farmer and the shipbuilder, or with a dozen other disciplines that must be brought together, and related to the history of Europe, if the age is to be understood.

No one can be master of all these trades. The historian must be content to be the pupil and interpreter of many of them. But he must do his best to bring them together, for the evidence seems obscure only because its modern study is inadequate and fragmented. The significance of excavated objects cannot be perceived until they can be related to the written record of the people who used them. Yet most of the texts are made up of half truths, for they are abstracts derived from lost originals, distorted by the ignorance or interest of their compilers. They await the kind of critical scrutiny that centuries of scholarship have lavished upon the texts of other periods. Because that work has not yet been undertaken the historian of the fifth and sixth centuries has special problems. He has no main 'reliable' narrative witness, like Tacitus or Bede, to justify him in dismissing other evidence as 'unreliable' or 'forged'. He must borrow from the techniques of the archaeologist, and must uncover a mass of separate detail, most of it encrusted and corroded by the distortion of later ages. He must clean off as much of the distortion as he can, try to discover what the original sources said and then relate their statements to one another, and to the rest of the evidence.

The aim is modest, and has been well expressed by Professor Ludwig Bieler.

> according to a widely accepted view, it is the historian's task to find out 'what actually happened'.... This, I believe, is impossible. The historian cannot do more than collect, assess and interpret evidence.

He has to sum up like a judge, and decide like a jury. He may not blankly refuse to decide, but he cannot proclaim certainty. He must give an informed opinion on what is probable and improbable, and return an open verdict when the balance of evidence suggests no probability. He may not insinuate like an advocate, whose plea that evidence falls short of absolute proof covertly invites his hearers to disbelieve the evidence. It is irrelevant for him to assert his personal belief or disbelief. There is a reason for every statement in every text, and for the place where every archaeological object was found. His business is to ferret out the reasons. He may conclude that an author lied or misunderstood; but falsehood must be demonstrated as carefully as accuracy, and may not be casually implied by labelling a statement 'dubious', without argument. But, unlike the verdict of the jury, his conclusion is constantly subject to appeal, and he must therefore clearly distinguish between what his evidence says and what he deduces from it, that others may easily correct his inferences in the light of new evidence and deeper understanding. If he fails to offer clear conclusions from the evidence he knows, he infects his readers with false beliefs and woolly notions; if he leaves no conclusion to correct, the importance of new evidence is easily missed. He must acknowledge his own sympathies as openly as a Tacitus or a Bede, for the historian who rashly pretends to be free of bias unconsciously surrenders to the superficial assumptions of his own day; and is therefore always misleading, and usually dull.

The evidence must first be collected. Most of the main texts are printed, but many are to be found only in large or specialist libraries. They cannot be studied unless they are assembled for constant reference and comparison; and this book could not have been written without the exceptional facilities generously provided by librarians, especially of University College London, and of the London Library, who permitted rare volumes to be retained on loan for years at a time. The difficulty of getting at the sources is one of the main reasons why the period is so poorly understood; for any historical study is lamed if it can only be undertaken by a few experts, whose judgement their readers cannot easily criticise. If the Arthurian period is to be studied seriously in the future, the first need is to make the sources accessible, no longer the secret lore of the learned. The first steps have been taken. The most important single texts, *Gildas*, *Nennius* and *Patrick*, will shortly be easily available, in text and translation, with comment; the rest of the main evidence is collected in my *Arthurian Sources* (forthcoming), where the separate texts of Annals, Genealogies, Saints' Lives and other sources are collated, and the scattered information about people, places and problems is assembled and assessed in detail. The study of this collected evidence prompts the conclusions here expressed, some of which are bound to seem abrupt and dogmatic until these publications appear.

The Age of Arthur interprets this evidence. It places most weight on contemporary statements, for in any age the contemporary cannot outrageously falsify the knowledge that he shares with his readers; for the same reason, texts written within living oral memory of the events they relate command respect. A modern writer may distort the actions and motives of contemporary individuals or distant peoples, but he could not assert that modern Britain is immune from war or ignorant of electric power; he might bamboozle an illiterate audience with a story that Napoleon fought Marlborough at Minden, but he could not pretend that Gladstone lived in the eighteenth century, for many men are still alive who know that Gladstone lived in their fathers' time. So when Gildas told his readers that theirs was an age of civil war and external peace, and that Vortigern and Ambrosius Aurelianus had lived in their fathers' time, he could not have done so if these matters of public knowledge were wholly untrue. But once the threshold of living memory is passed, after about a hundred years, the antiquity of a text is of small moment; many that were written a thousand years later follow their sources more closely than others written two or three hundred years after the event.

Interpretation rests upon bringing the evidence together, once the superficial deposit of later fancy has been removed, for it is no use discussing the meaning of the sources, until we know what they do and do not say, as exactly as we can. The history is narrated and described by bringing their separate statements together. Not much faith can be placed on a single statement by a single source; confidence grows when a number of independent sources each tell something of the same story. The proof of the pudding is in the eating. The evidence hangs together, and tells its own story. Innumerable separate details combine into a plain and credible tale, more coherent than any that an ingenious later historian could devise.

The tale is plain. But any account that is built up from a mass of small items of evidence seems complex at first sight. It is doubly difficult to explain the age of Arthur simply, for most of the names are unfamiliar. The historians of later periods, whose kings are conveniently numbered, may assume that their readers know that Henry VII reigned before Henry VIII; and many well known tales make it clear that Elizabeth ruled after and not before the Henries. But in the fifth and sixth centuries even the names of persons of comparable importance are known only to specialists, and their relation to each other in time and place is often clouded, compelling examination of the evidence. In order that the unfamiliar names, dates and events may be more easily understood, a short Summary of Events and a Table of Dates is provided.

The story that the sources tell raised a difficulty that was not at first foreseen. It had been intended to start from the relatively firm ground of the late Roman Empire, and to end in the middle of the seventh century, whose events Bede recorded within living memory. But it soon became apparent that much that has been written in modern times about the seventh and eighth centuries jars awkwardly against the earlier evidence. The reason is evident. Many of those who studied the early English were well acquainted with later medieval history, and looked back from the standpoint of Norman or Plantagenet England. But the processes of history move forward in time; men are influenced by the experience of their forebears, but they know nothing of their descendants' problems; and history looks different when viewed the right way up. It has therefore been necessary to discuss some later problems, where misconceptions about the Arthurian period and its immediate sequel have caused misunderstanding. This discussion does not set out to contradict what others have written; rather, it deals with different questions, for much that looked puzzling from an eleventh-century standpoint seems no problem at all in the context of the sixth century, while some of the assumptions that seemed natural to historians of the middle ages prove alien to thinking of earlier ages. It has also been necessary to discuss some aspects of barbarian and medieval European history that have not been systematically explored; and therefore to disregard some modern notions entertained about them. Such differences of approach do not assert greater wisdom or understanding; they are the result of fortunate chances that have given me the opportunity to read and sift more varied sources than most other individuals.

It has only recently become possible to attempt an overall history of the Arthurian age, thanks to a number of important publications that have pulled together several sections of the evidence. They rest upon much detailed work, whose conclusions cannot always be discussed within the limits of this book. It has proved necessary to stick to the principle expressed by H.M. and N.K.Chadwick in the preface to their *Growth of Literature*:

> if we had read more widely, we would not have completed this book . . . which might have been the better course. The amount of time at our disposal is limited; we have preferred to give as much of it as possible to the primary authorities.

It is therefore necessary to apologise to the very many scholars whose work is not here acknowledged, and has often not been adequately assessed. It is also impossible to acknowledge the many scholars whose kind advice has been freely offered on many details; my expressed gratitude must be limited to those whose unfailing patience my many queries have most heartily exploited, notably Professor Kenneth Jackson and Professor Idris Foster; Mr J.M.Dodgson and Professor D.M.Wilson; and Professor Christopher Hawkes; to Michael Gullick, who drew the maps to my specification, with limitless patience; and to Dr John

Wilkes, Dr Ann Ward and Miss Vivienne Menkes, who have kindly read and commented upon the typescript. None of them of course bear any responsibility for the way in which their advice has been treated. I am also grateful to the indulgence of the publisher, since the mass of unfamiliar names and concepts has made it necessary to use capitals, figures and punctuation for clarity and emphasis, in disregard of convention; and I am particularly indebted to the advice and help of Julian Shuckburgh and Sue Phillpott.

The interpretation here given of the Arthurian Age can be no more than a preliminary attempt to open up questions, and to make it easier for future specialist studies to relate their conclusions to a wider context. The book is therefore published in the confident expectation that many of its conclusions will soon be modified or corrected. It will have served its purpose if it makes such correction possible. It would be kind if readers who detect figure mistakes or errors of fact, in the text or the notes, would notify the author, via the publisher.

This reprint includes some corrections of substance. It has not yet been possible to correct minor misprints, spelling and punctuation which do not mislead.

John Morris

The aim of this book is to make the Arthurian period manageable. The term describes the years between the Romans and the English in the British Isles. The account is prefaced by a description of the later Roman Empire, and followed by a brief examination of the effect of English conquest. Understanding depends on how you use your sources. If you search for 'reliability' or 'forgery', 'truth' or 'falsehood', you will make no sense of this or any other period of human history. Almost all our sources are half-truths, distorted by interest or error; and in the rare instances of tales wholly untrue, woven from nothing, what matters is why the lies were told and believed. The business of source criticism is to find out why every word was written, and how each object got into the place where the archaeologist found it. That is how the interest and error of the ancient or modern writer is detected. As with any other kind of evidence, we are then left with no certainties, but with varying degrees of probability. Probability increases when two or more sources say the same thing in different ways from different standpoints. When the probabilities are assessed and put together, they outline an overall sequence of events that can be described and understood. Once an intelligible outline exists, others may in the future correct the detail and adjust the outline.

In the limp edition in three volumes, the first two are narrative. The main events described in these volumes are shown in the Summary of Events.

John Morris

ANALYSIS

CHAPTER EIGHTEEN

THE FIFTH CENTURY CHURCH

Before 410

The Christian religion scarcely touched Latin Europe before the late second century, and until the end of the fourth century British Christians are rare in the records of the Church. Alban of Verulamium, executed in 209, is the earliest known Latin Christian of the European provinces, though others doubtless existed. His fellow Christians in Africa and Egypt noted with pleasure and surprise that Christ was worshipped in distant Britain, even beyond the Roman frontier. But these stories have no sequel. A century later four British sees, probably metropolitan, were represented at Constantine's first church council at Arles. No more is known for another forty years; then the catholics of Gaul praised the steadfast orthodoxy of the British in the Arian crisis, and remarked upon their light-hearted contempt for the government; the bishop of London was perhaps among the few who held out to the end and suffered exile.

Bishops and clergy existed. Nothing suggests that they were more numerous than in northern and central Gaul. There Christianity was hardly known before Constantine, was still weak half a century after his accession, and did not widely prevail until the end of the century. The archaeological evidence in Britain consists of a number of buildings that may or may not be churches, and of a variety of Christian symbols. Hardly any of it can be closely dated, and it is probable that, as in Gaul, more of it concerns the fifth century than the fourth; and that Christians were strongest in the major towns. London was one of the largest cities in the western provinces, big enough to have contained a Christian community even in the third century that could afford a church building; but it is unlikely that in other towns the Christians were better placed than in Gaul, where, in provincial capitals like Tours, they were too few to build or maintain a church before about 350.

In the fourth century almost nothing is known of British Christianity, save that it existed. Its detailed history begins with the visit of Victricius, bishop of Rouen, about 396. He is the best known of Martin's admirers, and Martin, then still alive, was a controversial symbol. Sulpicius Severus' biography, probably published about the same time, emphasised his plebeian dress and habits, and presented him as the miraculously gifted champion of the weak against oppression, of the subject against the government, detested by well-bred established bishops who bowed to the will of emperors. Victricius, himself perhaps of British birth, extended Martin's reforms. Martin had preached to peasants, but Victricius was the first missionary, converting the peoples of the barbarian frontier districts, in modern Belgium, so that

> where once barbarian raiders and native robbers made woodland
> and coast unsafe, now the angelic choirs of the saints sing.

Victricius made a theory of Martin's egalitarian practice, proclaiming that

> men do not differ by nature, but only in time and place, in their
> occupations and ideas; for difference is foreign to divine unity,

and warning the mighty that

> divinity spits upon degree, breaks beyond time and place; . . .
> greater is the glory of your authority if you protect those who toil,
> defend the oppressed against their enemies.

Pope Innocent was disturbed, and warned Victricius that Rome condemned innovators, whose presumption violated the purity of the church by seeking the favour of the people rather than by fearing the judgment of God. But Victricius was heart and soul with the reformers. His letter, describing his journey to Britain, was addressed to Ambrose, apologising that his visit to Milan had thereby been delayed. His excuse is that he had carried to Britain the 'precepts of the martyrs'; he defined them by praising

> hands heavy with the relics of the saints, whence the crowds of
> monks, refined by fasting, are thickened.

He called himself the 'interpreter of the views' of the martyrs, in Britain, and explained that he had gone to Britain because

> my worthy fellow bishops summoned me to make peace. . . . I filled
> the sensible with love of peace, taught the teachable, overbore the
> ignorant, attacked the opposition.

Victricius does not spell out the issues in dispute, but his letter makes them plain. Ambrose and Martin were old and near to death; he was their foremost adherent in northern Europe, advocate of the veneration of martyrs who had defied unjust authority in their lifetime and inspired living men to similar independence; he was the organiser of monks who condemned and renounced secular society, the pioneer of the extension of Christianity from townsmen and gentlemen to peasants and barbarians. Pope Innocent protested that bishops should not interfere outside their own diocese or rouse plebeian support, but Victricius was the spokesman of all bishops everywhere who found strength in 'the favour of the people', and was the impassioned champion of equality among all men, irrespective of rank and station. He was invited to Britain by British bishops, who knew his views; they could not have invited him unless the reformers were already strong in Britain. They were a party within the British church, for he faced a stormy synod and fierce opposition; but he judged that his views had prevailed. The issue which divided the bishops was the impact of Martin's reforms, offensive to many established bishops in Gaul, and also in Britain. The synod strengthened the reformers, and perhaps made them the majority.

Victricius' visit powerfully affected the future Christianity of the British Isles. Echoes of his radical thought abound in the scanty records of the British church, whereas in the fuller record of Gaul Martin is honoured, but rarely imitated. There, urbane bishops akin to Martin's critics still predominated, and tamed the monastic impetus. But in Britain, the causes that Victricius championed prospered immediately. Lay monks were still rare outside the senatorial aristocracy of Rome and their dependants; yet, though few Britons of the early fifth century are known by name, half a dozen of them were monks, and by 411 wandering monks were common. Within thirty years of Victricius' visit, the shrine of St. Alban had become the centre of an important national cult, too influential to have been left without the protection of a church building; and lesser local martyrs' shrines abounded in Britain. The name of Martin was venerated; Bede describes a Canterbury church

> built in antiquity in honour of St. Martin, while the Romans yet inhabited Britain.

Nearly half the major towns of Roman Britain have a similar church; but it is impossible to tell whether their re-used Roman stones were first made into a church in 400, or in 1100, or in between, for no text dates any but the Canterbury church. Any or none may be as old; but some such churches existed, and one or two seem to have maintained schools, like Martin's at Tours.

Victricius' missionary work on the barbarian borders of his diocese was an innovation, and no tradition gives him contemporary imitators, except in Britain. Patrick, in the mid 5th century, knew of lapsed Picts; some had been baptised, hardly later than about 400. Bede was told that the southern Picts had been converted by a bishop born in Britain and trained at Rome, named Nynia, who built a church 'in the name of Martin' at *Candida Casa*, 'the White House', Whithorn in Galloway, so named because its stone construction was then unfamiliar to the British of the far north. It is likely that Bede's Nynia, better known as Ninian, is identical with Patrick's unnamed missionary who preached about 400.

At that date Whithorn can scarcely have been a bishop's see; Victricius was a bishop of Rouen who built monasteries in Belgium, and Ninian was evidently bishop of a recognised urban see, probably Carlisle, who also built a monastery by the barbarian border of his diocese. The name of the church proclaims the influence of Martin, and argues a date not long after his death; its place bespoke the influence of Victricius. Irish tradition knew it by the name of Rosnat, and knew it as an important monastic school from the mid fifth century onward, while British tradition gives a precise date for its foundation, 398, just after Victricius' visit. Excavation has uncovered the remains of a very early stone church at Whithorn; if it be not the church of Ninian, then a similar church awaits discovery nearby.

Barbarian missions, monks and schools, shrines and the veneration of Martin, are all novelties advocated by Victricius, and they concentrate in the ten years or so after his visit. In these years British ideas first made an impact upon mediterranean Christian thought. The ideas are fresh, logically formulated, expressed in clearer and more polished Latin than was then usual among Italian and African theologians. They are deeply tinged with a radical egalitarianism that echoes Victricius, but extends beyond his elementary concepts. Though most of these British works were published abroad, they reveal something of the Britain where their authors were brought up, so that its intellectual climate is better documented for the early fifth century than for the Roman past, or for generations to come.

The Early Fifth Century

Before the fall of Rome changed men's thinking, the British monk Pelagius was esteemed in Rome as the most polished writer of his day, a Christian Cicero. But the shock of the city's capture overwhelmed the comfortable Ciceronian past and drove men to seek new remedies. Some urged the wholesale rejection of secular society, on the model of the monks of Egypt. John Cassian instituted at Marseille the first Latin monastery on the Egyptian pattern, but his success was limited; imitators were few, and Cassian complained that the Gauls did not respond to the principles of monasticism; they preferred to receive gifts of land, living upon their rents rather than upon their own labour. A few houses were founded in remote deserted districts, especially in the Jura, but most of them became quiet and ineffective retreats for men of property, sheltered from the wreck of their orderly world. They made little impact on the Christianity of Gaul, and by the middle of the century were easily subjected to close episcopal control. In the words of Montalembert, the modern historian of the western monks, the monasteries of the west had declined into 'torpor and sterility' before the end of the fifth century.

The example of Egypt did not yet appeal; others pioneered new types of monastery. On the island of Lérins, off the coast of the French Riviera, the fruitful initiative of Honoratus established a select monastic community of high-powered intellectuals, devoted to the reform of the practice of the church. Lérins was heavily imbued with the ideas of Ambrose. Its aim was reform from above, by securing the election of learned monks to bishoprics in Gaul. Many were elected. Among them was another Briton, the third abbot, Faustus, who became bishop of Riez in southern Gaul; whose prolific writings are the foundation of later Gallic theology. In tune with the teaching of Ambrose, and with much of Martin's thinking, the Lérins reformers encouraged another form of monasticism, the institution of a celibate diocesan clergy, and cathedral monasteries multiplied. Among their closest allies were Martin's pupil Amator, who founded the cathedral school of Auxerre before his death in 418, and also his illustrious successor Germanus. The best-known of Amator's pupils and priests was another Briton, Patrick, who may also have spent some time at Lérins.

Monastic reformers planned for the future, but the present was urgent. The most important Christian reaction to the fall of Rome was the speedy triumph of the views of Augustine, bishop of Hippo in North Africa. Augustine's central thesis was simple; all men inherited the sin of Adam, and could only be redeemed by the grace of God. Logical conclusions followed like links in a steel chain. A good life and good works were of no avail without grace; salvation depended more on God's predestined gift of grace than on the individual's free choice between good and evil; babies were damned at birth, unless they received grace through the sacrament of baptism. Pelagius was horrified when these views were first published, especially at Augustine's prayer, 'Grant what thou dost command, command what thou dost will'. Pelagius saw Augustine as the innovator, against whom he defended the humanist, classical, traditional values that Christianity inherited from its Roman past.

At first Augustine's views aroused only interest and comment. But the disaster of 410 ended the world that bred Pelagius' gentler philosophy. Churchmen listened more keenly to Augustine; though the deeper implications were not immediately spelt out, responsible ecclesiastics sensed that the gentle individualism of the past must cause the church to fragment into as many diverse hostile units as the secular state, whereas the logic of Augustine made man's salvation dependent on sacraments administered by a duly ordained priest, obedient to bishops, metropolitans and popes, in a disciplined hierarchy that might preserve the unity of the church, though political authority dissolved. Augustine's first attack was unsuccessful, but he made considerable use of the extreme tenets of a radical wing among the Pelagians, and secured an imperial edict, over the pope's head, outlawing and banning their beliefs, in 418. The government's statements made clear its reasons for aiding Augustine; the radicals had 'split Rome into factions', they had excited the minds of the common people, and had sapped 'the authority of the catholic law', and with it the Majesty of God, itself 'the source of our imperial rule'. Their leaders went into hiding in Rome, and 'corrupted the minds of the ignorant' by distributing 'secret pamphlets'. The pope died, and plebeian riots at the ensuing election taxed the strength of the police; the successful candidate proved a strong supporter of Augustine, and the laws against the Pelagians were rigidly enforced by church and state.

All the known leaders of the radicals in Rome came from the British Isles. The government denounced Pelagius' most prominent supporter, Coelestius, as their chief inspirer, perhaps rightly. He was probably Irish; and an educated

Irishman in early fifth-century Rome probably came from an Irish colony in civilised Britain, perhaps from Demetia. But the authors of the surviving tracts are British, foremost among them a young man who wrote in Sicily, called the Sicilian Briton, since his name is unknown. His half-dozen pamphlets have a single starting-point, the text 'If thou wouldst be perfect, go sell all that thou hast'. He condemns social inequality more fiercely than any Christian writer since the second century, turning Victricius' philosophical propositions into vivid rhetoric.

> One man owns many large mansions adorned with costly marbles, another has not so much as a small hut to keep out the cold and heat. One man has vast territories and unlimited possessions, another has but a little stretch of turf to sit upon and call his own. . . . Are these riches from God? . . . If God had willed universal inequality, he . . . would not have permitted . . . equal shares . . . in the elements. . . . Does the rich man enjoy the blessing of fresh air more than the poor man? Does he feel the sun's heat more keenly or less? When earth receives the gift of rain, do larger drops fall upon the rich man's field than upon the poor man's? . . . What God himself distributes . . . is shared equally; what we own in unjust inequality is everything whose distribution was entrusted to human control. . . . Is there one sacrament, one law for the rich, another for the poor? . . . inequality of wealth is not to be blamed upon the graciousness of God, but upon the iniquity of men.

The viewpoint is not new. But it had not been put so sharply for two hundred years, nor ever in such compelling language; for the direct plain vocabulary and strong balanced periods have more in common with the Latinity of Caesar than with the turgid prose of late Roman theologians.

Wealth was not merely unjust; it was the cause of misgovernment and oppression:

> Look you now, I pray you, at the pride and arrogance of those who . . . would take on the power of a master where Christ took the form of a slave. With that proud ambitious spirit which covets all earthly glory for itself, the rich commonly sit themselves upon that tribunal before which Christ stood and was heard. What is this, Christian? . . . You sit upon the tribunal. . . . Under your eyes the bodies of men like you in nature are beaten with whips of lead, broken with clubs, torn on the claws, burnt in the flames . . . It is the rich, dripping with excessive wealth, whom the will to cruelty leads into acts of such savage wickedness.

He was scornful of the excuses that the Christian rich found in the scriptures to justify the retention of their wealth, and scorn rises to fierce satirical humour when he faces the rich man's 'explanation' of Christ's assertion that 'it is easier

for a camel to pass through the eye of a needle than for the rich man to enter
into the kingdom of Heaven'.

> 'But,' you say, 'it does not mean a camel, which cannot possibly pass
> through a needle's eye, but a *camelus*, which is a kind of ship's
> hawser'. What intolerable subtlety when human greed . . . grasps
> at the names of ropes to keep its earthly wealth! . . . It is a rotten
> argument that will do the rich no good. As if it were easier to get a
> huge rope through the needle's eye than that well known animal the
> camel! If you want an excuse to live estranged from heaven's
> throne with an easy mind . . . ships are no good to you, with their
> huge great fittings. . . . You had better try the weaving trade, and
> search for some kind of thread called *camelus*. Such idiocy may
> amuse men . . . but it will carry little weight with God. But you
> quote . . . 'What is impossible for men is possible for God'. Of
> course it is 'possible' for Him to let the rich into heaven, 'possible'
> to let them bring all their estates and their mobile property and
> their wealth into heaven too, and the camels with them into the
> bargain. If it were just a matter of 'possibility' no one would be
> shut out of Heaven, for everything is possible to God.

The Sicilian Briton was not a lone idealist, but the spokesman of a movement.
The rich were on the defensive against vocal plebeian critics.

> Listen to your rich man calling your poor man 'wretch', 'beggar',
> 'rabble', because he dares to open his mouth in 'our' presence,
> because in his rags he reproaches 'our' morality and conduct, . . . as
> if the rich alone had a right to speak, as if the understanding of truth
> were a function of wealth, not of thought.

He had evidently encountered poor men who voiced a protest, and rich men who
condemned them. He cried aloud the age old resentment against social injustice,
expanding ideas that the Fathers of the early church had cemented into the
structure of orthodox Christian theology; but he added an entirely new theoreti-
cal analysis:

> Mankind is divided into three classes, the rich, the poor, and those
> who have enough.

The problems of human society are to be solved by transferring the superfluous
property of the rich to the poor, so that everyone has enough. The argument
culminates in a practical slogan.

> Abolish the rich and you will have no more poor . . . for it is the
> few rich who are the cause of the many poor.

Nineteenth-century theologians rightly compared these views with modern
socialism, for the causal analysis and the proposals based on it are unique in

antiquity, whose Christian tradition went no further than simple denunciation of wealth and property as evil and un-Christian. But the disintegrating Roman empire was not a society ready for socialism. The Sicilian Briton's ideas were turned against him. Augustine seized upon his major work, *On Riches*, and used it against Pelagius, who disclaimed responsibility; Augustine reluctantly accepted his denial and blamed Coelestius instead. The government denounced him as the author of sedition and ordered his arrest, for the Sicilian Briton's slogan, 'abolish the rich', in Latin *Tolle Divitem*, has a rhythm that a crowd might chant in anger; and an organised urban movement that rallied behind it, under the leadership of educated lawyers who went underground to escape arrest, was disturbing enough to any ancient government. Pelagius was no radical himself, but the government made no scrupulous distinction between the views of one Pelagian and another; Augustine might justifiably argue that it was the loose liberalism of Pelagius that permitted alarming subversion to riot outside the control of ecclesiastical discipline. Pelagianism became heresy.

The controversy flared up and was settled in the short space of eight years. But the outlooks that then clashed were the most fundamental in all Christian thinking; they disputed whether man might commune directly with his God, or must depend upon the intermediary of a priest. Modern theologians have properly remarked that Pelagius' philosophy has much in common with the later Protestantism of northern Europe; in its own time it was near to the need of the monk, who sought solitary communion with God in the desert. The similarity is not an accident. Though the Pelagians were universally condemned in name, their teaching was preserved. Not a word survives of any other of the major early heresies, save what their orthodox opponents cite against them, or fragments salvaged from papyri. But some seventy Pelagian works were copied and recopied through the centuries, most of them in northern European lands where monasteries inspired by monks from the British Isles were most numerous, and where protestant reform aroused its earliest and most enduring response a thousand years later.

In its own day, Pelagianism was eclipsed. Faustus and the church of Gaul formally accepted its condemnation, but strict Italian Augustinians reproached them as 'semi-Pelagian'. They had cause, for in northern Gaul a mid fifth-century layman might still treat Augustine as a distant heretic of small importance. Gaul was upon the margin of controversy, and soon accepted the ruling of Rome. But in Britain Pelagianism was no heresy. Most of the Pelagian writers were British, and their works were still read and cited as orthodox a century later in Britain. Britain escaped the controversy.

The one Pelagian author who is known to have written in Britain, Fastidius, takes it for granted in 411 that his readers share his assumption, and expresses incredulous amazement at rumours that abroad men urged the dogma of original sin. His social outlook is that of Pelagius rather than of the Sicilian Briton, but he too gives ample witness that plebeian protest was strong in Britain. In the course of his address to a young widow he welcomes a new government, of men of property, which had recently ousted a previous government, also of men of property. The previous government had oppressed the poor, and some of its members had been lynched by crowds, acting in support of the new rulers. He instructs the new government, with heavy emphasis, that it must use wealth rightly for the benefit of the poor, without oppression. Exhortations to charity addressed to individuals are a commonplace of late Roman sermons; used to exhort a government and a ruling class they are unusual. European churchmen uniformly preached obedience to ruling emperors, condemning all rebellion, while they urged emperors to heed their bishops; even the conflicts of Ambrose with Justina and Theodosius centred on a power struggle between bishop and emperor, unconcerned with the rights of rich and poor. Though the plebs frequently rioted in the great cities of the Mediterranean, they made little impact upon theological writing; and, except where Martin's influence was strong, the peasants of Latin Europe were as yet scarcely concerned with the church. Salvian of Marseille deplored their oppression, and Germanus of Auxerre sought a pardon for peasant rebels in Gaul after their defeat, but the active pressure of the poor upon the government made little impression on Christian writers, except upon the British.

Nothing is known of the British church for ten years after the condemnation of Pelagius, and its reaction thereto is not recorded. There is little trace of Augustine's thinking in the later writings of the British, and there is no reason to suppose that any considerable body of British opinion welcomed it during his lifetime, though there is ample evidence that Pelagian views persisted. The attitude of the British clergy, now outside the empire, can have mattered little to Rome so long as it did not impinge upon the affairs of Italy and Gaul.

Germanus

Something changed about 428. The chronicler Prosper, a strenuous Augustinian, records that the Pelagian heresy was 'revived' by Agricola, a bishop in Britain. The words must mean that he and his fellows openly and vigorously asserted the heresy, and began to affect Gaul. Doubtless some unrecorded incident, the condemnation of a British bishop in Gaul or the like, sparked off a dispute hitherto latent. It was clearly of importance, for both the Pope and the Gallic bishops bestirred themselves, sending Germanus of Auxerre to Britain in 429. Like Ambrose, he had been a secular officer, in command of troops, and had been forcibly chosen bishop by 'all the clergy, the whole nobility, and the people of town and country' when Amator, Martin's pupil, died in 418. As austere as Ambrose, he 'turned his wife to a sister, and gave his substance to the poor', and became an outstanding champion of reform, a vigorous ally of Lérins and of its foremost leader, Hilary, now bishop of Arles and metropolitan of Gaul. He was accompanied to Britain by Lupus, the young bishop of Troyes, who survived to describe his experiences to Germanus' biographer, Constantius.

Germanus found in Britain the same active hostility of the poor towards the rich that the Sicilian Briton and Fastidius knew, and turned it to his advantage. The bishops began by preaching 'not only in the churches, but also in the streets and in the countryside', until they won 'the whole region to their opinion', so that the Pelagians, who had hitherto ignored them, were compelled to challenge them to public debate. The debate was not held in a church council, as was normal, but in public. Ordinary people came for the day with their wives and children, and the Pelagians made a bad impression because their clothing was ostentatious, their 'crowd of flatterers' offensive. The people voted victory to Germanus by acclamation; the victory was sealed by a curative miracle, and the *suasio iniqua*, the subtle evil, was wiped from men's minds. The word *suasio*, appropriate to the legal plea of a professional orator, carries an overtone that the heretics were clever intellectuals, refuted by the plain man's common sense of Germanus.

Germanus tried to win the population for the cause of unity with Europe and Rome against separatist bishops. The only other ecclesiastical occasion that the biographer describes is a visit to the shrine of St. Alban. Germanus had the tomb opened and placed within it

> relics of all the apostles and of various martyrs . . . since . . . the saints . . . of different countries . . . were of equal merit in heaven.

It was an extraordinary action; saints' tombs were commonly opened to verify, transfer or remove relics, but not to intrude alien bones. The biographer admits a 'pious sacrilege', though the British bishops may well have questioned its piety. Germanus' intent is plain. The shrine was of great importance; otherwise Germanus would not have made his dramatic gesture, nor would his biographer have selected the isolated incident for full description. The shrine was evidently already the centre of a national cult, which clearly warranted a church building and a monastic community for the protection of the relics. Alban was already the national saint, and Germanus' strong assertion that the saints of all countries were equal claimed the tomb as the common property of Christendom, not merely the pride and symbol of a heretical national church. But the fame of Alban was not successfully merged with the generality of martyrs whose remains now shared his tomb. The shrine and church remained and remain the church of St. Alban, not of All Saints.

What Germanus did not do is as significant as what he did. He was sent to Britain to root out the Pelagian heresy, and his biographer selected the most convincing incidents he could to show that he succeeded. He worked miracles; he took part in a military campaign, and therefore clearly had the support of the secular government, who were in no position to quarrel with the imperial power in Gaul, or with the churchmen it favoured. But his only ecclesiastical success was to be cheered at a public meeting, and to make a demonstration at the chief national shrine. He held no synod; no heretics were condemned and no bishops were deposed, though there can be no doubt that Germanus would have had the Pelagians condemned if he could, and that his biographer would have reported any success that he had. Though he is said to have rallied at least a part of the laity, especially the rural population, against their bishops, he is not said to have won ecclesiastical support of any kind. What is set down in his biography is that which his assistant Lupus remembered. It is direct contemporary evidence that Germanus failed, that the church of Britain remained united, uncompromisingly Pelagian.

Palladius

Rome reacted swiftly. Germanus' visit had been prompted by the pope's deacon, Palladius, whose office made him one of the most important ecclesiastics in Europe, a potential successor to the papal throne. Palladius now took the remarkable decision to absent himself from Rome, and to visit Britain himself. The pope had no power to impose a bishop or a legate on an existing see, and Palladius was therefore given the novel post of 'bishop to the Irish Christians'. It is quite impossible that the propagation of the faith among the pagan Irish could have been the whole, or even the main reason. Missions to the heathen were new; a native Goth or Abyssinian might receive consecration if he travelled to Constantinople or Alexandria, but no Romans were sent to barbarians. Victricius had pioneered the conversion of pagans on the borders of his own diocese, and Ninian in Galloway had set a precedent, as yet not imitated. It is likely that Germanus had already decided to follow that precedent, for the biographers of Patrick believed that he was a priest of Germanus at Auxerre, and that the post of bishop to the Irish had been proposed and approved, Patrick named thereto, before Palladius decided to go himself.

It was an astounding decision. The proper person for a new and uncertain mission was an obscure priest from a provincial diocese, like Patrick; the choice of the pope's personal deacon was as eccentric as would have been the despatch of the most eminent cardinal of the mid nineteenth-century *curia* to Arizona or China. So unusual an appointment requires explanation, and Prosper gives the reason. Pope Celestine

> in consecrating a bishop to the Irish, while he was striving to keep the Roman island catholic, also made the barbarian island Christian.

The main object was to rout the Pelagians in Britain; the conversion of the Irish was secondary. The creation of a new see enabled Palladius to establish himself in Britain, among the heretics. The see had been created for straightforward missionary work alone; its success was an integral part of the British government's political policy towards the Irish, and Patrick was the kind of man required. Palladius was not. Yet, though the bishops and rulers of Britain might be confounded and dismayed at the pope's choice, they could not gainsay it;

the best they could do was to try to ensure that Palladius spent as much as possible of his time on his official business in Ireland, as little as possible in organising an anti-Pelagian faction in Britain.

Palladius was not successful. Prosper, who knew him well and wished him well, wrote two or three years after his appointment. He claims that Palladius fulfilled his nominal duty, for though the bland statement that he 'made Ireland Christian' is a patent exaggeration, it was acceptable to Italian readers, if he was known to have visited Ireland and to have made a few converts. But Prosper does not even claim that he converted the Pelagians, merely that he strove to do so. Prosper says no more of Palladius or of Ireland, though his wording implies that the mission was over, no longer in progress. Irish tradition makes it short, believing that Palladius failed, and died within the year, on his way home.

The see existed, and after Palladius' failure there was no longer reason to vary its original purpose or to hold back the original nominee. Irish tradition is unanimous that Patrick landed about 432. Patrick himself relates that his appointment was delayed by controversy and opposition, but ultimately received the support of British bishops. Opposition is understandable. In addition to the handicap of a broken education, which he felt unfitted him for the post, he was, though British born, the nominee of the foreigners who had tried and failed to discipline the British church. Trained abroad, he was no Pelagian, and no theologian; in his surviving works there is no Pelagianism, but also no trace of Augustinian opposition to the Pelagians; he was plainly dominated by a single-minded devotion to his mission. His attitudes must have been as clear to those who knew him as they are in his writings, and he could only have seemed a second Palladius to men who had not met him. Grounds of opposition were not strong enough to warrant further dispute with Rome and Gaul; he suited the lay government, and Rome and Gaul had no reason to complain when British bishops endorsed their choice.

Later Fifth-Century Britain

The church of Roman Britain lasted ten or twenty years more, and kept its character to the end. When Patrick was again at odds with British bishops, about the early 440s, he reproached them as urbane prelates, 'learned, skilled at public speaking and all else'. It is the same judgment that Germanus and Lupus had made of their Pelagian opponents a dozen years before. The British bishops were products of the same schools and the same society as Pelagius and Faustus, Fastidius and the Sicilian Briton. Before the sudden disaster of the Saxon revolt, their world had been spared the barbarian inroads that had convulsed Italy and Gaul; it had been able to preserve its institutions and its culture undamaged; it had had no need to undergo the bitter experience of the Augustinian controversy, and could afford to retain the older humanist theology. Only when the outbreak of the Saxon revolt caused its world to crash in ruin did it begin to yield; Germanus on a second visit in the mid or late 440s secured the deposition of two bishops. It was a small gain, too late to matter to the church of Gaul or of Britain.

Contemporary records of the church last a generation longer than those of the state, and serve to explain secular society, for the opulent cultured bishops whom Germanus and Patrick encountered were the contemporaries of Vortigern and his councillors, products of the same society, educated in the same schools, housed in similar buildings, bound by the same institutions. They were also influenced by the same ideas, heirs both to the attitudes that the Sicilian Briton urged and to those that he condemned, and to the gentility of Fastidius and Pelagius. Their material world was destroyed by the Saxon rising and the fifty years' war that followed; but the ideas outlived the buildings and the institutions, for Arthur's victory came just in time to save some of them. Children who had been born and baptised just before the revolt, who had seen their first Christian services in sophisticated Roman buildings, on the mosaic floors of the Roman mansion at Hinton St. Mary in Dorset, in the chapel at Lullingstone villa in Kent, or in the churches of Roman British towns, were aged sixty or seventy when Arthur was emperor and the monastic reformers of the sixth century were growing boys. The continuity of ideas is obscured, Roman Britain and the Welsh monks are made to seem unrelated worlds, by the break in historical tradition, as savage in the history of the church as in the history of laymen. Yet the older teachers of Gildas and his fellows were themselves children of an undamaged Roman Britain. To the young, ruined buildings and tales of the life lived in them were meaningless ancient history, ghosts of a dead past; but old ideas of the relation of man to man and man to God still mattered.

The memorials of the church after the Saxon revolt are scattered chiefly among the Lives of the Saints. Their outlook is usually repellent, their stories superficially absurd; but their indigestible mash of fiction, fantasy and folk-lore is rooted in the ruins of contemporary record, and needs careful excavation, like the vegetation that covers material archaeological ruins.

Patrick

The earliest of the British saints is Patrick, and he is the only one whose own writings survive. His history has been obscured by his later eminence, which has inspired the most elaborate falsifications in the ecclesiastical history of medieval Europe. In the course of 7th-century controversies, centred upon the proper date for the celebration of Easter, the adherents of conformity with Rome took Patrick as their patron. Their principal contrivance was to assert that all the churches of their day in Ireland that were not already under the control of major monasteries, and many that were, had been founded by Patrick. He was therefore made to consecrate some 450 bishops and a corresponding quantity of priests, establishing himself in Armagh as primate of Ireland. Though Patrick's own writings admit no other bishop but himself, and do not name Armagh or any other place, and though the authors of the fiction admitted that Irishmen in their own day did not believe them, the victory of their cause won acceptance for their story, and the tragic later history of Ireland hardened it into an article of national faith.

One by-product of the fiction has recently confused the straightforward account of the early texts. A 7th-century writer compared Patrick with Moses, who lived for 120 years; symmetry gave him 60 years before he came to Ireland, 60 thereafter. All writers agreed that Patrick landed about 432, and early tradition entered his death at 459 or 460. But his 120-year life-span added alternatives; since he died in 460, his birth was entered at 340; and since he taught for 60 years after 432, his death was also entered in the 490s. The Annalists repeated all these dates; and from the two death-dates an intelligent 8th-century writer advanced the thesis that there were two Patricks, and suggested that the earlier was perhaps identical with Palladius. The thesis had little sequel until it was revived in the middle of the 20th century, by writers who overlooked Moses and the early birth-date, and transferred the landing and the death of the second Patrick, author of the *Confessio*, to the later fifth century. Yet no writer earlier than the twentieth century admits any date other than about 432 for Patrick's landing, and his own writings treat of urbane bishops and a settled municipal life in Britain that ill accord with the disasters of the second half of the century.

These views have attracted little support outside Ireland, but they have inhibited serious study of the earlier and sober accounts of Patrick. Apart from his own writings, only two informative texts are immune from the extravagance of the Armagh tradition, a mid 7th-century Life by Muirchu, and one that forms the basis of a still unpublished anonymous Life. All the other early accounts of Patrick must be discounted, for their incentive, clearly expressed, was to invent stories that were not believed at the time when they were written. They are sources rich and fruitful for the study of the churches of 7th and 8th-century Ireland, and of the traditions of their founders. A few among them may have been Patrick's converts, for some lived in his time in the regions where Muirchu records his preaching, but the fabricated texts cannot be used to argue for or against such connection, or to provide any information whatsoever about Patrick himself.

Patrick's own writings record that he was the son of a British landowner, whose ancestors had been Christian since the early fourth century. Their names suggest that they had been Roman citizens for at least two hundred years. At the age of sixteen he was captured by Irish raiders; he served as a slave for six years, and escaped by sea. When he returned to Britain he dreamt that a man named Victoricus, Victoricius, or Victricius in various manuscripts, who was possibly Victricius of Rouen, charged him to preach in Ireland. Many years later, he was consecrated bishop, with the support of a boyhood friend who seems to have been a prominent ecclesiastic. He wrote after a number of years in Ireland, refusing to answer accusations brought against him by British bishops in a formal meeting, reminding the British that though he would dearly love to visit his homeland, he also had friends in Gaul. He had travelled widely in Ireland, he had occasionally been imprisoned, but was normally tolerated by local kings, and had made numerous converts, including both slaves and the children of kings, many of whom had taken monastic vows. He calls himself the 'bishop established in Ireland', and refers to priests who served under him, but not to any other bishops.

Muirchu and the anonymous Life send him to Gaul between his captivity and his consecration, under Amator and Germanus of Auxerre, and state that Germanus intended to send him to Ireland before Palladius' appointment; his mission was delayed until Palladius' death. He then coasted Ireland to the territory of the Ulaid, where he made his headquarters at Downpatrick, paying one visit to the former Ulaid capital of Emain, where he founded Armagh, and another to the High King's court at Tara. Patrick's own words suggest somewhat wider travels, and there may therefore be some substance in the northern Irish traditions of his journeys in the texts that do not make him 'primate' of Ireland or locate him in a single centre, at Armagh or elsewhere. Muirchu does not make him consecrate any bishops in Ireland, but associates him with two British bishops in the consecration of an Irish convert as bishop of Man.

The Annals record that Patrick was 'approved' by pope Leo the Great, who ruled from 440 to 467, and had earlier succeeded Palladius as papal deacon. Patrick's *Confessio* rejects the jurisdiction claimed by the bishops of Britain, and refers to friends in Gaul. Leo's policy throughout Europe was concerned to weaken the power of metropolitans and synods, and to establish the direct dependence of provincial bishops upon Rome. It is probable that Leo 'approved' Patrick's rejection of British metropolitan supremacy and welcomed Ireland as directly subordinate to Rome, independent of Britain; possible that Patrick's complaint was carried by Germanus on his last visit to Italy in the late 440s. It is not probable that the episcopate of Britain was in a position to assert authority over Ireland after the outbreak of the Saxon revolt.

Patrick was not the first missionary, even in the north of Ireland; for when he claimed that he had penetrated to

> the farther regions . . . not previously reached by anyone who baptised or ordained priests,

he assumed that his readers knew that in the nearer lands someone had previously ordained and baptised. But he was the first regular bishop, appointed by Rome, and he made a considerable number of converts, including a number of highly placed younger men and women, at least in the north. He established an organised church, which his successors maintained. But the mass conversion of the Irish to Christianity in the next century was not the work of that church. Patrick, and the bishops who succeeded him, are almost unknown in the early traditions of the Irish monastic movement. The only modern scholar who has made a thorough study of documentation of early Irish Christianity, James Kenney, rightly remarked that for almost two centuries Patrick

> was not entirely forgotten, but . . . his memory had slipped into the background of old and far-off things.

His memory was revived and reasserted during the Easter controversy, when the framework of his episcopalian church was found to provide a means whereby the monasteries of Ireland might gain communion with Britain, Rome and Europe, without losing their independence.

Patrick wrote his *Confessio* while Roman Britain was still in being, just about the time of the Saxon revolt. When he died, towards 460, Roman Britain was destroyed, its political leaders were massacred, and a great part of their surviving relatives were emigrants in Gaul, while others were preparing to join Ambrosius' resistance movement. There is no further mention of British bishops in the lowland cities exposed to Saxon raids, though it is probable that Verulamium, London and a few other cities whose walls withstood the raiders still maintained bishops. In the west, less savaged by the wars, several bishops are named on both shores of the Severn.

The earliest of them, Docco, is the worst recorded of all the early British saints; he is named in a dozen unrelated English, Irish and Welsh texts, and in a couple of extremely corrupt Lives. Statements that do not appear to serve their authors' purpose are few and unconfirmed; but they match the circumstances of south-western Britain in the mid fifth century. Docco, also called Congar, is said to have belonged to one of the leading Cornovian families, young when they moved south to Dumnonia, probably about the 430s. He was apparently regarded as a son or grandson of an emperor Constantine, evidently the British emperor of 407. Whether he was a relative or not, he acted like one; for Constantine's known son Constans had taken monastic vows, probably a year or two before Docco's birth. In Dumnonia, Docco's home was his estate at Congresbury, that preserves his name, in Somerset, south of Bristol. There he lived as a monk, as some of his European contemporaries lived ascetic lives on their own estates. He maintained a school, as did Martin; at least three other monasteries bore his name, St. Kew in northern Cornwall, and the two Llandough's in Glamorganshire. St. Kew is attested as a fifth-century foundation; the others are perhaps as early. Somewhere about the middle of the century he is said to have been consecrated bishop, presumably in the chief town of a *civitas* where his monasteries made him known, either Exeter, or possibly Caerwent. His death is placed at 473, and he is said to have died an old man.

Later Fifth-Century Ireland

Docco was honoured in Ireland as the first author of the Irish Christian liturgy, and a number of notices suggest the reason. Patrick died about the same time as pope Leo, perhaps a year or two before, and his death left an organisational problem in Ireland that only Rome could solve. The law of the Church required that a bishop must be consecrated by two or more existing bishops; therefore, unless there were a number of bishoprics in a country, new bishops must either travel abroad for consecration, or hold office irregularly. In the generation after Patrick's death, the Irish record four or five new northern sees; either they were authorised by Leo in Patrick's lifetime, or by his successor after his death. The churchmen were either Irish, products of the church that Patrick founded, or British; and several of the prominent Irish leaders were trained in Britain, some by the abbots of Whithorn.

These northern sees derived from the concepts of Roman Europe, that assigned one bishop and one only to each political unit. In Europe the unit was the Roman *civitas*, but Ireland had no towns. The distribution of the late fifth-century bishops points to the commonsense principle evolved; a bishop is attested for each of the main kingdoms. There is no sign of a metropolitan. It is probable that the bishop of Armagh was from the beginning accorded some greater deference, but the earliest recorded claim to the title 'Archbishop' was advanced at Kildare in Leinster in the earlier seventh century, not at Armagh. The early canons of the Irish church attest a normal married diocesan clergy; Patrick had encouraged monastic vows, and speaks more often of the women than of the men who took them, but the church did not yet insist on celibate priests. Beside the bishoprics, two or three fifth-century monasteries are remembered in the north, together with a number of small cells of consecrated virgins.

Further south, traditions differ. Northern Leinster went its own way. Its earliest Christian record is dominated by the formidable energy of Brigit, whose large monastery and splendid church lay hard by the principal residence of the king. Her bishop, Conlaed, is depicted as a kind of domestic chaplain, necessarily employed to perform those ecclesiastical functions for which women were ineligible. The account is distorted by the prominence of Brigit in later legend; but the concept is early, set down a little over a century after her death, only just out of living memory. Brigit, who is said to have lived from 455 to 525, was a small child when Patrick died, but the inspiration that led her and Faencha and other young women of her day to take the veil was plainly his.

Brigit's house overtopped the rest; her miracles and activities are mainly concerned with cattle, butter, milk and other aspects of dairy farming, so that she appears as the patroness of women and of peace; she was also the champion of north Leinster. Other women practised women's virtues, and local patrons abounded, but Brigit became a national saint, second only to Patrick; and she reached her eminence earlier, within a century of her death. It seems evident that Irish society needed a female cult. In Ireland, as in European Christianity, congregations of religious women preceded the male monasteries; but they did not survive in Ireland, and separate houses for women play little part in later Irish monasticism. The choice among female saints was therefore restricted to those who lived in the late fifth century, and it must be presumed that among her contemporaries Brigit's personality excelled, attracting more numerous followers. It was perhaps a slight additional strength that she happened to bear the name of an ancient goddess, but the name Briga, in various forms, was almost as common in early Ireland as Mary in modern England, and the name by itself brought no closer identity with a mother-goddess.

Later tradition accommodated a female counterpart of Patrick. But the rest of the south remembered origins independent of Patrick. Ailbe of Emly, Ciaran of Saigir in Ossory, Declan of the Dessi, from the three main divisions of Munster, and Ibar of south Leinster went to Rome during the pontificate of Hilary, that lasted from 461 to 468. Another Irishman, Enda, and a Briton, Kebi, or Cybi, cousin or nephew of bishop Docco, visited Rome at the same time. The date was immediately after Patrick's death, which obliged Rome to consecrate one or more northern bishops to succeed him. The southern Irishmen had had difficulty in finding priests at home; Ailbe had British teachers, Ibar was a pupil of the Briton Mocteus of Louth, and Ciaran had had to go abroad to find Christian instructions; only Declan had found an Irish teacher, who had himself been trained abroad. A little later other Leinstermen, Eugenius and Tigernach, were sent to Whithorn for schooling.

Ibar and the three Munstermen were consecrated bishops in Rome and sent back to Ireland. Their biographers insist that they were consecrated before Patrick, and overcome the chronological difficulties by giving them life-spans of up to 300 years. Paragraphs in the medieval texts recount how they reached agreement with Patrick, with varying degrees of politeness, retaining southern independence without prejudice to Patrick's rights; these stories were plainly added in an age when the priority of Armagh was admitted in the south, but only grudgingly. The bishops founded sees, but Enda was a man of a different stamp, with other ideals. He was already a monk. In his youth he had been a dynastic chief. Leading his men home from battle, singing a victory song, he passed the cell of the virgin Faencha.

'That horrible yelling comes not from the grave of Christ,' she protested, and denounced Enda as a murderer.

'I keep my father's inheritance, and I have to fight my enemies,' he replied indignantly.

'Your father is in hell, his inheritance is crime and wickedness,' answered Faencha.

Enda was converted and joined the community. Soon after, raiding neighbours attacked his men; Faencha saw him put down the plank he was carrying as though tempted to help. She took no chances.

'You must get out of Ireland' she told him, 'or you will be seduced by the things of this world. . . . Go to Britain to the monastery of Rosnat.'

'How long must I stay there?' Enda asked.

'Till I hear good reports of you,' she retorted.

But from Britain he went to Rome, with Ailbe and 'Pubeus'. On his return he asked king Angus of Munster, who ruled from about 463 to 492, to grant him the desert island of Aran for a monastery. Angus was astounded, because the teaching of Patrick had enjoined that he should offer to clerics only 'good agricultural land near my royal residence'. But he agreed when Enda insisted. Few tales more clearly illustrate the basic differences between the bishops and the monks. Patrick's concept is the normal and proper attitude of the church of Rome and Gaul; bishops Ailbe and Declan followed it, and their churches were built by royal residences; most fifth-century bishops settled near royal centres, rarely more than a couple of hours' drive away, often within easy walking distance. Like most continental bishops, their duty was to guide kings. Enda's unusual attitude foreshadowed the future. The monk sought to escape from political society, not to reform it.

In the Life of Enda, the most eminent of the three companions was 'Pubeus'. Like several other island visitors to Rome, in the fancies of the biographers he was elected pope by the admiring Romans, but immediately resigned in favour of Hilary. As they left the city, Hilary gave the party sacerdotal vestments, and then recalled them; Pubeus protested, but Enda submitted, and Hilary foretold that thanks to his humility Enda would become chief of the three. Later, in Aran, a dispute arose as to which of them was *princeps*, chief, in the island; the polite redaction of the surviving text makes each defer to the other, Enda admitting that Pubeus was 'senior' and 'of higher authority', *auctoritate dignior*. The dispute was resolved by an embassy to Rome, consisting of a Finnian, of MacCriche, who was Ailbe's subordinate cleric in Clare, to whose territory Aran belonged, and of Erlatheus, bishop of Armagh, who died in 481. One story brings Ailbe with MacCriche to Aran. The pope, guided by a miracle, decided in Enda's favour.

The Life of Kebi is an exceedingly corrupt British text, but it is independent of the Irish tradition, and tells a similar tale. Kebi visited Hilary, who is confused with Hilary of Poitiers, dead a hundred years before; he returned to Wales in the time of king Etelic of Gelvissig, in the later 5th century. He crossed to Ireland with his aged 'cousin' Kengar, Docco, who died in 473. They settled on Aran, but after four years 'Crubthir Fintan' denied Kengar the cow that fed him and quarrelled with Kebi; though abbot 'Enna' for a time pacified him, Fintan succeeded in driving Kebi from Aran and Ireland, to make his permanent home in Llangybi, the Roman fort that bears his name on Holyhead, off Anglesey. The tale is packed with nonsense, but rests on a less banal original; the later editor had no idea who Hilary or Enda were, and took the Irish word *crubthir*, priest, for a proper name; he did not know that Fintan was a protégé of Mocteus of Louth in the late 5th century, or that these people were contemporaries of one another and of Etelic. These were statements that he found in his source. Yet the essence of the tale is similar to the Irish account; Kebi and Kengar were expelled from Aran after claiming disputed rights; as in the Irish story the superior authority of 'Pubeus' over Aran was disputed, and rejected after an appeal to Rome.

The name 'Pubeus' is unknown in Ireland, Britain or elsewhere, and is plainly a corrupt form; but it is a spelling natural to an Irish scholar who thought that Kebi was the Irish form of a British name, which should properly be rendered in Latin and in British by replacing an Irish K with a British P. It is not probable that Irish and British tradition remembered two separate people with similar names whose claims on Aran were both rejected by the same pope; it is more probable that the two traditions differently remembered the name of one person. The connection with Docco explains the context. He is the only late 5th-century British bishop known to monastic tradition, and he is honoured as the earliest episcopal patron of the monks, both by the Irish and by the British. He was the contemporary of pope Hilary, and the Roman church required that monasteries should be placed under episcopal supervision; it is likely enough that when Enda visited Rome, Hilary required that his intended monastery should be subject to an established bishop of south-western Britain rather than to untried Irishmen, consecrated to sees not yet formed; and it may well be that Hilary, faced with the problems of reorganising the Irish church on Patrick's death, sought and welcomed the advice of a British bishop who knew Ireland. Irish tradition distinguished the 'first order', Patrick's episcopalian church, from the 'second order', the monastic church, that multiplied in the sixth century. It named Docco as the earliest author of the liturgy of the second order. It may be that he was the author of the whole enterprise, and sponsored the visit of the five young Irish ecclesiastics to Hilary in Rome. But Welsh and Irish tradition agree that Aran, the first of the great Irish monasteries, soon threw off the tutelage of the British clergy.

These vigorous churchmen were Irish. Though they owed their organisation and perhaps their papal sanction to British help, their enthusiasm sprang directly from native tradition. They baptised the Irish as they found them, giving a Christian future to the weaknesses as well as to the strengths of their society. They were the heirs of Patrick's mission, but not of his outlook; his writings reveal his love for his Irish converts, but also his detestation of their society and his anxiety to replace it with the ideals of Christian Europe. But Conlaed and Ibar, Ailbe and Ciaran, became bishops of large Irish kingdoms, their priests spiritual heads of similar constituent kingdoms, and the clergy took on something of the colour of the society they served. The rugged Life of Ailbe's priest, MacCriche, portrays a wonder-worker whose supernatural authority was principally exerted to make good the military weakness of his people.

The Life is late and unhistorical, but the situation it outlines was real. It foreshadowed a danger that was long to haunt the Irish church, that the bishop or abbot might shrink to the status of the king's wizard, little more than the *magus* of pre-Christian Ireland, enlarged by the majesty of Roman Christendom. The danger was ultimately averted by the large monasteries; their ethic abhorred the violence of dynastic chiefs, and it was proclaimed when the dynasties were still relatively new, when their violence was keenly resented by humbler Irishmen. At first it was the women saints who led the struggle for peaceful living. Faencha told Enda that the virtues he respected were vices, and persuaded him. Darerca in the north, Ita in the next generation, and the many-sided cult of Brigit denounced violence and exalted maternity, dairy farming and all that belongs to the craft of women, against the bellicosity of men.

The bishops acted by practical example. Ciaran of Saigir intervened to prevent a war between the high king and the king of Munster, and the southern bishops found new outlets for the energy of men. The end of overseas raiding had accentuated internal warfare and the savagery of the chiefs. The bishops reversed the trend by reviving the ancient tradition of overseas voyages, called *Imramma* in lay saga, pilgrimage or *peregrinatio* in the language of the church. At first, not all voyages were peaceful. The followers of Senan and of the saints of the Shannon went with armies to Cornwall, and those who succeeded in establishing themselves brought with them the name of their own bishop, Ciaran, trans-literated to Pyran or Perran in Britain. But the military expeditions had little success, and were not repeated. Ailbe preached peaceably to the Irish of Demetia, and baptised the infant David. But the main stream of the voyagers looked westward. Ibar and Ailbe are said to have been the first who dreamed of looking for an undiscovered Land of Promise in or beyond the Atlantic Ocean, and to have sent men to seek it. The first explorers are not reported to have reached further than Iceland, but the traditions of Brendan in the mid sixth century tell circumstantial tales of the sunny and fertile lands of north America. Whether these tales draw upon vigorous imagination or upon actual experience, the decision of Ailbe and Ibar to look for new lands beyond the Ocean added a new dimension to European thought.

Throughout the 5th century, in north and south, the church of Ireland was held to have been organised by British Christians and their native pupils, its organisation sanctioned and approved by Rome. That organisation approximated, as nearly as was possible in a land without towns, to the structure of the church of Rome and Britain. It was based on territorial sees, with a few monasteries under episcopal control, most of them, apart from Enda's Aran, concentrated in and about eastern Meath, Brega, the central regions of the national monarchy. But almost nothing is known of the late 5th-century church in Britain, save for its work in Ireland, and for the existence of a few monastic schools. Political disaster had cut away the foundations of the urban church. The Saxon wars had destroyed the lowland society of the educated early 5th-century bishops, and, though men were doubtless consecrated to urban sees, the decayed towns no longer ruled the countryside. The only part of the lowlands that had escaped continuing warfare was the Severn estuary, Dumnonia and South Wales; there Docco and other unnamed bishops survived; but elsewhere the bishops of the highland areas of Britain, who served a rough rural and military population, can never have attained to the strength and status of their lowland colleagues.

CHAPTER NINETEEN

SIXTH CENTURY MONKS

Britain

Good order prevailed in Britain so long as the victors of Badon lived. Gildas approved of the older bishops and clergy who, like the lay rulers, had 'each kept their own station'. Evil had come quickly, during the 520s and 530s. Tyrannical warlords who overawed laymen also appointed their own creatures to bishoprics, thereby spreading indolence and corruption among the lower clergy. Until the end of the fifth century, men like Docco and Illtud had been reared in the manners of a steady pre-war civilisation. But the men born two generations later, the adults of the 520s, had known nothing of past gentility; they had experienced only the violence of their own time, and they behaved as their education had taught them.

In the past, a few individuals turned away from society to find comfort in monasticism. Fastidius and the Sicilian Briton had known some monks early in the fifth century, direct followers of the teaching of Martin and of Victricius. By the middle of the century their example was followed in south-west Wales. Brioc, born of Irish colonist parents in Cardiganshire about 468, sought solitude in Cornwall, and later in Brittany; in his old age he attracted numerous disciples, when the monastic movement blossomed, but in younger years he was a lone hermit. Samson's father Ammon was born within a few years of Brioc, in nearby Demetia, then still Irish. His parents were sufficiently acquainted with the history and ideals of the monks to give him the name of the father of Egyptian monasticism; their fathers were younger contemporaries of Coelestius, who was perhaps also Demetian, and the distinctive names used by this family, Anna, Enoch, Samson, Umbrafel, denote an evangelical outlook that was alien to the polite British bishops of Patrick's time, and to the churchmen who served the warlords in Gildas' day. Monks were known, but they were few. Some monastic retreats had been founded by landed gentlemen, during and before the wars, but they are represented as comfortable places, recalling the milder austerities of Latin Europe, akin to those whose outlook John Cassian deplored. They obeyed the bishops, and made no known impact upon churchman or layman; they were as 'torpid' as the monasteries of Gaul.

Samson

Reform was the work of a single generation. Many of the earliest and best-remembered leaders were students at the school of Illtud, at Llanilltud Fawr, or Llantwit, in Glamorgan. Samson, Paul Aurelian, Gildas, Leonorus and others entered the school at the age of about five; and stayed there a dozen years or more. Their motive, method and achievement is most clearly seen in the Lives of Samson and Paul, both of which survive in early versions and rest upon contemporary originals. Samson is independently attested; he was present at a church council in Paris, about 557, and Gregory of Tours dates the events that brought him back to Brittany to the last weeks of 560. He died soon after, in old age. The oldest surviving Life was written some thirty or forty years later, about the year 600 or shortly before, and rests upon a contemporary original, composed 'in an elegant style' by Samson's cousin, Enoch, who had obtained stories of the saint's youth from his mother. Enoch's nephew gave verbal detail to the author, who also visited Britain to collect additional information.

He tells a vivid tale, whose incidents depict the reformers as their contemporaries saw them more clearly than any later description. Samson's father was a Demetian landowner, and also an *altrix*, companion of the king, probably Agricola; at the request of

> a learned master who lived in the far north and was much sought
> after by many provinces,

young Samson was sent to Illtud's school at the age of five; the northern master was perhaps Maucennus of Whithorn, who seems to have visited Demetia just before 500. When Samson said goodbye to his parents at the school, he

> did not cry as children usually do when they are taken from their
> father and their mother

but immediately began to learn his letters. By the age of fifteen his learning was precocious, his fasting immoderate; and he knew some practical medicine. At an early age he was ordained priest and deacon by bishop Dubricius, and aroused the jealousy of Illtud's nephews, who feared that he might succeed their uncle as head of the school and so deprive them of their 'earthly inheritance'. He sought and gained a transfer to another monastery of Illtud's, newly founded by Piro on Ynys Pyr, Caldey Island, where his austerity and theological scholarship astounded his fellows.

One winter's evening messengers rode to Caldey to tell him that his father was gravely ill and not expected to live. Samson

> was obdurate, and answered 'Tell your master I have forsaken
> Egypt and must not return thereto. God has power to heal the
> sick'.... Piro was shocked ... and said, 'Why do you answer like
> that, saint? You ought not to do God's work carelessly. It is your
> business to care for the passing of souls'.... Saint Samson looked

at him, and stood still awhile. Then he answered 'God's will be done; for the Lord and for the winning of souls I am ready to suffer in all things . . . I will go.'

The old man recovered when Samson reached home; he and his wife, his brother and younger sons all took monastic vows; but Samson rejected his sister, 'given over to worldly pleasures', adding grudgingly, 'but we must maintain her, since she is a human being'. Most of the family property was given to the poor, a little retained; the sister was no doubt not the only dependent. But on his three days' journey home, accompanied by a young deacon, Samson's zealous severity occasioned an unhappy incident.

As they passed through a great forest, they heard a wild voice near them, shrieking horribly. The terrified deacon . . . let go the pack horse . . . and fled. . . . Samson . . . followed . . . and saw a hideous hairy witch, a decrepit old woman, with a three pronged spear in her hand. Samson, trusting in Christ, tied his horse to a tree . . . and chased her. The witch ran into the deacon and knocked him down. . . . Samson . . . cried out 'In the name of Christ Jesus I order you to stay where you are.' She stood still trembling, and dropped the spear, as Samson came up, asking 'Who and what are you?' 'I am a witch,' she answered . . . 'there is no one left of our family but I; my eight sisters and my mother are still living, but all nine are in another wood. I was married to a husband on this estate, but my man is dead, so I cannot leave the wood.' 'Can you cure the

---

Map 24

Main concentrations of dedications to

///   David and Teilo

\\\   Cadoc

||| Illtud

≡   Beuno

⊞   Tysylio

D   Houses of Docco

▫   Roman towns

•   Main monastic centres

+   Bishops' Sees

MAP 24 MONKS IN WALES

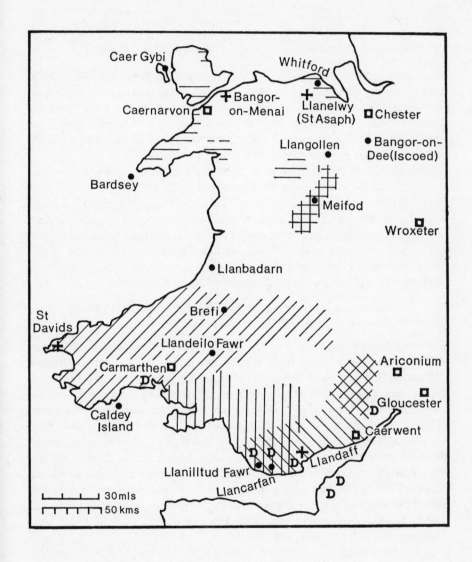

Caer Gybi

Whitford

Caernarvon — Bangor-on-Menai

Llanelwy (St Asaph)

Chester

Llangollen

Bangor-on-Dee (Iscoed)

Meifod

Wroxeter

Bardsey

Llanbadarn

Brefi

St Davids

Llandeilo Fawr

Ariconium

Carmarthen

D

Gloucester

Caldey Island

D

Caerwent

D D + D

Llanilltud Fawr

Llandaff

Llancarfan

D D

30 mls

50 kms

man you have knocked down?' Samson asked. 'I cannot and will not . . . do good' she answered. 'I call upon the name of Almighty God,' Samson replied 'to prevent you doing any more harm to anyone . . .' Immediately . . . she fell down and died. Samson ran back to the half dead deacon, who recovered in not more than an hour and a half, very grateful that thanks to Saint Samson the wicked witch's three pronged spear had not pierced his skin.

There must have been many half-crazed old men and women, as terrified as they were terrifying, subsisting in woodland shelters when their normal livelihoods were gone. Though witches were fearful and loathsome creatures, Samson's fatal curse caused murmurs. Bishop Dubricius, who was visiting Ynys Pyr, 'as he usually did at Lent', conducted a thorough enquiry; but he acquitted Samson, and confirmed his appointment as steward of the monastery.

Some time later, Piro drank more at dinner one night than his head or stomach could hold; forced to get up, wandering alone in the darkness in the *claustra*, the monastic enclosure, he fell down the well. He let out a *magna ululatio*, a great yell. The brethren came to his rescue and pulled him out alive, but the old man died of shock. None the less, in the eyes of Samson's cousin, he was 'a saint and a gentleman', *vir sanctus et egregius*. But his fate reinforced the preaching of the stricter moralists, and the chastened monks chose Samson to succeed him. Their comfortable standards are revealed in their praise of him, that

> no one ever saw him drunk, or even talking thickly; he never forbade the cup, but the cup never hurt him.

The praise implies that the cup sometimes hurt other Caldey monks; and within eighteen months monks and abbot alike regretted the election. Samson did not find among them the passionate ideal that he sought, the fervour of the few that Gildas 'longed and thirsted' to share; the Caldey monks were rather to be numbered among 'those of my own order' who shared the worldliness of the rest of the clergy. Soon the brethren came to consider that Samson was more of a hermit than a community monk, for 'in the midst of ample dinners and abundant drink he strove to fast and thirst'. He himself 'longed for the desert', and his opportunity came when 'some learned Irishmen returning from Rome' visited Caldey. With the bishop's permission, he accompanied them to Ireland, and stayed there a short while, somewhere in the north-east, performing numerous healing miracles. His patients included an abbot, who bequeathed his cell to him, and thereafter followed him as his disciple.

It was the turning-point in his life. Samson must then have been in his thirties, the date somewhere in the 520s. The travellers from Rome cannot but have told tales of Benedict of Nursia, a Roman noble who had withdrawn from secular life soon after 500, at the age of about twenty, to live in a cave on the banks of the river Arno; after a quarter of a century, as his fame spread throughout Italy and attracted numerous disciples, he found the banks of the Arno too accessible to the envious and curious, and removed, about the year 530, to his permanent retreat on Monte Cassino. Samson had long seen his own vocation as 'quitting Egypt', as two centuries before the monks had left the cities to live in the Egyptian desert. Their example had long been admired in his family. On his return from Ireland he left Caldey. He sent his uncle to take charge of his Irish cell, and himself withdrew to an abandoned fort on the Severn, but soon left it for a nearby cave.

He was not allowed to remain long in solitude. A synod appointed him, against his will, first as 'abbot of the monastery which Germanus is said to have founded', and then as bishop of an unnamed diocese north of the Severn. Throughout his life Samson, like Patrick, was guided by dreams and visions, and on this occasion a vision warned him to accept the bishopric. But soon afterward another vision told him to emigrate; he settled the affairs of his diocese, said farewell to his mother and his family, and excommunicated his sister, who was 'living in an adulterous union'. He crossed to Cornwall, to the monastery of Docco, at St. Kew, where he suggested to the abbot Iuniavus that he should stay for a while. With polite embarrassment Iuniavus answered

> beloved father, it is better for the servant of God to continue his journey . . . your request to stay with us is not convenient, for you are *melior*, better than us; you might condemn us, and we might properly feel condemned by your superior merit; for I must make it clear to you that we have somewhat relaxed our original rules. . . . You had better go on to . . . Europe.

Samson was 'stupefied at this doctrine'. It was the same unresponsive hedonism that he had met at Caldey, perhaps also in his brief episcopate, the same indifference that distressed his contemporary, Gildas. Samson

> dismissed his ship, loaded his books and spiritual vessels on to his waggon, and harnessed to his carriage the two horses he had brought from Ireland, and . . . made his way to the southern sea that leads to Europe.

His stay in Cornwall was somewhat longer than the wording suggests, for in Tricurium, now called Trigg, the district of north Cornwall in which St. Kew lies, he dispersed a crowd of the subjects of count Gwedian, who were celebrating heathen rites about a standing stone, and with his pocket knife carved on it the sign of the cross; and the Life of Saint Petroc reports that when he landed nearby he found Samson in residence in a cell on the Padstow estuary. After some dispute Petroc evicted him. Samson moved again, to Castle Dore by Fowey, the insular capital of the Cornovian ruler Conomorus, where a chapel bore his name a few years later, and still does. But soon after he sailed abroad.

In Brittany he became bishop of the kingdom of Jonas of Dumnonie, with his see at Dol, in the north-east. When Conomorus mastered Brittany and killed Jonas, his son Iudual fled to Paris, but was imprisoned by king Childebert.

MAP 25 MONKS IN CORNWALL

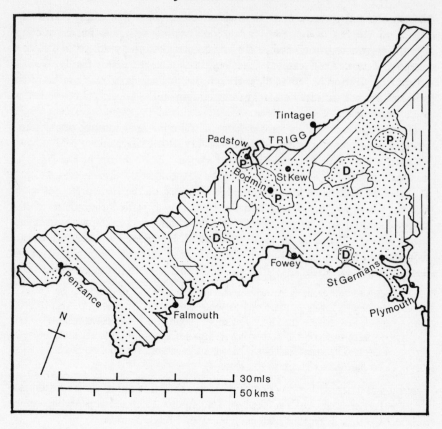

Parishes now or formerly named after

IRISH monks

The Saints of the Shannon

The Children of Brychan

Other Irish saints

BRITISH monks

D   David and Nun

P   Petroc

Old names not known

Samson, like many other saints of Brittany in Conomorus' time, also went to Paris. He is the only one among them who signed the acts of a church council held at Paris about 557, for thanks to his brief tenure of the Severn see he, unlike them, was a canonically consecrated bishop. He cured a court noble, whose support he enlisted, but found an enemy in the queen, whose machinations he miraculously defeated. In the end he prevailed, though the author of the Life was not aware that the occasion was the death of Childebert and the succession of Clothair. He came back with Iudual to Brittany in 560, and soon after died, 'his life and age completed'.

Paul Aurelian

Samson's biographer is mainly concerned with his life in Britain. Wrmonoc's Life of Paul Aurelian is chiefly concerned with Brittany, but contains some details of the saint's youth in Britain. The present text was set down in the ninth century, but uses a number of sixth-century spellings taken from a contemporary original Life. Paul's father was a landowner in Dumnonia who served as a military companion to a local king in Glevissig. The boy entered Illtud's school 'at a tender age' and left at sixteen because he felt the urge 'to penetrate the desert wilderness and live apart from civil society'. He settled with a few followers 'on a deserted site that belonged to his father's estates'. The fame of the hermit spread, and he was summoned to the court of 'king Mark, also called Quonomorius', who ruled 'different peoples who spoke four languages' from 'Villa Bannhedos', Castle Dore above Fowey, where Samson had been before him. Paul refused Mark's invitation to become the bishop of his kingdom, and crossed to Brittany, where he founded St. Pol-de-Leon and became 'bishop of the Osismi', the Roman name for the people and the bishop's see of the region. The date is plainly indicated. Mark Conomorus died in 560, Paul had then been long established in Brittany, but he crossed after Samson. His migration can hardly be much earlier than 540 or later than 550.

Samson and Paul were two among many hundreds of emigrant saints. Where dates are given, almost all are said to have crossed in the time of king Childebert, who reigned from 511 to 558. When dates are closer, they lie in the latter part of his reign. Leonorus died at the age of fifty-one, soon after 560; he was five when he entered Illtud's school, fifteen when he left. His migration cannot be earlier than 530, and was probably somewhat later. Winwaloe died in a year that was probably 583, and was already adult when his father reached Brittany. Teilo made a number of foundations in Wales before he crossed to Brittany in the hope of escaping the plague, about 550, and on the same occasion the aged Brioc hurried home to comfort his plague-stricken kinsmen in Cardigan, after he had been in Brittany for some years. Numerous other indications point to the same conclusion. The large-scale migrations to Brittany did not begin until after 530; Samson, Paul and probably Leonorus crossed the sea nearer to 540 than to 530. But there was an extensive migration well before the plague, and by about 545 many had crossed. Though new arrivals followed the pioneers later, the main weight of the emigration falls in the decade from 540 to 550.

The emigration to Brittany was one among several ways of achieving the ideals of new monks. Their aim was to get away from the 'society of man', to live alone with a few companions in caves or 'desert wildernesses'. Their Lives constantly cite by name the fathers of the Egyptian desert, especially Antony, and they deliberately imitated their practice and regulations. Very many found remote and deserted sites to hand in Wales and Dumnonia. Place names attest the scale of the movement and its locality. Sixth-century Latin usage calls the monastery *claustra*, enclosure, whence comes the English word 'cloister'. Its equivalent in Welsh was *llan*, whose literal meaning is enclosure. Well over six hundred Welsh towns and hamlets bear the name Llan, as do many hundreds in the Dumnonian lands and in Brittany. The numerous names that begin with *Tre-* or *Plou-* also derive from the terminology of the 6th century monks, and many of them were so named in the 6th and 7th centuries. The scale of the migration was large enough to entail a considerable transformation of society.

The saints did not set out to reform society. They gave it up as an evil to avoid. But, as in Egypt, the pioneers found that so many men flocked to the desert that they were driven to build a new society of a different kind, whether they liked it or no. Theirs was the first experience of a mass conversion to monasticism in the Latin west. Their experience differed from Egypt in one important respect. The eastern deserts were natural wildernesses that no effort of early man could make fertile; the deserts peopled by British saints were man-made, in lands depopulated by the decay of Rome; the effort of new cultivators easily reduced them to tillage and pasture.

The reasons that prompted men to move are not hard to see. Though the Roman civilisation of western Britain had not been physically destroyed, as in the lowlands, its strength had been sapped. It was a limb detached from a tree now dead. The unpredictable violence of the warlords weighed upon landowner, tenant and churchmen alike. At first, pioneer individuals who led a dedicated life in solitude were termed 'holy', *sancti*. The modern connotation of 'saint' did not arise until a later age, when the authority of Rome limited the use of the title in Europe to a restricted number of outstanding men long dead, and forbade its application to living persons; but in the fifth and sixth centuries, in Europe as in Britain, 'saint' was the normal and proper term for a living person of outstanding religious virtue. In late Roman Britain it applied not to monks in general, who were relatively few and unimpressive, but to men of notable piety who rejected the normal assumptions of lay society. The movement grew slowly, until a decisive moment, when public opinion approved the example of the *sancti* and began to see in them a possible protection against the ills that beset ordinary men. That moment was reached when the 'best councillors of the congregation' chose Samson for bishop, a man who had hitherto been regarded as an uncomfortable extremist even by his fellow monks; and when king Conomorus judged it wise to seek a monk, Paul Aurelian, as bishop of his kingdom. The date of both events is close to 540.

The turning-point coincided with the publication of Gildas' manifesto. It became the favourite text of the reformers, and accelerated their success. It denounced the *duces* who had usurped the authority of kings; and went on to arraign the churchmen who ought to have withstood them, but had connived at their crimes. Gildas protests that bishops and priests buy their places from the tyrants, and if they meet resistance in their diocese, they spend their substance on travelling overseas to seek consecration, to impose themselves on their country, proud and puffed up, on their return. They conduct services and preach in the churches, but instead of attacking the sins of the rulers and the people, they condone them and share in them. The evil extends even into the 'clergy of our order', priests who have taken a monastic vow. There are however a 'few, but very few' who have 'found the narrow way', whose life Gildas longs to share before he dies. These are the *sancti*, men like Samson and Paul Aurelian. The work was written late in the reign of Maelgwn, who died about 550. It cannot be much earlier than 540. But since the saints are still a 'very few', it cannot have been written after they inspired a mass movement in the early 540s. It was published just before the movement grew great, about the later 530s.

Gildas' book gave the new monasticism cohesion, and justified it in the face of existing society. The book succeeded because it came at the right moment, giving a voice to inarticulate men who were ready to reject that society. Such men were numerous. The Saints' Lives abound in tales of wicked persons who withstood the monks, but also record many who welcomed and protected them. Men of property gave them land; others led lay migrations in company with the monks, and some turned monk themselves. There were ascetics in small numbers elsewhere in Europe; but they became a mighty movement only in western Britain, because there men were able to heed them. In Italy, where the armies of Justinian were expelling the Goths, and in Gaul under the sons of Clovis, ascetics found no such response. There the ancient bond of landlord and peasant remained intact; the secular and ecclesiastical institutions of Rome were still strong. Benedict of Nursia thought and acted like Samson and Paul Aurelian. But he impressed Italy because he was exceptional. Few others imitated him and it was not possible to sprinkle the Italian countryside with hundreds of local copies of his monastery on Monte Cassino.

Almost nothing is known of the church that Gildas denounced. He says that until his generation ecclesiastics, like laymen, had 'kept their station'. The proper ordering of the church was still a diocesan episcopate, with monasteries subject to the bishops. The Saints' Lives record one such bishop, because he was well disposed to their aspirations. Dubricius visited Illtud, and Piro on Caldey Island, as a superior, investigating complaints and ordaining priests and deacons. The churches that bear his name are most frequent in the district called Ercig or Archenfeld, on the right bank of the Wye, opposite and below Hereford.

Archenfeld takes its name from the Roman town of Ariconium, Weston-under-Penyard, the other side of the Wye, nearer to Gloucester, but Dubricius' churches extend more widely, covering almost the whole of Gwent, the former *civitas* of the Silures; his see was probably its capital town, Caerwent, possibly Gloucester.

Episcopal sees had been designed to correspond with lay political states, Roman *civitates*. They functioned ill when the *civitates* ceased to be coherent states, and the remnant of their identity cannot long have survived the fall of Arthur's empire, shortly before 520. Gildas complains that kings appointed their own bishops, who sometimes sought consecration abroad if they could not get it at home. Though established bishops doubtless clung to their undivided sees, the kings might plead with justification that new political realities needed new diocesan boundaries; the principle of the church had always been one bishop for one state, and now that the Roman *civitates* had been replaced by new states, the bishops' sees should correspond to their frontiers.

Mounting pressure brought change. Samson was consecrated bishop north of the Severn. It may be that Dubricius had resisted the establishment of a new see designed for a royal nominee, but agreed to its creation if Samson was accepted as bishop. In Dumnonia, king Mark Conomorus sought Paul Aurelian as bishop of his own small kingdom, and bishop Wethenoc, whom Petroc encountered in the region of Bodmin and Padstow, had nothing of the status of a bishop of all Dumnonia, enthroned in Exeter. He too was clearly the bishop of a local king. By the 7th century, the new frontiers had become relatively stable; the greater abbots functioned as bishops of large kingdoms, Gwynedd and Powys, Cardigan, Demetia. But in the sixth century, the organisation of the episcopate was a matter of change, dispute and confusion. Once the monasteries were established, monks had little need of bishops; church order consigned to them certain necessary functions, chiefly the ordination of priests and the consecration of churches, but they were otherwise little esteemed, and are rarely mentioned unless they were monks themselves, or encountered them. Most early monks, like Samson and Paul Aurelian, rejected pressures to accept sees in Britain, and yielded only to the needs of colonists in Brittany. In south Wales, after Dubricius, only Teilo is regularly styled bishop; his chief monastery, at Llandeilo Fawr, commands the routes from Demetia to Glamorgan and Brecon; he was the patron of the reformers in Glevissig, and received grants from Agricola of Demetia. He was probably bishop of all Demetia, his nominal see Carmarthen, until in his old age the separate bishoprics of Glevissig and of St. David's were established. But Roman administrative divisions disappeared earlier, and a bishop of Gwent could no longer complain if his colleague poached within his diocese; each abbot had the effective power to choose the bishop whom he invited to ordain his priests, until established frontiers and hardening custom limited his choice.

The new monasteries became numerous in the 540s, and some of them were large. They were the first form of Christianity that the bulk of the countryside encountered at close quarters, for it is doubtful if the bishops and priests of the old sees had much effective contact with scattered local homesteads. The monasteries aroused eager support, and also fierce opposition. The numbers of single men who entered the new 'enclosures' as monks was in itself considerable; the Saints' Lives also emphasise that from the beginning monasteries, small and large, also maintained lay brothers, as Cassiodorus did in Italy, who brought their families to work the lands around them. Some monasteries, like Llantwit and Llancarfan, began upon the estates of large landowners who had turned monk. Others were built upon lands granted by a king or landowner, and the Lives have many tales of monks who were several times refused lands by wicked notables before a pious donor gave them ground. The original grant was often rapidly supplemented, and the Lives of the earliest founders, as well as later charter memoranda, frequently mention landlords' offers to make over estates, with their cultivators, to the monastery.

Grants of lands were doubtless often inspired by simple piety. But more practical consideration also operated. Once the monks had earned a wide respect among the population at large, they became powerful protectors. Kings and warlords might levy exactions upon lay landlord and peasant with little fear of opposition; but demands upon monastic lands and monastic tenants were sacrilege, not lightly to be risked when all men condemned it. Yet kings, and landlords who kept their estates intact, had good reason to resent the migration to the Llan. Each new recruit to the monastery, each estate placed under its control or protection, meant a loss of labour to the landlord, the loss of taxpayers and of army recruits to the king. Kings did not readily acquiesce, and the commonest miracles in the Lives of early saints are those that secure for the Llan a right of sanctuary and immunity from billeting, conscription and taxation. Commonly, in the fancies of the Lives, the evil king, Arthur, Maelgwn, or some local ruler, is blinded, swallowed up by the ground, or stricken with illness by the anger of the Lord; when he repents, the supernatural virtue of the saint cures him, and in gratitude he grants sanctuary or immunity. Miracles apart, the contest was a trial of strength between the old order and the new. The monks won early success because public opinion backed them, and their dependents enjoyed an enviable security against the exactions of royal government.

David

The monks sought solitude. Public support made them reformers, who transformed the character of the church and founded a new civil society within the kingdoms of the warlords. Their success divided them. There were many variant attitudes, but two sharply opposed outlooks crystallised, the practices of David of Demetia and those of Cadoc and Gildas. David is said to have been born in the 520s, and to have died in 589. He was baptised by Ailbe of Munster, who died in 528, and was taught by Paulinus, who was probably a pupil of Kebi and Docco, and was probably also the Paulinus who is styled 'defender of the faith, patriot, champion of justice', in Latin verses engraved upon his tombstone in a monastic churchyard near Pumpsaint, ten miles north of Llandeilo Fawr.

David was the pattern of the stricter monks, styled *meliores*, or 'better', the term that Iuniavus of St. Kew had apprehensively applied to Samson. Like Samson, his aim is said to have been to 'imitate the monks of Egypt'. His Rule rested on vigorous manual labour throughout the daylight hours, the evenings devoted to reading, writing and prayer. His mottoes were 'he that does not work, neither shall he eat', and 'comfortable ease is the mother of vice'. His monks therefore farmed without draught animals; their shoulders pulled the plough, 'each his own ox', their arms 'driving spades into the earth'. Their food was bread, cabbage and water, and David was therefore called *Aquaticus*, the water-drinker; there was 'no *meum* and *tuum*', no mine and thine, and even to speak of 'my book' was a punishable offence, since all was held in common. Unlike most other abbots, David resolutely refused to accept land or other endowments from laymen. 'Clothing was cheap, commonly of skins'; conversation was kept to the minimum, and discipline enforced absolute obedience. Aspirants to the strict rule were tested by being kept outside the gates for ten days, their patience tried by abuse from within, and thereafter by submission to a long probationary period before acceptance.

This extreme rigidity was a reaction against the comfortable ease of St. Kew and Caldey Island, and it also contrasted with the moderate conduct of Illtud. The *meliores* felt themselves to be superior, and provoked criticism as well as respect. In his later writings Gildas fiercely attacked them.

> Abstinence from bodily foods without charity is useless. The real *meliores* are those who fast without ostentation . . . not those who think themselves superior because they refuse to eat meat . . . or to ride on a horse or in a carriage; for death enters into them by the windows of pride. . . .

He accused them of social egalitarianism; it was a legacy of earlier British thought that he did not himself inherit; for

> they criticise brethren who do not follow their arrogant conceits. . . . They eat bread by measure, and boast of it beyond measure; they drink water, and with it the cup of hatred. Their meals are dry dishes and backbiting. . . . When they meditate their 'Great Principles' it is from contempt, not from love. They put the serf before his master, the mob before its king, lead before gold, iron before silver. . . . They set fasting above charity, vigils above justice, their own conceits above concord, their cell above the church, severity above humility; in a word, they prefer man to God. It is not the Gospels they obey, but their own will, not the apostle but their own pride. They forget that the position of the stars in heaven is not equal, and that the offices of the angels are unequal.

Gildas vigorously defended those whom the *meliores* attacked, the

> abbot . . . who owns animals and carriages, because he is physically
> weak or because it is the custom of the country.

Such an abbot was less sinful than

> those who drag ploughs about and drive spades into the earth with
> arrogance and prejudice.

What was virtue to David was vice to Gildas. Like Paul and Samson, Gildas had been brought up at Illtud's school. Illtud was a nobleman on his own estates who taught classical learning and the scriptures. He gently rebuked Samson's excessive asceticism, and gave no encouragement to Paul's urge for the desert, though he did not hinder it. Even the strict Samson is praised not as a water drinker, but as a moderate drinker of wine, whom 'no man ever saw slightly mellow'. Illtud is also said to have maintained a hundred labourers, and to have continued to receive the rent of his tenants. His school lies in a full Roman tradition, akin to that established in Italy in the next generation, about 540, by Cassiodorus, a learned noble who had been the minister of successive Gothic monarchs; his monks lived well upon the rents of their peasants, but they treated them benevolently, according to their founder's precept,

> teach your peasants good conduct; do not exploit them with new
> and heavy impositions, but call them often to your feasts.

Cadoc

Gildas was a conservative admirer of the old social order, of its privilege of rank and property. He deplored David's extremism, but he found himself on the defensive against the growing strength of the radicals, and was driven to reach commonsense compromise as more and more monks adopted the rule of David, or moved to houses where it was observed. He advised that

> abbots of the stricter rule should not admit monks from an abbot
> somewhat less strict; but similarly, less strict abbots should not
> restrain monks who are inclined to the stricter rule.

Sampson's outlook lay somewhat nearer to David's than to Gildas' and Illtud's. But the opposite pole to David was the monastery of Cadoc, Llancarfan, also called Nantcarfan, in Glamorganshire. The son of a local king, schooled by an Irish teacher at Caerwent, Cadoc sought ample estates with numerous rent-paying tenants, and kept his own labourers; unlike any other recorded British saint, he also maintained a hundred men-at-arms in the hill-fort above his monastery. He inherited his father's secular kingdom and ruled it without renouncing his abbacy, 'abbot and king over Gwynnliauc after his father', 'holding both the secular government and the abbacy of Nantcarfan', 'appointed by his father to rule after him'. The concepts of David and Cadoc clashed in the middle of the century. The Synod of Brefi is described in the Lives of both. In the David version, the saint accused his enemies of Pelagianism, perhaps with reason, and won a resounding victory. The Cadoc version admits defeat, excuses it by alleging that David deliberately and unfairly chose a time when Cadoc was absent abroad, and recounts Cadoc's fury on his return, that was cooled by his Irish pupil Finnian, but was ended only by the direct intervention of an angel. The opposing viewpoints were welcomed most widely by different social classes, among different nations in different regions; the adherents of David and of Teilo have left plentiful traces in the poorer uplands where Irish settlers were most numerous; but the tradition of Cadoc and Illtud is strongest in the wealthier Vale of Glamorgan.

The initial vigour of the British monks was confined to the decades about 550, and its strength lay in south Wales, Dumnonia and Brittany. Elsewhere reform was late and limited. In north Wales, Maelgwn resisted the monks; it was probably only after his death that Daniel came from Demetia to found the great Bangor on the Menai Straits. Most of north-west Wales traced its monastic inspiration to a dimly remembered mission from southern Brittany, headed by Cadfan, whose most important foundation was the monastery of Paternus at Llanbadarn by Aberystwyth. The few effective saints of Powys belong to the end of the century, and the monastery of Bangor-on-Dee was comparatively new when the Angles massacred its monks about 614. Throughout north and central Wales, places named Llan, followed by a saint's name, are rarer than in the south.

The Rest of Britain

Elsewhere in Britain traces of monks are fewer. Northern Britain knew a single outstanding leader, Kentigern. Exiled in youth, he is recorded as bishop of Senlis, near Paris, in 549 and again about 557. Some years later a change of government recalled him to the kingdom of the Clyde, where his principal monastery, Glasgow, became the nucleus of a great city. In southern and central England the traditions that might have remembered saints were lost when the British language gave place to English. A few notices survive. The story of Collen sends him east from Glastonbury and brings him to Southampton, though his best-known monastic foundation is Llangollen, on the Dee. The names of David and of Samson are remembered at a dozen places up the Fosse Way from Exeter to Newark, and thence to York; but they are absent on most of the central section of the road that was settled by the English in the fifth century. Irish monks are reported to have founded Abingdon and to have visited other pagan English peoples, perhaps in Norfolk. The Armorican British Winwaloe was remembered at the farther end of the Icknield Way, in Hertfordshire and in Norfolk; Cadoc is said to have preached on the further borders of the kingdoms of the Clyde, and to have established at least one monastery in a

MAP 26 MONKS IN THE NORTH

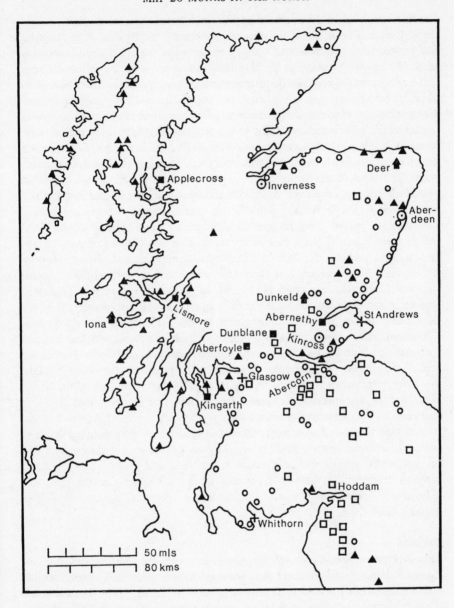

+ Bishops Sees

Dedications to ○ Ninian □ Kentigern ▲ Columba

■ Main centres of Irish monasticism ⊙ Other places

Pennine kingdom. In the north, bishop Wilfred 'listed the church lands . . . that the British had abandoned' and secured them for himself; British monasteries had existed there. In the south, enough remained of the old Roman monastery of St. Alban by Verulamium for king Offa to refound it in the eighth century.

The fragments of evidence do no more than prove the obvious, that a Christian church survived into the 6th century in most of Britain, ready to be reformed by the monastic pioneers. It was plainly feeble, the ghost of an urban church in a land where what remained of the towns had lost their grip upon the country. Even in Europe, where towns retained authority, the language of the church equated the country folk, *pagani*, with non-Christians, and for centuries churchmen had cause to condemn continuing heathen rites; for though no other organised religion remained, men who accepted Christianity did not thereby cease to be pagan. In Britain, Samson and others attacked heathen ceremonies and their successors were obliged to admit many pre-Christian observances, which were tolerated for centuries to come. The late Roman missionary adherents of Victricius and Martin had little time to evangelise the countryside or establish rural priests and churches before disaster overwhelmed them; and when the advancing frontiers of archaeology learn to recognise the religious beliefs of the early 6th-century warlords and their peasant subjects, they are also likely to uncover rites outrageous to the faith of devout Christians. Christianity was still the religion of kings and lords and townsmen, and nothing suggests that anything but the name had touched the bulk of the rural population before the coming of the monks. To most of the peasants, the monks brought not only monasteries, but Christianity itself. Thanks to the upheavals of the fifth century, the monastic reformers found their first response and strongest centre in the lands about the Severn estuary, the only region of Roman lowland wealth that the wars had spared; there, the example of the reformers inspired a mass movement in the 540s, but in less than a generation, before it had had time to arouse comparable enthusiasm in the north and in the fertile lowlands, English conquest cut short its expansion. After the conquest, monasteries and Christianity were carried to the north and the lowlands, not by the British monks, but by their Irish pupils.

Ireland

The fervour of British monasticism was soon spent, cut short by the agony of national defeat; but in Ireland the monasteries were to retain an inexhaustible vitality for centuries, and to impart it to most of Europe. The Irish and the British movements grew up together, each constantly renewing the inspiration of the other. The traditions of both countries acknowledge their mutual debt without rivalry. Christianity itself had come from Britain, in the time of Patrick. After him Mocteus, Mael and many others of the first Irish Christian leaders were British; the earliest Irish abbot, Enda, was schooled in Britain and guided in his novel experiment by British monks. But from the beginning the Irish

MAP 27 MONKS IN IRELAND

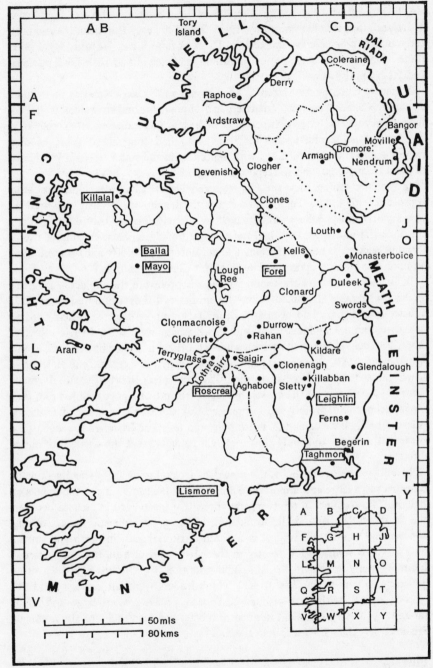

Chief Foundations of ● The 6th Century; ▭ The 7th Century.
Inset, the Irish National Grid

also inspired the British; it was the visit of Irish monks, and a few years' stay in Ireland, that enabled Samson to break free of the easy European traditions of early British monasticism and to found a mass movement. He and David both came from the most Irish region of Britain, and David had both Irish teachers and Irish pupils, as well as British.

Monastic Christianity blazed as fiercely and as fast in Ireland as in Britain, and at the same time; for Irishmen had similar reasons to welcome the re-forming preachers. The Irish colonists in Britain had experienced the material and intellectual sophistication of Rome, and had transmitted some of that experience to their kinsmen at home, especially in the south. Ireland was ready to learn from Rome, and to respect its religion.

In the later 5th century, the Christian religion of Rome meant bishops, who consorted with kings. To most Irishmen the bishops necessarily appeared as new style Druids, wizards strengthened by the power of a Deity mightier than the ancestral gods; but they had not the stature of prophets, capable of transforming society. Then, in Britain and in Europe, as in Ireland, monks were a minor excrescence upon the fringes of the Christian church.

In Britain in the 530s the monks voiced the protest of the subject against the violence of tyrants. Irishmen suffered a similar evil. For a hundred years Irish attacks upon Britain had been stilled; military captains had used their arms at home, to found kingdoms great and small, whose wars wasted their subjects. Abortive recent attempts to revive assaults on Britain had been beaten back by the brief power of Arthur's empire, and returning warriors increased the violence at home. Soon after, the successes of the British reformers made their faith the main form of Christianity on the coasts that faced Ireland, and gave visible proof that monasteries could protect the humble against the worst excesses of arbitrary rulers. The Irish welcomed their example, and for most Irishmen the monastery became the first and only form of Christianity that touched their lives directly.

Thanks to their early links, the monks of Ireland grew from small groups of eccentrics to a large and important community at the same time as the monks of Britain. The accounts of the two generations that intervened in Ireland between the death of Patrick and the foundation of the great monastic houses chiefly concern the labours of bishops, in a dozen territorial sees, in north and south; of a very few monasteries, mostly in the north; and of a number of scattered hermits, many of them British. Irish tradition rightly distinguished these generations, named the 'first order', whose leaders were 'all bishops', and the 'second order', with 'few bishops and many priests', when large and small monasteries were established in great numbers, and many tens of thousands of Irishmen left their homes to join them.

Finnian

The Irish records are much fuller than the British, and give the same close dates many times over. The 'second order' began in the last years of king Tuathal, who reigned from 532 to 544. The 'master of the saints', called the 'abbot of the second order', the 'best of the saints', was Finnian of Clonard. He died in the plague, about 550, after many years' work. He was baptised by Abban, nephew and companion of bishop Ibar, who had died in 499, and he was educated by Foirtchern, Patrick's royal convert, who was born about 440, the grandson of Loegaire of Ireland and of Vortigern of Britain. Finnian was an almost exact contemporary of Samson and of Gildas, born about the years 490 to 500, very near to the time of Badon. At the age of thirty Finnian went to 'study with the elders of Britain', and on his return brought two British monks with him. He was well received by king Muiredach of south Leinster, who reigned about the years 530 to 560, and set out on a missionary tour through Leinster and Connacht, preaching the ideas that he had learned in Britain, at first founding a few small monasteries, at one of which, Mugny, he is said to have stayed for 'seven years'.

After his travels, Finnian established his permanent home at Clonard and made it the nursery of Irish monasticism. The date cannot be far from 540, since a previous incident is dated to the reign of Tuathal, and is therefore later than 532; it was also some considerable time before his death about 550. The place was central, on the borders of Meath and Leinster, about twenty miles from the royal capital of Tara, and the same distance from Brigit's great house at Kildare, previously the largest monastic centre in Ireland. The area was peculiarly suitable, and deliberately chosen, for many of the principal houses founded by Finnian's pupils, Durrow, Birr, Clonmacnoise, Clonfert, Terryglass and others, lie close together, south-west of Clonard, concentrated in a small area barely thirty miles square, which straddles the frontiers between the four provincial kingdoms of Meath and Leinster, Connacht and Munster. Unlike their fifth-century predecessors, the monks chose a territory as withdrawn as possible from the seats of power of the main kings, and its many monasteries early made it a compact region, the heartland of the new society. In eastern and central Ireland men responded to its promise, but in the west, in Donegal, Connacht and western Munster, no major mainland houses are recorded till the seventh century, and then they are few.

Finnian's teaching was reinforced by the success of his monastic colleagues in Britain. 'The saints of Ireland came from every point to learn wisdom from him' at Clonard. The claims made by the authors of his Life are also accepted by the biographers of his pupils. Many of them came to him from other teachers, Columba of Iona from Gemman, Columba of Terryglass from Colman Cule, Ciaran of Clonmacnoise, the 'smith's son', from Enda's Aran. They, and many others who left a great name in Ireland, were for a few years contemporaries at Clonard. Women came too. Finnian had to assign a king's daughter for a short time to the care of the embarrassed Ciaran, 'until we can build a house for virgins'. The house was soon built, and placed under the care of Finnian's mother and sister. His pupil Dagaeus, and others later in the century vigorously encouraged double monasteries for both sexes.

Finnian's monks lived by their own labour, not on rents. He was

> full of knowledge, like a scribe most learned in teaching the law of God's commands. . . . With great tenderness he healed the minds and bodies of those who came to him. . . . From a pure heart he loved others. . . . He ate nothing but bread and vegetables, and drank nothing but water, save that on feast days he partook of a little wheaten bread, a small piece of fish, and a cup of beer or whey. . . . He never slept on a bed, but on the bare ground, with a stone for a pillow. . . . He was kind to others, austere and harsh to himself.

His diet and habit are akin to the rule of David, though the tenderness, emphasised again and again in the Irish tradition of his pupils, is not matched in the tradition of David in Britain. The Irish-language Life of Finnian tells a picturesque tale, that while in Britain he was called upon to adjudicate between David, Cathmael (Cadoc) and Gildas, contestants for the 'headship and abbacy of the island of Britain', and decided for David. The setting is unhistorical, for the controversy did not mature until after Finnian's death; but it enshrines a historical truth, for the discipline that Ireland learnt from Finnian was nearer to the rule of David than to the attitudes of Cadoc or of Gildas.

Finnian died in the plague, not much more than ten years after the foundation of Clonard. Several of his pupils had already left him. Ciaran, born about 517, and Columba of Iona, born about 521, were in their twenties, Columba of Terryglass probably somewhat older. Their lives were modest, but less austere than Finnian's. Ciaran went to an island in Lough Ree, and left it to found Clonmacnoise a year before his death, in 550. Tradition makes Ciaran's Clonmacnoise less strict than Clonard. He performed a miracle with wine brought by 'merchants from Gaul', but wine was a drink as alien to Finnian as to David, and so was the commercial agriculture that made such imports possible.

The plague wasted the Irish saints even more severely than the British. But the survivors outdid the energy of their predecessors, and the movement was spread by Finnian's pupils and by their pupils thereafter; the heirs of Columba of Iona were to win the greater part of the English to Christianity and monasticism. Fintan of Clonenagh was a pupil of Columba of Terryglass, and Comgall, who lived from 515 to 605, studied at both Clonenagh and at Ciaran's Clonmacnoise before he founded the great Irish school of Bangor in 559. There his outstanding pupil was Columban, who left Bangor for Gaul in 590, at the age of fifty, to found the monasteries of Luxeuil and Bobbio and to initiate the monasticism of the Franks and Lombards. Columban's numerous surviving letters are almost the only contemporary words that survive from early Irish monasticism, and are our only authentic guide to the outlook and aims of a sixth-century Irish monk, born within a year or so of the foundation of Clonard. That outlook is in essentials the same that the medieval Lives attribute to Finnian, Comgall and their fellows.

Columba

The greatest of the second generation monks was Columba. He was born an heir to the throne of Ireland, and in adult years his tremendous personality over-shadowed his cousins, to whom the throne passed. Royal status as well as his personal stature set him apart from other men and other monks. Tradition contrasted him with the plebeian Ciaran, with whom he is said to have quarrelled in youth. The Columban version emphasises that the dispute turned on con-flicting views, both widely held, and not on personalities alone, for Ciaran died at the age of 33 leaving a golden memory, but Columba's long life was stormy; he is made to comment

> Blessed is God who called Ciaran from this world in his youth.
> If he had lived to old age, he would have aroused many men's hostility.

Columba cannot have been much more than twenty when he came to Finnian, and in his early years he did not forget his birth. He placed his first principal monastery at Derry, in his own territory, hard by the court of his royal cousin. Plain monks might well trust a man of Ciaran's plebeian origins more readily. Yet though some might fear, many more men joined the monasteries of the royal monk than those of any lesser founder. By the time of his decisive quarrel with king Diarmait in 561, he commanded by far the largest body of monks in Ireland, as well as the largest secular army. He fought for the rights of an in-dependent church against a king who opposed its claims. But the armies that won the battle of Cuil Dremhni were those of his dynastic relatives and their allies. Columba was personally present at the battle, praying for his own side against his monastic rival Finnian of Moville, who prayed for his enemies. Men believed in the power of prayer and attributed both the Ui Neill victory and the fearful slaughter to the greater efficacy of Columba's prayer. There was a real danger that the Christian saint might inherit the authority of the Druid, and also of the pagan king, that one man might become both head of the church and master of the secular kingdom.

Adomnan, writing a century after Columba's death, reports the sequel. Columba was excommunicated by a synod 'on certain pardonable and excusable charges', wrongly as the future showed.

> When St. Brendan of . . . Birr . . . kissed him, some of the elders protested . . . , 'Why do you . . . kiss the excommunicate?' Brendan answered, 'I have seen a column of bright fire going before the man of God whom you reject, and angels accompanying

him'.... They did not then dare to proceed with the excommunication.... This happened at Telltown.

Adomnan elsewhere sets down what he considers 'excusable charges'; among his list of Columba's merits, he includes the claim that

> in the terrible clash of battle, the power of his prayer obtained from God that some rulers should be victorious and other kings be conquered.

Prayer so used seemed a virtue to Adomnan in Iona a century later; but it was a dangerous offence to Columba's contemporaries. The tradition of Derry is more prosaic, told with greater detail and less apology.

> When the news of the battle came to the ears of the saints of Ireland, Columba was assailed as the author and occasion of so great a loss of life. A general meeting decided that it was proper for him to perform a solemn penance, to be determined by Saint Lasrian.... Lasrian enjoined him to leave Ireland and his family, and to spend the rest of his life in exile abroad, where he might win more souls for Christ than he had caused to die in battle. Columba sadly undertook the penance prescribed, saying to Lasrian 'So be it'.

Lasrian of Devenish was the eldest of the Irish saints. His wisdom and the courage of Brendan solved an intolerable dilemma. Events had passed almost beyond the control of personalities, for the pardon or the punishment of Columba equally threatened to destroy the monks. Their movement had been born in protest against dynastic warfare and military violence, but now the greatest of the monks was seen to have caused slaughter on an outrageous scale; yet all men knew that he had fought chiefly to uphold the churchman's right of sanctuary. It was impossible to ignore his offence, but also impossible to abandon the cause he had defended. Excommunication threatened a still greater danger, underlined because the synod was convened at Telltown, in the territory of his enemy Diarmait. To have condemned Columba then and there invited the convocation of a counter-synod in Ui Neill lands, whose opposite anathema might threaten a religious war fought with sword and spear. If Columba's action were condoned, then the churchman's prayer became a military weapon necessary to the armament of all kings; if he were excommunicated at Diarmait's behest, the church submitted to the will of the High King on earth.

Exile without excommunication, voluntarily accepted, removed an appalling danger. Columba remained head of the community of Columban monasteries; his exile stilled the threat inherent in his royalty, and warned future churchmen against over-involvement in the political ambition of kings. The lesson was learnt, and the records of the next century are rich in stories of monks and abbots who deemed it proper to aid their kings with prayer in defence of their own subjects against enemy invaders, but condemned their own rulers when they attacked their neighbours. This was the attitude that Irish monks were to bring to Northumbria, and to teach to Bede, and that the Irish and the English were to impress upon the churchmen of Europe.

Gildas in Ireland

More than twenty years had passed since the initial outburst of monastic enthusiasm. The monks had met and overcome the enmity of great kings, even before Columba's wars. As in Britain, they had run foul of the lesser lords whose manpower they took away, and had been denounced as seducers, *seductores*. Now the monasteries were established beyond challenge; but rapid spontaneous growth had brought differences of outlook, practice and discipline, whose danger the crisis signalled. It was time to take stock and consolidate.

The Irish looked abroad for guidance. The tradition of Gildas, preserved in Brittany, held that he was summoned to Ireland by king Ainmere to 'restore ecclesiastical order'; he taught the Irish 'the rule of regular discipline', and put emphasis on the recruitment of new monks from among 'the poor as well as the nobility', and on freeing those 'enslaved by the tyrants'. Irish tradition also held that after Columba's exile

> the elders of Ireland sent trustworthy envoys with a letter to Saint Gildas. . . . When he read their letters, and also Columba's . . . he commented 'The man who wrote this is filled with the holy Spirit.' One of the envoys answered 'Yes, he is. But he has none the less been censured by a synod of Ireland, because he ordered his family to flight, when they were in danger of death.'

Irish tradition also attributed its liturgy to Gildas, together with David and Docco. Among the British, the Cambrian Annals enters Gildas' journey to Ireland under the year 565, two years after Columba's exile. The tradition survives independently in the three countries, and is confirmed by contemporary notices. Thirty years later, Columban cited to Gregory the Great a ruling given by 'Gilta' to 'Vinianus', Finnian. Columban reported Gildas' advice to an Irish monastic leader. He was a contemporary, and also a first-hand witness. Aged about 25 in 565, the year in which Gildas is said to have visited Ireland, he was a monk at Comgall's Bangor. Comgall was a close associate of Columba, deeply involved in the crisis, and visited him in Iona, also in the year 565. In making such a visit in that year he cannot but have conveyed Gildas' views to Columba, or Columba's to Gildas, or both. Bangor was already a pre-eminent monastery, that must have entertained Gildas during his visit. It is likely that Columban then met Gildas personally and heard his advice himself. Parts of the advice are extant, in a number of extracts from the letters of Gildas, preserved in Irish texts, that deal with various problems of monastic discipline, and also in the Penitential, or monastic Rule, that bears Gildas' name and is probably substantially his work.

The Rule of Gildas contrasts sharply with the Penitential ascribed to David. David's rules are limited to prescribing heavy punishment for grave sins, sexual offences, murder, perjury, drunkenness, usury and the like. They had little influence on later Irish regulations. But Gildas' Rule and the late sixth-century Penitential of Finnian, perhaps the Vinianus to whom he wrote, underlie the seventh-century Rules of Cummian, and of Columban, which form the main basis of later Irish monastic discipline. Unlike David, Gildas ignores murder, perjury, usury, and concentrates on a score of commonsense rulings concerned with the normal problems of day-to-day monastic life.

> A man who nurses anger long in his heart is in death . . . for anger
> breeds murder. . . . A monk who thinks another has wronged him
> must tell his abbot, not as an accusation, but as a genuine effort to
> heal the breach.

Penances are lighter, and vary with the circumstances of the individual and of the monastery, as well as of the offence; the punishment of three hours' standing night vigil is to be enforced only

> if there is plenty of beer and meat in the monastery, and the man is
> of strong physique; if the food is poor, let him recite twenty-eight
> or thirty psalms, or do extra work.

Common sense enjoins masses for good kings, not bad ones, and prompts the final tactful exhortation,

> if a monk sees one of the brethren breaking rules, he must tell his
> abbot. He should not be deemed an informer . . . provided that he
> first tries to persuade the wrongdoer to make a private confession
> to the abbot.

In his letters Gildas pleaded with the clergy to accept the authority of a superior without dispute, and with ecclesiastical superiors not to despise their clergy. The language and detail of the regulations imply that they were first devised for Britain; but they were preserved in Ireland, by Irishmen who adapted them from Gildas. Their controlled and disciplined austerity discountenances fierce asceticism, and matches the concept of the abbot's rule patterned by Finnian of Clonard, 'kind to others, harsh and austere to himself'.

Irish monasticism easily accepted a workable blend of the divergent interpretations of the monastic ideal. It lacked the tensions that had sharpened conflict in Britain. It had inherited no Roman legacy of wealthy landowners who lived a monastic life in their own mansions; it was equally free of the zealous radicalism that was provoked by the great inequalities of wealth in Britain, and was continued by the traditions of David. Gildas' tolerant conservatism discouraged extreme asceticism, but the society of Ireland did not permit the opulent ease that had distressed Samson and David. The quiet, simple and affectionate life derived from Finnian and Gildas was now guaranteed against secular interference; unembarrassed by the cares of administering monastic estates, the monks were able to develop an astonishing outburst of creative energy.

Art

Their energy was many-sided. Bold inventions in agriculture changed the economy of much of Ireland. Contemplation of the universe prompted searching enquiry into scientific phenomena, as uninhibited as any speculations since those of Hellenistic Greece. Irish ideas were to disturb the received dogma of the church, but they stimulated the education and the learning of Europe for several centuries. Probably towards the end of the sixth century, and probably a little earlier than in Britain, the monks pioneered a vernacular alphabet, and began to write down both the scriptures, and thereafter the stories and traditions of their homeland, in the spoken language of the people. Irish became the first medieval European language to be written. Ireland needed literacy, for it had less Latin than Britain; but Irish example soon taught the British and the English to write their own tongues.

Literacy brought important consequences; but the outstanding intellectual achievement of the sixth-century monks was their art. Dagaeus, who probably died about 586

> ingeniously and wonderfully constructed for the abbots and other saints of Ireland bells ... staffs, crosses, reliquaries ... cups ... and book covers ... sometimes plain, sometimes decorated with gold and silver and precious stones.

He spent some time at 'the little monastery called the school' at Devenish where he 'taught reading and writing and manual skills', and thereafter passed 'many years' at Bangor, where, among other works, he

> wrote an outstanding Gospel, and made for it a marvellous case.

The Book of Durrow was written not many decades later, and the splendid manuscript art, that Dagaeus is held to have initiated, matured through the succeeding centuries.

A few books and some ornaments survive to illustrate the splendour of early Irish monastic art. But their greatest pride was in the churches that these works adorned. Most of the great churches have been altogether rebuilt in later ages, and in the few early buildings that remain the rough exterior masonry, now unplastered, and the bare interior give little idea of their original magnificence. One vivid picture is preserved in words. Cogitosus, the biographer of Brigit, described the great church of Kildare as it was about 650.

> I must not omit the miracle which attended the repairs to the church in which rest the bodies of Bishop Conlaed and the virgin Saint Brigit. They are placed in elaborate monuments, to right and left of the decorated altar, and are splendidly bedecked with gold and

silver, jewels and precious stones, and have gold and silver crowns hanging above them.

As the numbers of the faithful of both sexes grew, the church was extended, both in area at ground level and in height projecting upwards, and was decorated with paintings. It has three oratories within, divided by painted walls, under a single roof that spans the larger building.

In the eastern part, a cross wall extends from one wall to the opposite wall, decorated with pictures and covered with linen. In its ends are two doors. Through the southern door the Bishop enters with his regular choir and those deputed to celebrate the rites and sacrifices to the Lord; through the other door, in the northern part of the cross wall, the Abbess enters with her girls and faithful widows to enjoy the feast of the body and blood of Jesus Christ. Another wall extends from the eastern part as far as the cross wall, and divides the paved floor of the buildings into two equal parts.

The church has many windows, and on the south side one ornamented gate, through which the priests and the faithful people of the male sex enter the church, and another gate on the north side, through which the congregation of virgins and faithful women enter. So in one great basilica a large people may pray with one heart to Almighty God, in different places according to their orders and ranks and sexes, with walls between them.

When the workmen set on its hinges the old door of the north gate, through which Saint Brigit used to enter the church, it could not cover all the newly constructed gate . . . unless a quarter were added to the door's height. When the workmen were deliberating whether to make a new and larger door, or whether to make a picture and add it to the old door . . . the leading craftsman of all Ireland gave wise advice, to pray that night to the Lord, with Saint Brigit. . . . Next morning the old door . . . covered the whole gateway.

Kildare was one among many great churches; many others are likely to have been as lavishly adorned, in the sixth century as well as the seventh.

Travel

The creative energy of the Irish monks was not confined to their homeland. Irishmen had travelled abroad for centuries, usually in arms. Peaceful travel had long been natural to pious Christians of all nations. Deep reverence drew churchmen and kings to Rome and Jerusalem, and humbler pilgrims also travelled easily. The curious document from fifth-century Gaul entitled the 'Pilgrimage of Aetheria' is a chatty letter written home by a middle-aged nun who toured the holy places of the east. Her journey was somewhat more strenuous than a modern tourist's, but her simple curiosity, her interest in her fellow-guests at the houses where she boarded, and her relentless questioning of her guides differ little. Pilgrimages like hers, to Rome or to Jerusalem, were normal, and wealthy Christians constructed numerous *xenodochia*, or lodging-houses, to accommodate the stream of pilgrims. Such relatively light-hearted tours lasted through the sixth and seventh centuries, and many tales in many Irish Lives name pilgrims, while several report attempts by senior abbots to discourage them. They had good reason, and so had monks in other lands. In the eighth century Boniface urged archbishop Cuthbert of Canterbury to get his synod and his princes to

> forbid matrons and nuns to make frequent journeys to Rome. Many of them die, and few keep their virtue. In most towns of Lombardy and Gaul, most of the whores are English. It is a scandal and disgrace to your church.

Boniface perhaps exaggerated; the scandal doubtless arose because the tourists ran out of money on their way home; and the eighth century was perhaps more depraved than the sixth and seventh. But Rome was a magnet that attracted tourist pilgrims in some numbers from the fourth century to the eighth. Fewer could afford the greater expense and effort of a visit to Jerusalem. But Gregory of Tours has a pathetic tale of a British monk who set out for Jerusalem in 577, clad in sheepskins. He got no further than Tours, where the brethren wondered at his extraordinary asceticism. But after eight years his excesses deranged his mind; he seized a knife and made violent attacks upon several people, whom he evidently mistook for the devil. Gregory had to chain him for two years until he died.

Exploration

Travel was normal. The evangelical journeys and the migrations of dedicated monks had a deeper purpose than those of the tourists. The sixth-century British pioneered. About 550, a British hermit, John of Chinon, encouraged the Frankish queen Radegund to renounce her rank and establish her monastery at Poitiers; she left her royal ornaments with him, lest she be tempted to return to the world. When Columban settled in the Vosges forty years later, he was saved from starvation during his first winter by Carantocus, abbot of Saulcy, in the Haute Saône. His name is British, but the monks he had recruited included natives, since his steward was called Marculf. No Lives and no traditions remember these British monks abroad; a few chance mentions notice their existence. In northern Gaul they were evidently numerous, for many scores of churches and places, from Brittany to central Belgium, are or were named after their leaders, and a substantial number also settled in northern Spain, where they preserved their identity for centuries. But in most of Europe, the memory of the British monks was overwhelmed by the larger and later influx of the Irish and the English.

The energies of Irish travellers at first sought a more ambitious goal outside Europe. The southern bishops Ailbe and Ibar are said to have been the first to send men to seek the Land of Promise, whither the pious might emigrate, across the Atlantic Ocean. The voyages continued, and Adomnan records three unsuccessful explorations of Cormac Ua Liathain in the northern ocean. A considerable fanciful literature concerns the explorers; most of it, in Irish language texts, is a jejune repetition of banal wonders that plainly bored its authors; but several of the Latin texts, especially those that concern Brendan of Clonfert and his companion, the British Malo, contain vivid detail. The stories are evidently travellers' tales conflated under the name of an individual. In one version, Brendan made his first voyage in large coracles containing up to forty men apiece, but the virgin Ita warned him:

> You will not find the promised land in the skins of dead animals. Seek out a shipwright who knows how to build you a timber vessel.

Brendan found the necessary skills and wood in Connacht, and

> the shipwrights and workmen asked that their only wages should be that they should be allowed to sail with the man of God.

He was told stories of a previous voyage made by Ternoc, apparently from Iceland, and made the same voyage himself. In the first account, the saints

> sailed westward.... We encountered a fog, so thick in all directions that we could hardly see the prow from the stern.... After what seemed like an hour, a great light shone around us and we saw a spacious land, full of plants, flowers and fruits.... We disembarked ... and explored the island, and after fifteen days' effort failed to find its further shore.... On the fifteenth day we encountered a river flowing from east to west.... Then appeared a man in great splendour, who told us ... 'The Lord has revealed to you this land, which is to be given to his saints at the end of time. By this river you are in the middle of the island. You may not go further. Return whence you came.' ... He accompanied us back to our ships on the coast ... and we returned through the same fog to the Island of Delight, where our brethren waited for our coming.

This was the tale Brendan was told. He made the same voyage, taking forty days to reach the fog bank and spending forty days on the island, whose climate reminded him of autumn in Ireland. But when he reached the river, it was a youth who appeared to him, and told him,

> this is the land that you have sought so long. Yet you may not discover it now, for the Lord has desired to show you his secrets in the ocean. Go back to your native land, and take with you as many of the fruits of this island and its jewels as your ships can carry.... For after the lapse of many centuries, this land will be made known to your successors, at a time when there will be a great persecution of the Christians.

Brendan is later made to prophesy that 'Britain will cleave to a great heresy before the day of judgement'. These extraordinary prophecies naturally suggest to the critical reader that he is confronted with a nineteenth-century text composed after extensive Irish migration to the American continent. But the manuscripts are assigned to the thirteenth century, or, at latest, early fourteenth, long before the voyage of Columbus, and both derive from a common original, which itself draws on an earlier lost Latin Life. The substance of the story dates to the ninth century. These tantalising tales invite speculation as to whether the Irish reached North America in the 6th century. They might be true, for though much might be the product of a lively imagination, details like the fogbanks in the area of Newfoundland are less imaginary; Iceland had an Irish population when the Norwegians arrived, in the 9th century, and the study of blood-groups suggests that it was larger than Norse tradition admits; seamen who could reach Iceland might as easily sail on to Newfoundland and beyond. But the question has little more than romantic interest. The Irish tales specifically assert that there was no settlement in the Land of Promise, whose permanent discovery was postponed. The importance of the stories lies less in speculation about their possible truth than in the fact that they were told and believed. If they were believed in Ireland, they were certainly known in Iceland, to hand for the Irish of Iceland to tell to Leif Erikson, before he sailed for Vinland. The Irish stories were well known in the middle ages, and contributed to the hopes of undiscovered land that made men willing to sail westward with Columbus to seek it.

Brendan's travels were not confined to the ocean. His journeys in Ireland involved him in violent dispute with king Diarmait. He warned him:

Your kingdom is brought to an end, and will be given over to holy churchmen.

Deeds evidently followed words, for

fifty royal towns were emptied at his word, and remained unpeopled, for their inhabitants had offended the holy man.

A boy was drowned through Brendan's fault, and the saints of Ireland decreed a penance, to be fixed by the virgin Ita. She sent him abroad, as Lasrian had sent Columba, though not for life. He visited Britain and Brittany, recruited British disciples and miraculously read Gildas' Greek texts, as easily as though they had been written in Latin. These fragmentary notices evidently condense passages in the original that the editor judged unfit to repeat. They imply that Brendan was involved in wars like Columba's. Detail is not preserved, for Brendan's endeavours in Ireland are known only through the standard collections of polite medieval Lives, and similar Lives of Columba also leave out his stormy vicissitudes. Other older tales survive of Columba, because he was a great prince, and founder of many houses. Brendan was not.

Missions

Voyages continued, but the great age of exploration is limited to the first generation of the monks. Brendan retired from the sea and from wars, and settled at Clonfert about 560; and his young companion Malo settled in Brittany in or about the same year. The lure of the transatlantic lands had appealed to hermits who longed to abandon the world. But monks of the second generation set a different ideal. Lasrian enjoined Columba to 'win more souls for Christ', but there were no souls to be won in the empty ocean. A few missions to the heathen are recorded in the early years of the movement. In the last years of the 5th century, a monk of Leinster on his way to Rome founded and named the monastery of Abingdon in the centre of a pagan English kingdom. The story was transcribed in circumstantial detail by the medieval Irish, who normally take small account of Irishmen abroad; it was preserved because it was in Irish eyes a minor incident, the occasion of a few miracles in the Life of a saint whose important work was performed in Ireland. It is confirmed by the medieval English monks of Abingdon, who had even less incentive to regard a fifth-century Irish founder as an honourable distinction. Their tradition told them that the history of their house began with 300 monks established on the 'hill of Abendoun' by the Irish Aben, 'in the time of the British', after the Romans, but before the English mastered Britain; their account noted archaeological confirmation, by the frequent excavation of 'crosses and statues', but placed its emphasis on the first English foundation, in the 7th century, when the monks and the name were transferred from the hill to the riverside. The detail of their story is corroborated by modern archaeological discovery. The Irish were well aware that the British were Christians, but they knew that 5th-century Abingdon was the centre of a pagan kingdom. The medieval English also knew that in British times, before the English conquered, Abingdon had been an English 'royal seat, where the people used to meet to deal with the . . . business of the kingdom'. Yet no one knew that they were right until 1934, when a sewer trench exposed a major pagan English burial-ground, a mile to the south-west of the Abbey.

The two independent accounts, that both show accurate knowledge of fifth-century history, agree too closely for coincidence. There is nothing unusual about the story except its early date, half a century before the main monastic movement matured; for other pagan English kingdoms permitted British and Irish monks to preach within their territories. The East Angles received Winwaloe of Brittany; the South Saxons tolerated the ineffectual cell of the Irish Dicuil at Bosham; and Malmesbury was founded and named by Maeldubh, another Irishman, among the west Saxons, about the time of their conversion to Christianity. No Lives record how and why these missionaries came, but one Irish tale preserves some details of the visit of Columba of Terryglass to an unnamed pagan Saxon kingdom. On his way home from Tours in the 540s he stayed with a king whose children had just died; 'he turned to the ashes and prayed, and called two sons and two daughters . . . back from the ashes to life.'

The children asked to be allowed to return to the life of the just in heaven, so 'they were baptised and slept again in their grave'. The miracle is a conventional consolation story, where the saint's comfort to the parents, that the children are better off in heaven, is coloured by a temporary resurrection, so that the children may personally assure the parents that they agree, and may be baptised to guarantee heaven. The use of the word 'ashes', *cinis*, emphasised by repetition, is startling. If it were deliberately invented, the author would have made much of his hero's unique miracle, for many saints revived corpses, but no other restored a cremated body to life. But the Irish knew nothing of pagan Saxon cremation, and it is not easy to see how the words got into the text unless they derive from a contemporary, more rational story that involved cremation. Such tales are all that was remembered of missions to the sixth-century English; though there were doubtless other forgotten incidents, it is likely that the missionary effort was slight before the later sixth century, without great effect.

The lasting impact of Irish monasticism upon foreigners begins with the exile of Columba of Iona. From the beginning it was two-edged. Irish monks converted pagans to Christianity; they also converted more mundane Christians to the monastic ideal. Columba emerged from his crisis greater and stronger. Exile transformed him into the 'dove of peace'. At first, exile was hard and bitter, a greater loss than the renunciation of the throne; in the poems ascribed to him he is made to sing of

> the homeless land of my sojourn, of sadness and grief.
> Alas, the voyage that I was made to make . . .
> For the fault that I went myself
> To the battle of Cuil. . . .
>
> I have loved Erin's land,
> Its waterfalls, all but its government. . . .
>
> Death is better in reproachless Erin
> Than everlasting life in Britain.

But it was in Britain that his name won everlasting life. He settled in the island of Iona and was welcomed by the Irish colonists, who had recently been subdued by the pagan Picts. He did not rally the Irish for a holy war of Christians against the heathen; he went alone to convert the Picts, and in time they were converted. Their conversion transformed the north. No longer alien barbarians, marked off by a separate culture and a hostile faith from the British of Clyde and Forth, they became one among several states who shared a common culture. Columba kept the northern powers at peace for most of his lifetime and enabled them to set in motion the processes that were to form Scotland. But he was much more than the national patron of northern Britain. His successors at Iona undertook the conversion of the English, and in the next century the Irish and the English began to infect Europeans with their monastic experience. Columba was the mightiest of the monastic founders within Ireland, the first to carry their example overseas; he left behind him successors who transmitted that example to the furthest regions.

Monasticism was born and nurtured by the British of the Severn lands, but grew to maturity in Ireland. There, the monk's urge to seek deserts ever further removed from the seats of kings blended with the national tradition of the Irish, that had long encouraged their adventurous youth to win new homes overseas. They had colonised Britain until Vortigern checked them; thereafter they explored the Atlantic, and found it barren; then their energy carried the faith that swept their country to the nations of Europe. Ireland remained the homeland of monastic enthusiasm and learning for centuries; Europe welcomed what had been a limited and local form of Christian organisation, and developed it into a principal institution of the medieval church.

CHAPTER TWENTY

THE SEVENTH CENTURY CHURCH

The Conversion of the English

Columba's government moved contemporaries and later ages by its impressive austerity, discipline and simplicity. Its greater glory lay in the future and, if a great man's stature is fitly to be judged by the quality of his successors, then Bede's cautious judgement must stand:

> whatever may have been the character of the man himself, it is quite certain that his successors were outstanding in their abstinence, their love of God, and in the discipline of their organised life.

He died in 597. In the same year Augustine landed in Kent, sent by Gregory the Great to convert the pagan English. The history of English Christianity is told in sources utterly different from those that preserve the records of Irish and British monks. Bede, born in 672, grew up within living memory of most of the events he recounts. He is also one of the world's great historians, ranking with Thucydides, Tacitus and Shakespeare in his ability to select an incident that describes an age and forms a judgement.

There are ample other sources. Lives of English saints are fewer, but several of those that survive are contemporary, and have been preserved in their original form. Bede and the Saxon Chronicle provide dates that in the 7th century need little question; and the English church was soon in regular contact with Europe, whose documented history confirms the main story. But though the nature of the sources changes, there is no break in the nature of the story that they tell. Bede has much to say of Irish Christians, something of British, and his picture of their outlook and behaviour does not differ from that which lies beneath the native texts. Change there was, for Christianity brought the English into the European community, and the conversion of the English profoundly affected the native British and Irish. But the Christianity of the British Isles is a continuing whole, and the absorption of the English appears as a new starting-point only if its earlier history is disregarded.

Augustine and Edwin

Augustine was well received. The men of Kent were converted at the instance of their king, who had long been married to a Christian Frankish princess.

Bede in a sentence calls Augustine's life austere and simple, but he paints him as a proud authoritarian priest, conscious of the majesty of a constituted hierarchy. Appointed bishop by the pope, he expected instant obedience from the British abbots of the west, though they had lived long without organised contact with Rome. He knew nothing of their previous religious experience, and showed no wish to understand it. At first, a large party among the British were ready to submit. But the advice of a wise and humble hermit persuaded them to test the manner of Augustine's authority. At their second meeting they were to arrive after him. If he rose courteously to greet them, they would know him as a true servant of Christ, and hear him obediently. But if he sat enthroned like a master, they would despise him as he despised them. Augustine sat, and the British rejected him. Bede's story is doubtless over simple in its detail; the deep distrust plainly required more than a single polite gesture to allay it, and the shrewd hermit no doubt suggested his test because he anticipated Augustine's reaction. But the philosophies that the story portrays are accurate enough.

At first, Kentish Christianity is not known to have reached further than nearby London, and it was rejected when its royal patron died. But within a decade it revived, and was carried to the north. Edwin of Northumbria married a Kentish princess and received bishop Paulinus from Kent. Bede describes the dark, stern, hook-nosed prelate, remote and intense, simple and compelling. After hearing him, at the old pagan capital of Goodmanham by Sancton, in the East Riding, one of Edwin's councillors epitomised the strength of the Christian appeal to the barbarian.

> This present life on earth seems to me, my king . . . as though we were sitting at supper . . . in the winter time, warmed by a bright fire burning in the middle of the hall, while the storms of wintry rain and snow rage without; when a single sparrow flies swiftly in through one entry and out by the other. In its little time indoors, the winter weather touches it not, yet its brief moment of security lasts but a second, as it passes from the winter to the winter, escaping our sight. So seems the life of man in its little season; what follows, and what went before, we know not. Therefore, if this new teaching brings anything more sure, we should follow it.

These deep emotions were reinforced by the robust materialism of the high-priest Coifi, who proclaimed:

> I am convinced that our old religion has nothing good and no advantage about it. For no man has been more zealous in the worship of the gods than I; yet there are many who gain larger gifts and great dignities from you, my king, and prosper more in all they aim to do and to acquire. If these gods of ours were any good, they would rather have helped me, who have served them eagerly.

Coifi then mounted the king's charger and speared the idols he had served, though weapons and stallions were taboo to priests, and commanded the assembly to burn down the temple. So violent a profanation, undertaken with impunity, on the authority of the high-priest and with the cómplicity of the national assembly, jolted men's minds into an irrevocable breach with the old faith. Edwin was baptised on Easter Eve 627, in a hastily constructed timber church at York, soon to be replaced by a stone building, and the rest of the Northumbrians were baptised in crowds in the ensuing years.

A few years later Edwin was destroyed by the British king Catwallaun, aided by the Mercians. Catwallaun's aim was the expulsion of the enemy, 'exterminating the whole English race within the boundaries of Britain' without regard for age, sex, or religion. He proved a 'barbarian crueller than a pagan', and was shortly driven out by the sons of Aethelferth, who had adopted the Christianity of Iona while in exile among the Scots. In the disaster, Paulinus hastily took ship for Kent, with the queen and the church plate. Only James the Deacon stayed, to teach Gregorian plainsong in quieter times, to converts who remembered his courage in adversity.

Oswald and Aedan

Oswald and Oswy, the sons of Aethelferth, naturally applied to Iona for a bishop. Iona had preserved its austerity, sending exemplary humble monks to serve the political communities of the north, so that Bede called it the 'head' of all the Scot and Pict houses, 'presiding over the ruling of their peoples'. Its authority was the stronger because it depended upon no enforceable royal grant, but upon the affectionate respect and free consent of entire populations; and it was stable because custom enjoined, as in many other Irish and British monastic communities, that the abbacy descend among the heirs of the founder's family. In 634 the abbot of Iona was a grandson of Columba's cousin, and also third cousin to the reigning High King of Ireland.

The first bishop was defeated by the 'indomitable barbarism' of the English, but his successor, Aedan, less 'rigid with unlearned listeners', preferred 'nourishment by the milk of milder doctrine, leading gradually towards the higher and more perfect commands of God'. His apostolic simplicity contrasted both with the land-hungry monks of Wales and with the ceremonial dignity of Roman priests. Bede observed:

> what chiefly won men to his teaching was that he lived with his monks the life that he preached. He made no effort to acquire worldly advantage. . . . all that kings or rich men gave him he cheerfully gave away to the first poor man he met. He travelled everywhere . . . on foot, never on horseback unless he had to. . . . Timidity or obsequiousness never restrained him from criticising the sins of the rich, and he never gave money to great men.

Aedan's gentle dignity blended the best traditions of the British and Irish, the austerity of David, without the arrogance that had disgusted Gildas; the wisdom of Illtud, without the embarrassment of inherited estates; and the authority of Columba, without the violence of his earlier years.

Aedan's church was spread by the conquering armies of Northumbria, who made themselves masters of England. When the West Saxon king was persuaded to accept Christianity, his Northumbrian suzerain stood sponsor at his baptism; the kings of the East Saxons and the Mercians went north for baptism by the banks of the Tyne. In the south and the midlands, as well as in the north, monasteries modelled on Iona proliferated, often double houses, for women and for men, on the pattern of Whithorn, of Finnian of Clonard, and of Dagaeus of Bangor. Barking and Chertsey near London were among the greater foundations, and Irish teachers established themselves in ruined Roman forts or towns, at Burgh Castle by Yarmouth and elsewhere. Churches were constructed in the central squares of the Roman towns, ancestors of the medieval cathedrals, and at other centres of government. They were often impressive buildings; at Brixworth near Northampton, possibly a principal royal centre of the south Mercians, an

---

Map 28

+   **EARLY BISHOPS' SEES**   □   **NORTH ITALIAN CHURCHES**

MAIN MONASTIC FOUNDATIONS   **DEDICATIONS TO BRITISH SAINTS**

■   of Irish origin   C   **Cyngar (Docco)**

●   of Anglo-Irish origin   D   **David**

O   of English origin   G   **Gulval**

✕   of British or Roman origin   M   **Melor**

⊗   possibly of British origin   S   **Samson**

     W   **Winwaloe**

MAP 28 MONKS IN THE ENGLISH KINGDOMS

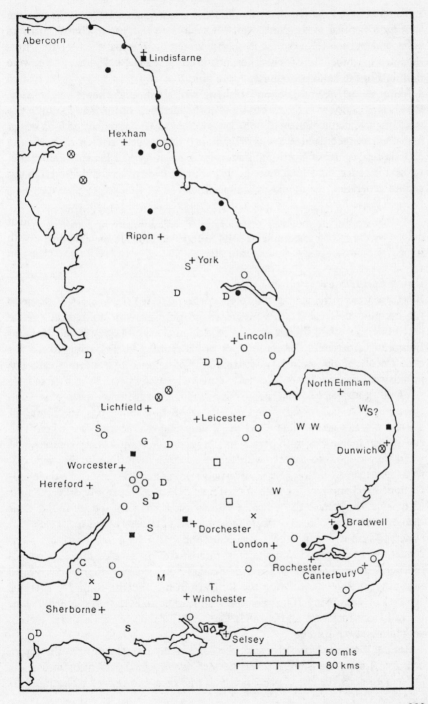

Abercorn

Lindisfarne

Hexham

Ripon

S York

D

D

Lincoln

North Elmham

W S?

Lichfield

S

G

D

Worcester

Hereford

S D

D

W

Dunwich

Bradwell

London

Dorchester

Rochester

Canterbury

C
C

M

Sherborne

Winchester

D

S

Selsey

50 mls
80 kms

Italian architect imposed upon the midland countryside a large basilica, of the type most familiar at Ravenna, which has survived as a parish church, with its aisles and portico removed. It is almost unique in Europe north of the Alps, though a few other similar churches, notably at Wing in Buckinghamshire, were built in English lands at about the same time.

Many of the new abbots and bishops were Irish, and they brought some monks and clergy with them; but most of the members of the new communities were English, many of them of noble or royal birth. The simplicity of Iona was at first unchallenged. Aedan avoided Paulinus' metropolitan church of York; the ecclesiastical centre of Northumbria was established on the island of Lindisfarne, where the concepts of Iona more easily endured. Bede observed that even in the second generation the monks of Lindisfarne

> owned no money and no cattle. . . . They refused to accept land or estates for the building of monasteries, unless constrained thereto by the secular government. This custom continued in the churches of Northumbria for a long time after.

Rome and Easter

But there were many among the English who preferred the majesty of Rome to the humility of Ireland; they found their spokesman in Wilfred. A prelate determined to establish and uphold in Britain the visible power of organised European Christianity, he chose York as his centre and took pains to list the endowments of his churches, securing a royal charter to confirm them. His intransigent determination forced the issue to a speedy decision in England.

The dispute was new and many-sided; so long as the monasticism of western Britain and Ireland stayed within its remote Atlantic homelands, the church of Europe was not greatly interested in its unorthodox practices. But when Irish and British monks began to preach in Europe in the early seventh century, and when they came into contact with the mission of Augustine in England, differences began to matter. Successive popes reminded the Irish that their old-fashioned reckoning of the date of Easter and their provocatively different style of tonsure threatened the unity of Christendom; and the popes found their theology Pelagian. The Irish were uninterested in theology, and made no effort either to refute or to uphold the philosophy of a long-dead heretic. Their concern was with practical morality, the defence of the monk's simple piety and independent conscience. Wilfred demanded conformity with the disciplined hierarchy of Rome, and made the Roman tonsure and the Roman Easter the symbols of submission. The issue was simple in outline, complex in detail; how far must the monastic church of Britain and Ireland change in order to gain communion with Europe?

Among the British and the Irish the controversy lingered on into the eighth century. Among the English it was decided at the Synod of Whitby in 664. Its immediate occasion was a plain practical nuisance, for Oswy of Northumbria and his Kentish queen were obliged to observe Easter on different dates. Bishop Colman defended Irish usage on the authority of the third-century bishop Anatolius and of Columba. Wilfred disputed the mathematics attributed to Anatolius and impugned Columba as a false prophet, but he based his case upon the universal practice of Christians elsewhere, obedient to the successors of Peter, to whom Christ gave the keys of heaven; to which the king replied simply and shortly, 'I will not quarrel with such a doorkeeper'. Northumbria accepted the Roman Easter. Colman withdrew to Ireland with the minority among the English and the Irish. Like Aedan, he had been both abbot of Lindisfarne and bishop of the Northumbrians. The twin functions were now separated; an Englishman succeeded to the abbacy, the Irish Tuda to the bishopric.

Whitby was a commonsense compromise, excluding the extremists of both sides; for Wilfred also spent much of his life in exile. He strove not merely for outward conformity with Rome, but to create a church conceived in the Roman manner, headed by potent bishops who sat beside the kings, and to eliminate the anarchic, spontaneous independence of the Irish monasteries. He continued his fight, and failed. When Tuda died, the underking of Deira put Wilfred in his place, with his see in the royal city of York, and sent him to Europe for consecration. But while he was away Oswy took control of York and installed as bishop an English pupil of Aedan, Chad of Lastingham, whose name was British. Oswy sought to combine the best of both churches, to gain communion with Rome and Europe, but to retain the Irish piety and the independence of the new English church; for Chad was

> dedicated to humility, abstinence and study; he preached in town and country, in cottage, village and fort, not riding, but walking on foot like the apostles; for he was a pupil of Aedan, and endeavoured to instruct his hearers according to Aedan's principles and practice.

When Wilfred returned, Oswy refused to accept him; he retired to Ripon, whence he was summoned as bishop to the new frontier kingdom of Mercia.

Theodore and Wilfred

The conflict of opposing philosophies was resolved by Rome. The see of Canterbury was vacant, and the pope made an extraordinary appointment; his nominee, Theodore, was a Greek of Tarsus in Asia Minor, an elderly scholar, seventy years old when he arrived in 669. The aged academic seemed altogether unfitted for his task, too old to tackle it before he died. But he lived to the age of eighty-eight, and shaped the English church for all time. His tact successfully blended the pious energy of the Anglo–Irish monasteries with episcopal discipline, and did so by encouragement rather than by command. When Wilfred complained that Chad's consecration was uncanonical, Chad replied,

> I will gladly resign. I never thought myself worthy, but I agreed to do as I was ordered, for obedience sake;

for he much preferred the quiet of Lastingham. Theodore removed the complaint by consecrating him canonically, but advised him to ride henceforth, gently enforcing his advice by helping him into the saddle with his own hand; for the spiritual needs of a vast diocese were inadequately served by the slow progress of a walking bishop. Wilfred's grievance was appeased by an exchange of diocese; Wilfred went to York and Chad to Mercia, establishing his see at Lichfield, in 669, barely fifteen years after the English conquest of the region.

Wilfred was given the opportunity to prove himself; within eight years his overweening pride had brought about his downfall. He endeavoured to assert the Roman concept of a great bishop who stood behind his king and guided him to greater glory. His ambition deeply affronted both the secular and ecclesiastical morality of Irish and Northumbrian Christianity; but he at first found an eager ally in Egferth, the new king of Northumbria, who succeeded his father Oswy in 670. Wilfred's close companion and biographer, Eddius, attributes to the favour of Wilfred the military successes of the king, who 'filled two rivers' with the corpses of 'vicious Picts', reducing them to 'slavery', and slew the Mercians in 'countless numbers', thereby making Wilfred 'bishop of the British, the Irish, and the Picts as well as of the southern English'. Bede, who was a boy at the time, expressed the monastic attitude; he condemned Egferth's second Pictish expedition as 'rash', undertaken 'against the emphatic veto of his advisers, especially of . . . bishop Cuthbert'; and denounced his invasion of Ireland as a

> wretched devastation of an inoffensive people, who had always been
> distinguished by their friendship towards the English nation,

also undertaken against the protest of 'the most reverend Father Egbert'.

Wilfred made his worldly ambition as evident at home. Eddius called him 'head of the church', *caput ecclesiae*, and delighted in the splendour of his abbey at Hexham, adorned with

> magnificent ornaments of gold and silver, and altars decorated with
> purple and silk.

Irish monasteries took pleasure in beautiful and valuable ornament, for the greater glory of God, but Wilfred made them symbols of the bishop's glory. The king soon came to resent his

> worldly glory and wealth . . . his vast army of retainers, equipped
> with royal livery and weapons

and exiled him in 678. Like Cardinal Wolsey long after, he had served his king too well. Archbishop Theodore endorsed the king's action, split the great northern diocese, and opposed Wilfred's appeals to Rome.

The contest was decided. Though Wilfred's determined resistance won him a brief return, the structure of the Anglo–Irish church was secure. Wilfred proclaimed that his life's aim had been to 'root out from the church the foul weeds sown by the Irish'. He failed, for the Northumbrian laity as well as the churchmen preferred the Irish plant to Wilfred's. When Egferth's rash expedition cost him his life, they chose as their successor his half-brother Aldfrith, born of an Irish mother, reared in Ireland and Iona, in the full knowledge that he was an eminent scholar, patron of the monks, resolutely opposed to aggressive wars and to prelacy. His guidance consolidated the monastic church, built upon the Irish principles of the simplicity and independence of Iona. Northumbrian art and scholarship equalled its Irish original, outshining the cathedral monastery of Canterbury and the enfeebled survivors of Roman Britain, Whithorn and St. Albans. The English converts brought discipline, and during the years of Wilfred's struggle, Benedict Biscop and Ceolfred introduced the rule of Benedict of Nursia, patterned in their new foundation at Wearmouth and Jarrow, in 674. One of their early pupils was Bede, who entered the monastery in 680. He was not only a great historian, but a philosopher and a mathematician as well, perhaps the most influential European scholar of the early middle ages. The quiet strength of Bede's wisdom is the measure of the church that the Irish built in England.

The Irish founded the Northumbrian church, but the English organised it, under the guidance of archbishop Theodore; and the Northumbrian church was the principal influence in the conversion of the rest of England, outside Kent. Its early organisation, before the time of Theodore, was modelled on the practice of Iona. But the organisation of Iona already seemed strange to Bede; writing ninety years after Aedan had come to Lindisfarne, he remarked that

> it is the custom of the island to have a governor who is an abbot and a priest, to whose authority the whole province, even its bishops, must defer, a most unusual form of organisation. Therein they follow the example of their first teacher, Columba, who was not a bishop, but a priest and a monk.

Bishops and Abbots

The early ecclesiastical organisation of the British Isles surprised and surprises all who are accustomed to the Roman hierarchy of Europe. The British, the Irish and the English each came to Christianity from a different starting-point; each was dominated by the great number of their monasteries, that were still not matched in Europe, and each adapted itself to Rome and Europe in a different manner. In Wales the greater abbots of each kingdom served as bishops, at St. David's in Demetia, Llanbadarn in Cardigan, Bangor in western Gwynedd, and later St. Asaph in eastern Gwynedd; the successors of Tyssilio in Powys and of Teilo in Ystrad Tywi are at times styled 'bishop'; and in Glevissig the kings were served by three principal abbots, while the seats of bishops varied with the union and division of the political kingdom until a permanent see was settled at Llandaff, by Cardiff, probably in the 9th century.

Fifth-century Ireland was also provided with territorial bishops, with seats near the royal residences of major kingdoms; and at first they and their priests constituted a normal married clergy. But as monasteries multiplied in the sixth century, more and more monks became bishops, and some great abbots, like Maedoc and his successors at Ferns in Leinster, became bishops of their kingdoms, as in Wales. But such examples were few. Most of the dynasties sought bishops for their own kingdoms, and some obtained them, nearly always accepting monks. The bishop who was a monk remained under the discipline of his abbot. The office of bishop was less esteemed; the greater eminence of the abbot was so generally admitted that Irish usage sometimes describes the Pope as 'abbot of Rome', and Christ as 'abbot of Heaven'.

This was the ecclesiastical organisation that Columba brought to Iona, and Aedan to Northumbria. In the far north, one bishop sufficed for the Picts and one for the Scot colonists; and when the Scot king acquired the Pictish throne, a single bishop seemed natural and adequate for the combined kingdom until the coming of English and Norman influence; and as far as is known, a single bishop also governed the church of the Clyde. So at first in Northumbria, Aedan was both abbot of Lindisfarne and bishop of the Northumbrians, and sent his monks where they were needed, as priests or as bishops; so Cedd, brother of Chad, was sent as bishop to the East Saxons, and in the tradition of Aedan was also abbot of a monastery, sited far from the royal residence, in the ruined Roman fort of Othona, Bradwell-on-Sea. But political and ecclesiastical problems soon eroded Irish precedent; when Irish monks became the first bishops of the Middle Angles and the Mercians, they remained subject to an abbot who was also the Northumbrian bishop; but when their kings rejected Northumbrian political supremacy, they could no longer tolerate Northumbrian primacy over their church. Moreover, since the early initiative of Gregory in Kent had made the metropolitan of Canterbury primate of all the English, the authority of Rome required that bishops should be subject to him, not to a remote island abbot.

The political events of the 660s and 670s enabled Theodore to find a convenient solution, that reconciled ecclesiastical hierarchy with practical needs. The Mercian kings brought all the southern English under their political control, but failed to reduce the Northumbrians. In 664, while the kingdoms still disputed sovereignty, the Northumbrian abbacy and bishopric were divided, so that the southern monks who obeyed the abbot of Lindisfarne no longer owed allegiance to the national bishop of the Northumbrians at York. Permanent solution was reached a few years later. After a fearful battle in 679, Theodore's insistence persuaded the Northumbrian and Mercian kings to forgo claims to sovereignty over each other, and to accept the lower Trent as their lasting frontier. Ecclesiastical organisation matched the political agreement. The northerners and the southerners were each provided with an archbishop; the Northumbrians acquiesced in the nominal precedence of Canterbury; since the superior might of the Mercian armies was admitted in Kent, the Mercian kings remained content with the ecclesiastical primacy of Canterbury, save for a few years, when the vanity of Offa sought and obtained the rank of archbishop for his own Mercian bishop at Lichfield. From the time of Theodore, the secular and ecclesiastical government of the English was divided between the empire of the Mercians and the kingdom of the Northumbrians. The solution satisfied the church, for the old causes of divided loyalty dwindled; thirty or forty years after the conversion of the southern English, Irish clergy from Lindisfarne were no longer needed; kings might be served by a new generation of home bred English bishops, untrammelled by personal ties with a rival kingdom. The problems of the past had been by-products of the contrasting structure of the Irish and the Roman church; among the English they were solved by the compromise of Whitby and the tact of Theodore. The English church retained its independent monasteries, but it accepted territorial bishoprics subject to metropolitans, in conformity with Roman usage. In remote Wales conformity was of less moment, and the externals of Easter date and tonsure that symbolised conformity were not accepted until 768, on the initiative of Nennius' teacher, bishop Elvodug of Gwynedd.

The Irish Church

The problems of Ireland were more complex. There was no metropolitan see whose authority an Irish equivalent of Theodore might exercise, and deep differences divided north and south. The majority of the southerners early favoured conformity with Rome, but most of the north long resisted. The monasteries were grouped, not as in northern Britain, under the tutelage of a single great foundation, but in a dozen different substantial groups, with a large number of small independent houses as well. Organisational unity of some sort was urgent, and partisans on both sides felt the need of a metropolitan episcopate. The earliest candidate, put forward about 650, was the southern see of Kildare, in northern Leinster. But the claim of Kildare was wholly alien to the north, and is not mentioned save in the contemporary literature of the controversy. The ultimate basis of organisational unity was prepared by bishop Aed, of Sletty in south Leinster, who ostentatiously placed his own church under the patronage of Armagh. Armagh was not only the principal bishopric of the north. It was the senior bishopric of Ireland, named first in the early 7th-century papal lists. It had been founded by Patrick, and remained the most important of his monasteries. Its abbots had commonly been bishops, who were regarded as the successors of Patrick, and Patrick had been consecrated in Rome, first bishop of the Irish, and in his own day sole bishop. He was the only man who had ever been supreme bishop of all the Irish. The half-forgotten memory of Patrick was revived, and employed to unite the contending parties under his neutral name. The extraordinary fictions of Tirechan and his imitators pretended that in the middle of the fifth century Patrick had been recognised as metropolitan by nearly 500 bishops, and had founded innumerable churches all over Ireland; no one believed these absurd stories, but they were happily accepted by northern patriots, and prudently endorsed by the southern champions of unity with Rome.

The southern partisans of the Roman Easter offered allegiance to a northern metropolitan before the north conformed; and the honorary primacy of Armagh was proved to be inoffensive, not irksome to the independence of existing monasteries. At the end of the seventh century, the efforts of the principal northern champions of conformity, Adomnan and the English-born Egbert of Iona, induced their colleagues to accept simultaneously the Roman Easter and the primacy of Armagh; with it came the priority of Patrick over Brigit and the southern saints, and the enhancement of episcopal authority. The struggle was long and slow. Adomnan failed to convince his own monks, and Iona itself did not conform until 716, after his death. The conflict ended with an episcopate independent of the monks, directed by its metropolitan, concerned with the guidance of kings and the spiritual needs of laymen, while monasteries concentrated upon their art and learning, and upon the despatch of missionaries to foreign lands.

Monks in Europe

Columban was the first of the insular monks to make a weighty impact on Europe. For a quarter of a century he had served his abbot, Comgall, Columba's close friend. When he landed in Gaul in 590, he had behind him their experience, and the teachings of Finnian, David and Gildas; he quoted Gildas with respect, and may have known him personally. His stern simplicity shattered the conventions of Frankish Christianity. When he strode into the court of one Merovingian king and denounced his lechery and misgovernment to his face; when he adjured another to forswear his earthly crown for the greater glory of a tonsure; when

---

Map 29

- Churches and monasteries
    of British origin or inspiration

● Monasteries
    of Irish origin, inspiration or influence

O Monasteries
    founded by Boniface, Willibrord and their English, Irish
    and German associates

? Churches and monasteries
    possibly of Irish or English origin, inspiration
    or influence

MAP 29 MONKS ABROAD

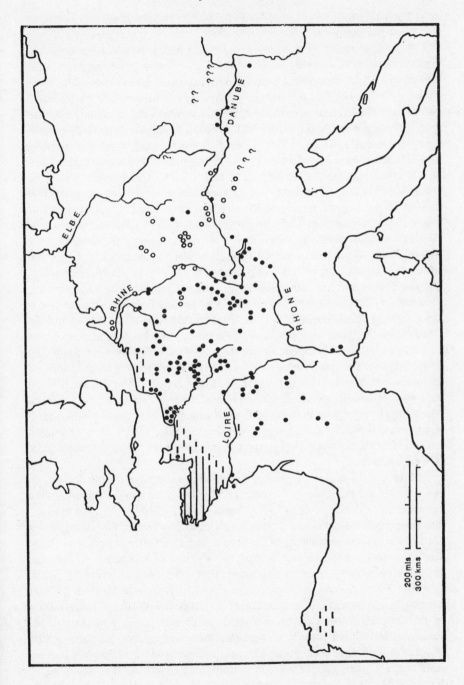

he publicly rebuked their formidable grandmother Brunhilde for crimes that all men knew but did not mention, then he sharply and openly expressed a disgust that their subjects had harboured in silent resignation. When he politely but firmly lectured pope Gregory the Great upon his mistakes in theology and in the government of the church, the pope and those accustomed to his authority were baffled by a sincerity that was neither subservient nor defiant. The Merovingian government deported him, but they could not suppress the monasteries he had founded, nor prevent him from founding Bobbio among the Lombards of Italy.

Columban enthused a number of Merovingian notables, as well as humbler men. He was soon followed by an increasing number of Irishmen from Ireland and Northumbria, and of English men and women. The English Willibrord evangelised Holland. The Irish Fursey spent ten years in East Anglia before moving to the neighbourhood of Paris. The Frankish queen founded Corbie under Fursey's guidance, while his brothers, his pupil Cellan of Peronne and their companions established some scores of houses between the Seine and the Meuse. Frankish noblemen entered these houses or founded their own; Didier, treasurer of Clothair II, and Eloi, mint master of Dagobert I, established monasteries and became bishops; their friend Iudicael, ruler of the British of Armorica, became a monk. The daughter of an East Anglian king founded Farmoutier-on-Brie, and the English wife of Clovis II refounded Chelles. St. Ouen and St. Vandrille were counts of the palace who were inspired by Columban to found houses, and his other disciples, among them St. Gall in Switzerland, St. Valery in Picardy, St. Omer of Therouanne, recruited many more Franks. Monastic fervour swept eastern Gaul in the middle of the seventh century as intensely as in contemporary England, or as in Ireland and Britain a century before. Merovingian society was in decay and ready for inspiration; the inspiration came almost entirely from the Irish and Anglo–Irish monks, with some contribution from the British, but with hardly a trace of influence from the earlier monasteries of Gaul or Italy.

The force of the movement west of the Rhine was expended during the seventh century. Beyond the Rhine it was constantly renewed for many centuries. In the eighth century the English and Irish began to evangelise the heathen German and their further neighbours. Boniface of Devon became archbishop of Mainz and apostle of Germany. Many of the bishops and abbots whom he directed were Irish; the most remarkable among them was Virgilius of Salzburg, who outraged orthodox opinion by teaching that other worlds besides our own exist in the universe. From Austria, later generations reached eastward. An Irish Colman became the patron saint of Hungary; others preached in Poland; and Brandenburg in Prussia perhaps owes its name to an Irish Brendan. The Scandinavian invasions of Ireland temporarily stemmed the flow of emigrants, but the monastic impetus revived thereafter. In 1076 Donald Rafferty, or Domnall mac Robartaig, head of the monasteries of Columba at Kells, sent his cousin Muiredach, better known as Marianus Scottus, to found the Irish house of St. Peter of Regensburg.

His vigorous successors established a chain of *Schottenkloster*, 'Irish Monasteries', at Vienna, Nuremberg and elsewhere, their furthest outpost at Kiev in the Ukraine. The Irish house at Kiev was destroyed by the Mongol invasions of the 13th century, but most of the monasteries in Germany remained Irish until the Reformation; a few, notably Erfurt and Regensburg, though in deep decay, continued as Scot houses into the 19th century, into an age when men had forgotten that Scot had once meant Irish and accepted emigrants from Scotland as the proper inmates of the *Schottenkloster*.

The quality of the Irish monks in Europe was as remarkable as their expansion in time and space, from north America to the Ukraine. Though evangelists continued to convert remote heathens, many of the Irish in western Europe transferred their emphasis from preaching to learning. From the seventh century to the eleventh the terms Irishman and scholar were virtually interchangeable; and until the Norse invasions, the English fully shared their scholarship. When Charlemagne needed schools to train the administrators of his revived western Roman empire, he induced Alcuin of York to become their first director; for Alcuin was the foremost scholar in Europe, York the finest library, Charlemagne the most munificent patron. At the central palace school Alcuin was assisted by the Irish geographer and astronomer Dicuil, and succeeded by the Irish grammarian Clemens; and in the next generation, the schools of Italy were directed by the Irish scholar Dungal of Pavia. These Carolingian foundations were the remote ancestors of the later schools of Paris and northern Italy, whence sprang the universities of medieval and modern Europe. Contemporaries, hostile and friendly, noted the comparative strengths and weaknesses of their teachers; the success of the schools stemmed from a blend of English discipline and administrative ability with Irish initiative and imagination.

The qualities that the Irish brought to Europe were those that their native monasteries had formed. To Europeans unacquainted with the origins of monasticism in Britain, the irruption of Irish monks seemed an act of God, as unpredictable as an earthquake, unexplained and in little need of explanation. Chroniclers noted that individuals were Irish, or pupils of the Irish, but did not wonder why they came, or why Europe responded to their coming. The story of the rise of monasticism in the British Isles is plainly told by the Saints' Lives, the Annals and related documents, once they have been stripped of the fancy dress in which medieval editors disguised them. The monastic explosion was not due to chance or wonder, but to the specific circumstances of early sixth-century western Britain and Ireland.

Seventh century Europe remarked that reforming monks came from Ireland and Britain. But nationality did not then arouse the powerful loyalties and resentments of modern nationalism. Large scale monasticism in the west originated among the British and the Irish, and its first and most notable founders in Europe were Irish and English. But they immediately drew to them many Franks, Germans and others, who shared and upheld their outlook, and in time their successors adopted the Rule of the Italian Benedict. Franks and Englishmen were received into monasteries in Ireland as readily as Irish and Englishmen settled in Germany. Men of Irish and English birth were long active in Europe in the movement that their countrymen had initiated, and were more numerous in some monasteries than others. But the common character of the movement rested upon its beliefs, not upon the birthplace of the men who made it. There were differences of emphasis; men often tended to settle among or near those with whom they had most in common, and the speech and background of their fellows were among the influences that brought men together. At some specific times and places men of one nation were more numerous than those of others; but no significant distinctions can isolate Irish or German, English or French monks from one another. All were deeply indebted to the British, Irish and English pioneers; the nationality of later generations marked only differences of detail.

Early monasticism, however disciplined, was by its nature subversive. In his communal life the monk owed strict obedience to his abbot; but the community was a necessary convenience, and in the monasteries of the 6th and 7th centuries each monk normally lived apart in his own cell, preserving the hermit's isolation within the community. The ideal of monk and hermit was direct access to God, in solitary communion that was often rewarded by heavenly visitation, in a dream or a vision, without the intermediary of the priest; but the hierarchy of the secular church, modelled upon the political society of men, interposed the priest between God and man, and thereby made the priest, however humble, in some degree an ecclesiastical politician. The monk was a student; though he must conform to the observances of his community, in his cell he was free to meditate on matters divine and human. The priest must accept the assumptions of the established authority he served; the monk might question them, and often did.

The early history of Christianity in the British Isles is a continuing whole; it is the first chapter in the history of European monasticism. In Europe the established church survived the barbarian invasions and tamed the first advocates of monastic meditation. The monasteries of Egypt had flourished in waterless deserts, and the efforts of late Roman ascetics to transplant them to the green lands of the west were unsuccessful; similar initiatives were no better received in the ensuing centuries. Cassiodorus, Benedict of Nursia, Radegund and other ascetics of Gaul and Italy who shared the aspirations of the British reformers were individually honoured, but inspired no large-scale movement on the model of Egypt, and did not prompt their contemporaries to enter and found monasteries in great numbers. But in Britain the destruction of the Roman economy and its institutions also brought down the established church; the failure of the church left men defenceless in face of dynastic violence and prepared them for Christian reform. The first and only European monastic movement that matched the scale and rapid growth of the original Egyptian monasteries was that which began in Wales in the 530s, and spread to Ireland, and thence by way of Iona to the English; and thereafter sent its missionaries to Europe.

The greater part of the early monasteries of Europe north of the Alps were founded by Irish, English or British monks, or by their native converts; to them most of the peoples beyond the Rhine and Danube frontiers of Rome, save for the eastern Slavs, owed their first conversion to Christianity. In the second and third generations the undisciplined enthusiasm of Irish founders no longer sufficed, and these houses sought an orderly rule; most of them ultimately observed the Rule of Benedict of Nursia, to form the nucleus of what was later termed the 'Benedictine Order'.

The monasteries of medieval Europe owe their being to Arthurian Britain. Most of the early houses were founded by men from the British Isles, or by those whom they inspired. The tenuous ancestry of British monasticism reaches back through Illtud and Docco to the teachings of the Sicilian Briton and Pelagius, of Victricius and Martin; but though it derived from the fourth-century Christian experience of Rome, it was spared the harsh necessities of Augustinianism. It won men's hearts because it adapted an older and kinder Roman Christianity to the needs of the shattered remnants of Roman Britain, and of the barbarians who had entered its ruins. Though the wars of Ambrosius and Arthur destroyed almost all that they fought to defend, their victory preserved one element of the Roman past, its radical, individualist and humanist Christian tradition. Though Arthur and his captains could not rebuild their old society in the land they had recovered, the ideas that they strove to defend did not wholly perish.

CHAPTER TWENTY-ONE

LETTERS

Language

In any society, education and literacy rest upon language. Most modern European peoples have achieved simplicity; they are monolingual, communicating in one language each, that is both written and spoken. Other modern societies, especially in Asia and Africa, are multilingual. They use more than one language, and are often handicapped because the language they know best is not written. But some societies are bilingual, equally at home in two languages. In the narrow zone of Switzerland where French and German overlap, neighbours in conversation may switch language unconsciously, and in some villages in Brittany French and Breton alternate as easily, though only French is written. The mark of a fully bilingual man, rare today, is that he does not notice which language he is speaking.

In early medieval Europe, most men were monolingual and illiterate; but the educated were multilingual, speaking their own language and Latin, writing in Latin alone, but keeping the languages apart. But in the Roman empire, language was more complex, bilingualism commoner. In the west, at the end of the empire, a few writers describe the relationship of Latin and Celtic. In the late 4th century, St. Jerome visited Trier on the Moselle, now in Western Germany, and also Ankara, now the capital of Turkey, but then the chief town of the Galatians, who were descendants of the Gauls who had invaded Asia Minor nearly 700 years before. He described what he observed.

> I have seen Ankara, capital of the Galatians. . . . The Galatians, apart from the Greek language that the whole east speaks, have their own native tongue, that is almost the same as that of Trier; and . . . just as the Africans have somewhat altered the Phoenician language, so Latin itself is varied in different districts at different times.

Trier was typical of northern Gaul. Soon after 400 Sulpicius Severus issued a sequel to his Life of Martin, in the form of a Dialogue; a participant from Latin-speaking Aquitaine gibed at a student from Tours in the north.

> Go on. Talk in Gallic or Celtic if you like, so long as you talk about Martin.

Gallic was the speech of all classes, not only of the rustics, for seventy years later

Sidonius, a great nobleman of the Auvergne, congratulated his younger relative
Ecdicius, because

> if our nobles have been inspired with a love of elegant language and
> poetry, if they have decided to abandon their hideous Celtic speech,
> it is thanks to your initiative.

Sidonius doubtless exaggerated Ecdicius' personal influence and the speed of
change, but he wrote of his own time, for readers who knew what languages they
and their fathers spoke. Gallic lingered among the nobility into the middle of the
fifth century, and doubtless lasted longer among the peasantry; it outlived the
Roman empire, and was effaced by the Latin dialect that grew into medieval
French only when Christianity spread into the countryside. But, as Jerome
remarked, it penetrated local Latin usage; a few Gallic words survive in French,
like *alouette* or *pièce*, and Gallic constructions pervaded the Latin of Gaul.
Sidonius strove to attain a classical purity, as far removed as possible from
popular idiom, but he nevertheless used *quod* and *quia* as the modern French use
que, and his *vir litterarum*, 'man of letters', perpetuated by the French *homme de
lettres*, is as alien to classical usage. The idiom that he heard in contemporary
speech occasionally penetrated his polished writing.

In Britain, Celtic and Latin were similarly related. British, akin to Gallic, was
everywhere spoken, and Latin was widespread. The pens used for writing on
wax tablets, called *styli*, are found in numbers in towns, and are not uncommon
in the countryside; they are evidence not only of literacy, but of Latin, for British
was unwritten. Several tablets survive, recording small-scale business trans-
actions, and London artisans could write Latin jokes on wet clay in good grammar
and a legible hand. In at least the larger towns, in London as in Trier, and
among the nobility, men were fluent in both languages, and many were fully
bilingual. As in Gaul, the languages interacted; British imported and passed on
to modern Welsh a very large number of Latin words, used for the commonest
objects of everyday life, that often displaced equally serviceable native words.
Up to the middle of the fifth century, British, like Gallic, was on the road to
absorbing so much Latin that it must soon yield to a spoken Latin language, but
the destruction of Roman institutions halted and reversed the process, for in
Britain spoken Latin died away, and the native speech endured.

The impact of the native idiom on Latin was less than in Gaul. Kenneth
Jackson's study of the Latin loan words concludes that, to a European ear,
British Latin

> seemed stilted and pedantic, ... upper class and 'haw-haw'. ...
> British Latin peculiarities ... tend to agree with the pronunciations
> recommended by grammarians. ... Schoolmasters ... succeeded
> in ... enforcing certain archaisms. ... The standard of Latin
> language, thought and culture was capable of being a high one.

The precise observation is followed by a more dubious conclusion, that British

Latin was the language of 'the well-to-do landowners of the Lowland Zone', contrasted with their 'half barbarian' peasants, who learnt their Latin from their lord's bailiff. The inference underestimates the rural pens and the artisan's literacy. It does not explain why the 'archaisms' of the pedant and the bailiff 'succeeded' in Britain while they failed in Gaul, nor why they prevailed in Snowdonia and Cornwall, where lowland bailiffs were unknown.

The standards of British Latin are more simply explained. It was old-fashioned because it was recent. The sophisticated wealth of aristocratic Romanity spread later in Britain than in Gaul, during the fourth century, and British Latin had no time to evolve colloquialisms on the scale of Gaul. The Latin of the fifth-century British writers, Pelagius and Faustus, the Sicilian Briton and Fastidius, is not merely 'archaic'; it is a clearer and more graceful Latin than the turgid prose of Jerome, simpler than the resonant rhetoric of Augustine, more fluent than the language of their pedestrian contemporaries in Italy and Gaul. By contrast, Patrick, whose education was interrupted, was throughout his life ashamed of his rough Latin, that he had to acquire in Gaul. The only known comparable non-literary work preserved from Gaul in his time, the travelogue of Aetheria, emphasises the contrast. Her constructions are better disciplined, for she passed her life among Latin speakers, while Patrick lived long among the Irish, but the paucity of her vocabulary and her insensitivity to sound and syllable are akin to his, infinitely removed from the polish of educated British Latin.

The writers of the early fifth century cared for language, and bequeathed their standards to the British of the south-west, who retained the leisure and the schooling to prolong a cultivated literacy, that the war destroyed elsewhere. Docco, Illtud, Paulinus and others passed on their tradition to their own pupils, among them Gildas, whose original experiments in the use of language were followed by the heady, zestful Latin of many of the later Irish and English monks. But in their day, as in the rest of Europe, Latin was spoken only by scholars. It died from ordinary conversation and the future lay with the native speech. The Celtic languages are exceptionally conservative. The Celtic name for the Baltic in the 2nd century BC, '*Mori Marusa*, that is, Dead Sea', is recognisably similar to the modern Welsh for Dead Sea, *Mor Marw*; when the Romans first encountered the same place name, Sorbiodunum, at Salisbury in Wiltshire and also on the Danube, current pronunciation dictated exactly the same spelling, though the Celts who named both places had parted company some seven centuries before; after fourteen centuries of separation Breton remains readily intelligible to Welsh children and is easily acquired by adults; Welsh has changed much less than English since its earliest sixth-century poems were written.

But, because the languages are conservative, change is sudden and sharp when it comes. Spoken British was jolted by the catastrophe of Roman Britain, and the transformed language is commonly called Welsh, in contrast to earlier British or 'Brittonic'. The change, centred on the end of the sixth century, seems somewhat sharper than it was, for it is also a change from old-fashioned

Latin spellings, hardened by custom, to new spellings devised when the native language was first written. Latin Cun-o-belin(us) became Kynvelyn, Maglos became Mael, and a host of other changes matured at much the same time. But oral change there was, evidently maturing first in the north, for English ears heard southerners pronounce names in -*maegl* as late as about 580, when Taliesin in the north was already composing poems in Welsh; though they were doubtless not written down until some decades later, their rhyme and metre make them products of the transformed language.

These changes coincided. The population ceased to speak Latin after Roman civilisation was destroyed; British turned into Welsh in the same years in which the Irish, British and English languages were first written, in the decades on either side of 600. Vernacular literacy gave a new orientation to education and literature, lowering the barriers between the learned and the unlettered. The earlier Irish annalists wrote sentences half in Irish and half in Latin with no more embarrassment than any other fully bilingual people, and continued to do so into the 11th century. They wrote as they spoke; and some schools sought to preserve Latin from contamination by forbidding their pupils to talk Irish to one another, or to converse with the local Latinless population. The Welsh and the English kept their languages and Latin apart, but the same scholars wrote as easily in the vernacular as in Latin, in an age when no European scholar could write in German or French, Italian or Spanish, even if he wished to address the unlearned. Their multilingual training gave them a far wider public than Europeans could reach; it enabled them to learn more from and about their own society, and to preserve customs, beliefs and social and historical traditions that in Europe died out or were suppressed.

Education

The schools of late Roman Britain resembled those of the rest of the empire, and are described by the Sicilian Briton. When his relative urged him to bring his daughter home for schooling, he told him to think of her as of a boy, who is normally sent to school away from home; in another context he cited the analogy of a school, where the pupils strove to reach the top form, *gradus*, but did not thereby leave the lower forms empty. The boys' boarding school, divided into forms, was normal, though most of the students lived out in lodgings. Literacy was commonly enforced by the cane, despite the protests of the most distinguished academics, but with lessening effect. In the early empire, westerners of breeding had been reared to fluency in Greek as well as Latin. In the 4th century Greek was still taught in the greater cities, Carthage, Trier, and doubtless also London, but the wide scholarship of Jerome was a rarity; most boys left school with one language only, like Augustine, to whom Greek remained a foreign language after a long education in Africa and Rome, or like the great eastern orator Themistius, who knew no Latin. Britain was exceptional; Augustine complained that Pelagius prevailed in debate in Jerusalem by reason of his fluent Greek, whereas Augustine's representative, the historian Orosius, failed because he had to rely on a faulty interpreter.

In the last days of the empire British education was reinforced by adaptations of Martin's monastic school; Whithorn in the far north was founded early in the 5th century and later emerged as a major school; and Coelestius, who was probably Irish and perhaps from Demetia, was educated in a monastery, probably in Britain, before he practised as a lawyer in Rome, not long after 400. Illtud in the later 5th century inherited and developed the experience of Europe and of Britain. Like Paulinus of Nola, Cassiodorus and other Roman noblemen, he withdrew to live a personal monastic life on his own estates; but unlike them, he maintained a school, whose pupils boarded with him. As in Martin's school, the pupils were sons of laymen, whose parents expected most of them to return to the world after a long schooling. Illtud's teaching techniques were ancient, for five year old infants learnt their alphabet from twenty pieces, termed *eleae* and *tesserae*, as the great Roman educationalist Quintilian had prescribed four centuries earlier, insisting that primary schooling must begin with the handling of physical letters, cut from ivory, bone or wood.

Illtud's school is described in the Lives of Samson and Paul Aurelian, which both draw on first-hand accounts. They illustrate the gentle wisdom with which he guided his pupils. When visions of the Egyptian hermit Antony prompted the sixteen year old Paul, heir to a great estate, to seek a desert solitude, Illtud probed his motive, warning that

> our thinking may have three origins, either from God, or from the Devil, or from ourselves; from God . . . by the infusion of the Holy Spirit . . . as it now seems to you in your case; . . . from the Devil . . . by hidden traps, shrewd and subtle . . . ; or from ourselves, when our ordinary natural thought recalls to our conscious memory things we have experienced or heard in the past.

He made him take time to reflect, but did not restrain him when he freely decided. When Samson, a year younger, fasted to excess, to the damage of his health, Illtud restrained him; years later, when Samson was already a senior, he too felt the impulse to solitude and

> was seeking to escape from the cenobite community without causing offence to his master.

Illtud then took the initiative, made him speak his mind, and arranged a transfer to the newly founded house of Piro on Caldey Island. The practical lessons on how to deal with human frailty that Gildas later imparted to the Irish were those that he had learnt in youth from Illtud.

Illtud's was the best known of the early schools, but it was not the only one. Paulinus soon after, and probably Docco a little earlier, were regarded as great teachers, and Tatheus maintained a well-reputed school in Caerwent. Some texts call the schools *Gimnasia*, and Winwaloe's is described as *scolasticorum collegium*, a college of scholars. Detail is rare in the later Lives; Cadoc taught the infant Malo to write his letters on a wax tablet; the cane, not mentioned in the tradition of Illtud or of other Welsh schools, is recorded at Ninian's Whithorn and at Servanus' school in Fife. Very many Lives stress that the schools taught both sacred and profane letters, 'both disciplines', or 'liberal studies'. The exception is Demetia. The Life of Teilo goes out of its way to denounce the 'figments of the poets', and the 'history of antiquity'; though David's Life remembers that in youth he learnt *rudimenta* as well as the scriptures, and was instructed by Paulinus in a 'tripartite' discipline, teaching plays no part in the record of David's adult work. In Demetia the tradition of David and Teilo prevailed, and there is little later sign of profane letters.

The first Irish monks had to travel to Britain for Christian schooling, for their own secular schools were pagan and were tight technical institutes devoted to the training of professional scholars in a set tradition immemorially old. In the 5th century, Enda and Darerca, Tigernach, Eugenius and others were taught at Whithorn, and many more 'went abroad' or 'visited Britain' in their youth. A few early teachers in Ireland had Roman names, like Boecius and Natalis, and may have come from Gaul or Britain, but the first influential school in Ireland was that of the British-born Mocteus at Louth. Like Cassiodorus in Italy, but unlike Illtud, he exempted his pupils from agricultural work; but the exemption seemed odd, even improper, to the Irish, and most of the early monks were proud to grow their own food. The first great native Irish school was founded at Clonard in the 530s by Finnian, who had previously gone for some years to 'study with the elders of Britain'. He was universally regarded as the 'teacher of the Irish saints', as well loved as Illtud in Britain; and from the middle of the century new monastic schools multiplied, many of them founded by Finnian's pupils.

The Irish schools differed from the British in that they were coeducational from the start. Patrick had brought to Ireland the experience of Christian Rome; the church of Italy had discovered that women were at first readier to withdraw from the world than men, and had early learnt that prudence and economy more wisely housed widows and unprotected single women in supervised hostels than in scattered lodgings. In later 5th-century Ireland the houses of Brigit, Darerca, Faencha and other women were more prominent than monasteries for men; and several early monks, like Enda, had been obliged at first to live with a minority of men attached to a community of women. The claims of women to equal monastic right were well established when the first schools opened, and Finnian of Clonard and his pupil Ciaran of Clonmacnoise are reported to have attached houses for girls to their monastic schools; though there was opposition, coeducation prevailed, stoutly defended by Dagaeus, the father of the art and craftsmanship of the Irish schools, who taught in turn at a number of the major monasteries.

A few Lives report the inevitable occasional problems. In her youth,

Darlugdach with difficulty resisted the temptation to steal from the bed she shared with Brigit to meet her lover. She lived chastely to succeed Brigit, but other men and women yielded to temptation; their sins are recorded when they went abroad to repent and returned to become austere abbots in their later years. A grave scandal disrupted the school of Whithorn in about 550. Drusticc, daughter of the king of the Picts, bribed Finnian, the future founder of Moville, to induce a fellow student with the British name of Rioc to her bed; but he sent a young Irishman from Cork in his place. The girl is also said to have tried to seduce Finnian. Both were expelled; the authorities are said to have used violence against Finnian, and the students retaliated with violence against the abbot. The story is no more likely to tell the whole truth than accounts of other scandals in other times. It outlines a situation often repeated, when a disciplinary incident sparks off a major clash; but it carried deeper undertones, for the girl was more than a king's daughter. The succession to the Pictish throne passed through the woman; if she had married Finnian or Rioc, the son of an obscure Irishman or Briton would have acquired a title to the kingship, as yet not held by any foreign-born king.

Yet scandals were infrequent. The double monasteries and their schools survived and multiplied. In both Britain and Ireland, numerous children are reported to have begun a ten-year curriculum at the age of 5 or 7, and intending priests continued their schooling until they were ordained deacon at the age of 19 or 20. In the monastic school, in contrast with Patrick's secular education, spoken and written Latin began in infancy, so that children grew up fully bilingual. At first, parents of means were expected to make an initial down payment. Some poorer schools were also sometimes compelled to invite the families of the district to make voluntary contributions to their funds, and some students are reported to have received free meals from nearby laymen. But most of the major monasteries had land and manpower enough to feed their pupils, and their status grew when the Convention of Drumceat incorporated the old learning within the Christian framework. Their influence encouraged the monastic schools to add both classical Irish and classical Roman learning to divine studies, so that the hostility to profane letters, advocated with success in Britain by David and Teilo, found fewer adherents in Ireland.

Educational opportunity made the Irish rather than the British houses the main centres of Christian learning. In the 7th century, students from Britain and Gaul began to frequent the Irish schools. Early in the century, Agilbert, later bishop of the West Saxons and of Paris, left his native Gaul to spend a long time in Ireland 'in order to read Divinity', for Ireland offered an advanced education that he could not find at home. Bede was amazed at the open-handed ease of the Irish educational system in the middle of the century, remarking that

there were many Englishmen in Ireland, both noble and plebeian,
who left their homeland in the time of bishops Finan and Colman

either to read Divinity or to live more continently. Some soon bound themselves to a monastic vow, but others preferred to travel around the cells of different teachers for the joy of reading. The Irish welcomed them all, gave them food and lodging without charge, lent them their books to read and taught them without fee.

Societies that find the means to offer higher education to all comers, native or foreign, without fee, with expenses paid, and without requiring proof of qualification, are not numerous in human history; and are more easily paralleled in Asia than in Europe. For the next several centuries Ireland prospered by the excellence of her schools. Men trained in Ireland were in demand throughout Europe; monied men as well as penniless students came to learn in Ireland. The freedom and the vigour of the schools was designed for learning, but it also brought material reward. Love of learning inspired a superb art, whose products, on paper and in metal, were exported in considerable quantity and earned a rich return by the receipt of corresponding gifts. At home, as in most societies, technological skills leapt ahead when a high standard of art and design was universally expected, and when its craftsmen were generally respected. Advances in mechanical engineering, in plant and animal biology, and above all in the cheap application of technological knowledge, rapidly increased agricultural and manufacturing production; the sudden widespread exploitation of waterpower, by devices long known and long unused, and the intensification of arable farming, were initiated by the same monasteries whose skills illuminated manuscripts and worked beautiful metal objects; both were the direct consequence of the educational system, whose expense was borne by rulers, who were compelled by public opinion to make land and resources available.

Irish inventiveness took its skills to Europe, especially to Italy and Germany, while its eagerness to learn enabled it to borrow and bring home something of the technological novelties that Slavs, Avars and others had brought to central Europe from further east. Inventiveness had its quirks, but common sense curbed the unfruitful and harmful; when at Ruadan's monastery of Lothra the commercial exploitation of a new and over-stimulating distilled drink threatened to overshadow the primary purposes of devotion and education, the pressure of other monasteries compelled Ruadan to limit the man-hours spent upon a specialised product of doubtful value to society.

Technological advance was an unforeseen fringe benefit. The business of the schools was to think and to teach, for the physical protection of a sacrosanct cloister was the only shield that could preserve the human intellect from the hideous violence of secular society. The same shield was welcomed abroad, by men who needed defence against the brutal administration that the uncouth rulers and lords of Europe had inherited from Rome. At first, the Irish came themselves. But other nations soon endeavoured to imitate and equal their learning. Among the English, double monasteries multiplied from the 660s onward; Benedict Biscop and others encouraged houses of purely English foundation and travelled to Italy to bring back books, that their *scriptoria* copied and circulated; Aldhelm tried without success to persuade English students that they could find at Canterbury in Theodore's time a Greek and Latin education as good as any to be had in Ireland. In Gaul, Columban brought the learning of Comgall's Irish Bangor to the Vosges at the end of the 6th century. The movement that he began swept Gaul in and after the 640s, as the original monastic reform had swept Britain and Ireland a hundred years earlier. Large numbers of monasteries founded by the Irish and English and by their native Frankish adherents also established libraries and copied books; if Agilbert had been thirty years younger, he would have had no need to go to Ireland to advance his education. Some Franks and many Englishmen still studied in Ireland, for the Irish libraries and learning were older than their own, and a journey to the land whence their monastic Christianity had come was in itself a pilgrimage. But the substance of Irish education had already spread abroad, and was in the next century carried to Germany.

The Irish brought not only books, but also men who loved to copy them, and did so with surpassing skill and beauty. They brought with them an understanding of what books were for, and a training in how to use them. The new education arrived when it was most needed, just after the old learning of Rome was dead beyond recovery. Half a century before the rash of new foundations, Gregory of Tours began the preface to his *History of the Franks* with a lament.

> Culture and education are dying out, perishing throughout the cities of Gaul. . . . There is no grammarian to be found, skilful enough in dialectic to depict the present age in prose or verse. You often hear people complaining 'Alas for our times; literacy is dying among us, and no man can be found among our peoples who is capable of setting down the deeds of the present on paper'.

The monks came just in time to replace the dying education of antiquity with a new learning, alert to seize upon what suited the needs of its own day.

Latin Literature

Latin learning persisted in the schools, at least in south-western Britain; but the work of one writer alone survives from 6th-century Britain, Gildas. The style of his letters is simple and vigorous, but his book, intended for publication, is an astounding and original development in Latin literature. Its construction is 'firm and monumentally wrought', put together 'on the grand scale, conscious and calculated'. The style and concept of language is altogether new. Gildas knew and studied the controlled elegance of the early 5th-century British writers, and the rhythmical rhetoric of his contemporaries in Europe. He rejected both. He learned more from poets than from prose writers, writing for the ear rather than the eye, striking at his readers' feelings. His paragraphs are an ordered series of impressions, painted in gaudy and unusual words, unusually arranged; their

sentences run on in 'shapeless splendour' like the exhortation of a platform
orator. Their impact is forced upon the reader by a wealth of colourful adjectives
and images, the words placed together by sound and syllable, in defiance of the
ordinary conventions of word order. When he contrasts Maelgwn's poets with
Christian choirs he opens with powerful alliteration, *arrecto aurium auscultantur
non Dei laudes*, 'the excited ears of the auditors are seized not by praises of God';
soft words compare the 'gently modulated tones of Christ's soldiers', *tironum
voce sauviter modulante*, with the frenzy of the warband's bards, *spumanti
flegmate proximos quosque roscidaturo*, 'bedewing all near him with foaming
phlegm'.

Gildas' extraordinary style is unique. He was born beyond the Clyde, outside
the frontiers of Rome, and sent to a good southern school because his father was
an eminent military captain. His unsophisticated enthusiasm was fired by the
possibilities of a long cultivated language, hitherto politely disciplined. His style
appears as his alone, elaborated without precedent or parallel. Yet what he wrote
was no literary exercise, but a political pronouncement of major importance, that
was intended to move the hearts and minds of great numbers of readers, and
achieved its aim. Gildas wrote as he did because he judged that a work so written
would be welcomed and understood; and he judged rightly. His book was
plainly designed to be read aloud to large audiences, as well as in private arm-
chairs; it presupposes a considerable audience who could still understand some
Latin, even if they could not read it. His work may have stood alone in his own
day; but it may also be that he was the foremost among a school of new-style
writers, that grew up among the pupils of Illtud's and similar schools, whose
other writings have not been preserved.

What Gildas inherited from the British Latin authors of the past was above all
a care for language. His idiom was original, without known antecedents. But it
had a long sequel. Bizarre words, often newly concocted, put together for oral
effect without regard to the precepts of grammarians, became a widespread
literary form, termed 'Western Latin', that long flourished in Ireland and found
occasional European imitators, like Virgilius Maro, though living Latin soon
ceased in Britain. The Irish taught the new style to their English pupils, notably
Boniface and Aldhelm, whose far-reaching influence established it firmly in the
tradition of English Latin. But Western Latin was chiefly a literary exercise, and
begot an extremist fringe, termed 'Hisperic', whose elaborate conceits defeat
understanding.

Western and Hisperic fashions endured for a few centuries, but they contributed to one important permanent development. The experiments of Welsh
and Irish poets exploited the regular and frequent use of rhyme, within lines and
at their end, in Latin, in Irish and in Welsh. Rhyme was not new to Latin, but it
was hitherto weakly developed. It well matched the alliteration of classical Irish
verse and, from the 8th century onwards, monastic poets who called themselves
the 'new writers' pioneered new metres, whose roots lay both in the late Latin

hymn and in classical Irish. Their innovation was not confined to form; and was earlier matched in vernacular Welsh. Delicate and lovely lyrics described the beauties of the countryside, that monks had leisure to observe; their contemplation extended to humanity, to the sadness of withered age and the splendour of youthful vigour. The descriptive verse of Roman poets had commonly appealed to the intellect and the ear; Irish and Welsh observation appealed to the eye, using words as a painter uses colour. The new poetry of the Welsh is almost entirely confined to the vernacular, but the continuing bilingualism of the Irish scholars rooted it in Latin as well, and imparted its concept to the English. Their successors made their themes the familiar common stock of European verse; but in early Christian Ireland they were new and unique.

The ornament of Western Latin and Hisperic extravagance enlivened the Latin of the southern English, but the Northumbrians outgrew their Irish teachers, and under the guidance of Benedict Biscop and king Aldfrith they matured their own monastic learning. The finely chiselled austerity of Bede's Latin silently reproves the riotous imagery of Gildas and Aldhelm. It learnt from Europe, but its roots were English. It also permeated Europe, for Bede's wide scholarship placed him among 'the most widely read authors of the early middle ages', an influence as potent as the Irish on form and style. In prose as in verse, the literature that Irish and English monks brought to Europe was powerful, and helped to renew the vitality of languishing Latin culture.

Welsh Literature

Welsh vernacular literature was a new creation. Four hundred years of Roman civilisation had drowned all memory of the bards and the ancient learning of pre-Roman times. The past was altogether gone. When national sentiment required historical legends, early in the 6th century, Welsh scholars had to look to Roman historians, and from a late Roman mis-spelling of Cunobelinus, the last great pre-Roman king of the south-east, they contrived 'Belin, son of Manocan', who had ruled in London; for the real Cunobelinus was forgotten. In four centuries, the Welsh had lost all memory of the past when they had not been Roman, though for fifteen centuries they have remembered that they are not English.

The first mention of a bard in Britain is beyond the Roman frontier, at the court of Coroticus of the Clyde in the mid fifth century; and Gildas inveighed against Maelgwn's bards three generations later. None of their works survives, and a text preserved by Nennius dates the beginning of Welsh poetry to the mid 6th century, in the north, when Talhaern Tataguen sang in Outigern's time. He then names Aneirin and Taliesin, to whom some extant works are attributed, probably rightly, and Bluchbard and Cian, 'called Gueinth Guaut', whose name is Irish. Irish literature is drenched in the remote past, but the surviving works of the early Welsh know no history; all concern the present. The poets depended on royal patrons. Rhyme and alliteration abound in their diction, as in the Irish tradition that the 'new writers' later formulated. The oldest poems date to the end of the 6th century, but they were doubtless not written down until some decades later; for nothing suggests that the Latin schools of 5th- and 6th-century Britain encouraged or designed a vernacular alphabet. Deliberate intellectual effort was needed to adapt Latin letters to the sound of native speech, and it is probable that that effort was first made in Ireland, in the later 6th century, where Latin and writing itself were both novelties.

The Welsh may have owed the mechanics of writing to the Irish, but the content of their writing was their own. The odes that Taliesin and Aneirin addressed to their dead kings are finer literature than any that a trained Irish poet sang about the heroes of his own day; though they are the work of royal minstrels, they have nothing of the polished flattery of court poets in other societies. The poets mourned a world they loved, and that they knew was dying; Aneirin's *Gododdin* describes the grandeur of a final ruin; Taliesin found in Urien and his son a personal magnetism that won his affection; and Cynddylan also aroused in his unknown poet a like admiration and respect.

The epics of the northern British became the classics of the Welsh. For many centuries a succession of great poets wrote songs in praise of their own day. Lyric verse began early, with an isolated poem copied by chance into the manuscripts of Aneirin, sung to a child.

> Dinogad's coat is coloured bright
> I made it from marten skins. . . .
>
> When your Dad went a-hunting
> A spear on his shoulder, a club in his hand,
>
> He'd call his fast dogs
> 'Giff! Gaff! Catch, catch; fetch, fetch'. . . .
> Whatever came near your father's spear
> Boar or wild cat or fox
>
> Unless it had wings it could never get clear.

Later Welsh medieval verse is rich in love poems, and in nature poems that owe much in form to the Irish; but they remained vigorously secular, their delight in life keener than the quiet observation of the monks.

Since Welsh tradition had no history earlier than the fifth century, the poems of the sixth century became the starting point of historical verse and myth. The Merlin Cycle, the *Armes Prydein* and many other medieval poems plundered the older epics to weave mystic, nervous prophecies of an ultimate reconquest of the lost lands of England; and in so doing they preserved in allusion something of lost early epic. The concept of constructing a long past history told in detailed stories was in itself Irish. But its main vehicle was prose.

The Welsh story-teller had greater need of foreign borrowings than the Irish. The principal collection of tales is grouped in the text commonly called the

Mabinogion. It comprises a mythological cycle, the 'Four Branches of the Mabinogi', properly so-called, whose form and content is heavily indebted to Irish mythological tales, their setting transferred to West Wales; an Arthurian cycle, whose core probably derives from the same sources as the Norman romances; and a few historical tales. Some of them, like Lludd and Llevelys, are late attempts to picture conquering kings of pre-Roman Britain who ruled from London, but others are finer literature. One of them, the 'Dream of Maxen Wledig', is among the best told tales in the early prose of any land.

Maxen was emperor of Rome, comelier, better and wiser than any emperor before. . . . Maxen slept, and he saw a dream. . . . Valleys he saw and . . . rocks of wonderful height. . . . Thence he beheld an island in the sea, facing this rugged land. . . . From the mountain he saw a river, and at the mouth of the river he saw a castle, the fairest that ever man saw. . . . He went into the castle, and in the castle he saw a fair hall. Its roof seemed to be all of gold, its walls of glittering precious gems. . . . Golden seats he saw in the hall, and silver tables. He saw two fair haired young men playing at chess . . . a silver board for the chess and golden pieces thereon. Beside a pillar in the hall he saw a hoary headed old man, in a chair of ivory, with the figures of two eagles of ruddy gold thereon. Bracelets of gold were upon his arms, and many rings upon his hands, and a golden torque about his neck; and his hair was bound with a golden diadem. He was powerful to look upon. A chessboard was before him, and a rod of gold, and a steel file in his hand, and he was fashioning chessmen.

He saw a maiden sitting in a chair of ruddy gold. No more easy was it to gaze upon the sun at its brightest than to look upon her, by reason of her beauty. . . . She was the fairest sight that ever man beheld. . . . The maiden arose, and he put his arms about her neck. . . . But when he had his arms around her neck, and his cheek rested upon her cheek, then through the barking of the dogs . . . and the clashing of the shields . . . and the neighing of the horses . . . the emperor awoke from his dream.

He was the saddest man that ever was seen. . . . The wise men of Rome said . . . 'Send messengers . . . to seek thy dream'. . . . So the messengers journeyed . . . and came to the island of Britain . . . to Snowdon . . . to Arvon. . . . They saw the youths . . . the hoary headed man . . . carving chessmen . . . and the maiden. . . . The emperor set forth with his army . . . and conquered Britain . . . and came to Arvon . . . into the castle and into the hall. And there he saw Kynan the son of Eudav and Adeon the son of Eudav playing chess; and Eudav the son of Caradawc sitting on a chair of ivory fashioning chessmen . . . and the maiden . . . upon a chair of ruddy gold . . . and that night she became his bride.

The next day in the morning, she asked her maiden portion, to have the island of Britain for her father, with the three nearby islands . . . and the three chief castles . . . Arvon . . . Caerleon and Carmarthen. . . . Then Helen bethought her to make high roads from one castle to another; and for this reason they are called *Sarn Helen*, the roads of Helen of the Hosts.

Seven years did the emperor stay in this island. . . . So the men of Rome made a new emperor. . . . So Maxen set forth towards Rome . . . and sat down before the city. . . . A year was the emperor before the city, no nearer to the taking of it than on the first day. . . . Then came the brothers of Helen from the island of Britain, with a small army, and better warriors were in that small army than twice as many Romans. . . . They came to the city, and set their ladders against the wall, and came into the city . . . and none could give it to the emperor but the men of the island of Britain. Then the gates of the city of Rome were opened, and the emperor sat upon his throne.

Then the emperor said to Kynan and Adeon, 'I give you this army to conquer what regions you will'. . . . So they . . . conquered lands and castles and cities. . . . Then Kynan said to his brother 'Will you stay in this land, or go home to the land from whence you came?' He chose to go home to his own land, and many with him; but Kynan stayed with the others, and dwelt there . . . and the men of Armorica are called Britons. This is the dream called the Dream of Maxen Wledig, emperor of Rome, and here it ends.

The tale is a straightforward historical narrative, its main facts accurate, their context altogether unknown and misunderstood. Maximus was a fourth-century Roman emperor, who conquered the city of Rome with the help of an army from Britain; his wife, described in her lifetime by Sulpicius Severus as the pious woman who waited silently upon St. Martin while her husband discussed theology with him at dinner, may have been British. The story used a description of Roman Segontium by someone who had seen its buildings and its furniture before time wore them, and who knew something of his remoter ancestors' ornament and dress. It is possible that a part of Maximus' army settled in Armorica. The context is amiss, for the author supposed that Maximus ruled Rome before he came to Britain, and led the Roman army that conquered Britain.

The 'Dream of Maxen' and the legend of Belin embody the Welsh concept of early history. It was formed early in the 6th century, when Rome died with Arthur. It already pervaded the outlook of Gildas; though he knew of Roman armies and governors, law and gentility, he had no notion that Britain had once been an integral part of Roman civilisation; though he saw the scale of Roman buildings he did not associate them with Rome, but with the *cives*, the *Cumbrogi*, his fellow-countrymen. The past was forgotten, but the present needed a past. It was learned from Roman writers, but recorded in the manner of the Irish. The Cambrian Annals begin as a text of the Irish Annals, into which some British notices are inserted; its account is supplemented by genealogies modelled on the Irish, and by tales drawn from Irish mythology.

Later Welsh literature was built on history and mythology. They were consolidated in the 8th and 9th centuries. The documents collected by Nennius took British history back to the 5th century and prefixed it with an Irish account of the origins of the peoples of the British Isles. They included a satisfactory explanation of the coming of the British themselves. It was a convention of the age to supply national names with a fanciful etymology, and to personify them. Early in the 7th century Isidore of Seville had explained that the British were so-called because they were *bruti*, 'stupid'; some twenty or thirty years later the Irish annalist Cuanu accepted his unflattering view, admitting that the British were 'odious' (*exosus*), but personalised their founder as Brutus, great-grandson of Aeneas the Trojan, legendary founder of the Latins.

Brutus the Trojan was welcomed in Britain and long retained his fame. When the English mastered the island, he acquired three sons, Loegrius of England, from *Lloegr*, the Welsh word for England, Albanus of Albany, the heartland of the future Scotland, and Camber of Wales. The fancy was so universally accepted that later national leaders of Scotland did not dispute its substance, but protested only that it erred in detail, wrongly making Loegrius ancestor of the Plantagenets, and thereby entitling them to supremacy.

The nonsense filled a vacuum and pointed to a need. When once the Welsh had learned to record their history, they took care to see that their known national heroes were not again allowed to lapse from memory, and enshrined the rest of their history in a continuing literature, deeper in their consciousness than elsewhere in Britain. The rest of the peoples of Britain forgot or suppressed their history. The language and the memories of the British of the Clyde were preserved in Wales, forgotten at home; the faint traditions of the Picts are preserved only by the Irish, and the Scots project romantic medieval institutions back into a mythical past; among the English, the legend of Brutus the Trojan survived until the 16th century, and even today tradition distorts national history by beginning in the middle, with the Norman conquest. For nearly half of their known history the English are disguised as 'Anglo-Saxons', remote blondes with their legs in thongs, a quaint and irrelevant prelude whose study may safely be relinquished to a few specialists, while the Roman and pre-Roman past is normally abandoned to archaeologists and younger school-children.

Welsh literature has given the Welsh a saner and more balanced understanding of their origins than the romanticism of the Scots or the cultivated ignorance of the English. It has helped the Welsh to retain their identity, even when most of them have forgotten their language. History was its starting point, but from the 6th century onward it has continued to produce great verse and prose in each generation, so that even today the bulk and quality of Welsh literature is not less, in proportion to the numbers of those who read the language, than that of any other European nation. In spite of the language decline, it has also created a modern literature that is no less Welsh because it uses the medium of the English language.

It remains free and natural, unembarrassed by the artificial stage brogue that hampers the modern Irish; for though the serious Irish writer who would develop a national idiom must tread cautiously, lest he look like an English comedian aping the Irish, the Welsh writer is less exposed to such risk. The immediate impact of Welsh literature is handicapped because it has not yet come to terms with the comparatively recent fall in the numbers of those who read the language with ease and pleasure; but the riches of many centuries give it powerful reserves, and when it finds translators worthy of its content, it is likely to enlarge the dignity of national sentiment far beyond the bounds of the spoken language, and to enrich the literary inheritance of Europe.

English Literature

English vernacular writing began almost as early as the Welsh and Irish, but it matured more slowly. The earliest known text is the law code of Aethelbert of Kent, published in about 600. Its title, the oldest surviving words of the English language, is spare and terse. *This syndon tha Domas, the Aethelbirht Cyning asette on Augustinus daege*, 'there are the Laws that King Aethelbert fixed in Augustine's days'. The promulgation of laws in the spoken tongue caused wonder; more than a hundred years later Bede singled them out as the only benefit of Aethelbert's reign that he found worthy of remark. It was to be many centuries before any vernacular laws were written down in Europe; though later Kentish kings added new codes, and Ine codified the laws of Wessex about 690, Bede, in about 730, emphasised a desirable innovation, evidently not yet imitated in Northumbria.

No literature but law is known from Kent. Written verse is first recorded in the north. Caedmon bore a British name. He was an elderly layman who lived near Whitby, about 670. He often dined out, in company that was evidently predominantly English, where the lyre was passed round from guest to guest. He regularly left the dinner and went home before the lyre reached him, since he could not sing, perhaps because he could not yet trust his mastery of English. But one night it was his turn to undertake the job of policing stables, that evidently belonged to the monastery, and in the small hours divine inspiration prompted him to compose a hymn to the Creator. He subsequently entered the monastery, and in his old age men copied his verses into books, and perhaps on to stone.

Few other English poets are known before the 9th century. The excellence of Bede and the brilliance of Aldhelm kept Latin the language of literature; king Aethelbald of Mercia and other poets chose it as the natural language of verse. The Mercians and the West Saxons, like the Irish, wrote down traditional historical verses, notably *Beowulf* and the *Widsith*. But in the 9th century quantities of Latin literature were published in translation, and the learning of Wessex pulled together earlier monastic record into the Saxon Chronicle; its form and its earliest entries are Irish, but towards the end of the 8th century its terse notices are interrupted by the dramatic story of king Cynewulf's murder; thereafter an increasing number of long passages in resonant prose transform its character, and from the 10th century its entries include numerous poems of simple dignity. Thenceforth other authors strengthened the tradition of English writing, so that it survived the darkness of the northmen, and re-emerged when the English regained literacy in the 13th and 14th centuries.

Irish Literature

The Irish, unlike the Welsh and English, inherited an immensity of ancient tradition. Ireland was the first large territory outside the Roman empire to become Christian. It had no Latin; Christian scholars were therefore compelled to write the Irish language in Latin characters, that the scriptures might be communicated. They were also compelled to come to terms with the old learning while the old learning was compelled to make use of the new technique of alphabetic writing. The learned orders of 6th-century Ireland retained the ancient names of *drui*, *bard* and *faith*; Roman writers had used the same words six centuries and more before to describe the religious orders of the Gauls, *druides*, *bardi* and *vates*, which in their view were already older than the learning of the Greeks. The superior order of the Druids, who included learned 'philosophers' and *theologoi* who understood the words of the gods, was then divided into specialised colleges. Caesar was impressed by the number of their pupils, who travelled from afar to study for twenty years or more, memorising immense quantities of verse, for the Druids refused to permit their sacred lore to be committed to writing, though they permitted the use of Greek letters for 'public and private records'.

In Christian Ireland the name of *drui* was restricted to a class of minor scholars; bishops and abbots assumed the duties of the *theologoi*, but the colleges of learned men, termed *filid*, remained. The secular schools of the 7th century comprised three main faculties, classics (*leigind*), law (*fenechas*), and poetry and philosophy (*filidhecht*). Students were expected to study for at least 12 years and the graduate *filid* were divided into seven classes, the lowest qualified to recite 20 stories, the highest 350, which he was expected to 'synchronise and harmonise'. Many of these tales survive, in more recent versions, and the titles of hundreds more are recorded.

The pagan Irish had no alphabet, but they adapted Latin letters to a script termed *Ogam*, wherein each letter was represented by notches cut against or across the edge of a squared wooden stick; no sticks remain, but many stone memorials are so inscribed. Ogam remained the chief form of learned record until the middle of the 7th century; then Cennfaelad is said to have written down the learning of the schools 'on slates and tablets', evidently of wax, and to have fair-copied them into 'vellum books'. Columba had persuaded Christian Ireland to accept the ancient learning half a century or more before, but

Cennfaelad's innovation opened its preserves to monastic scholarship; the Annals preserve many of the ancient verses that he copied; and together with Aileran, and with his own cousin's son, Flann Fina, the future king Aldfrith of Northumbria, he is remembered among the principal doctors of 7th-century Irish learning.

The volume and antiquity of the old learning swept over Christian Irish literature. The early Irish historians were sceptical, protesting that the tales they rendered were 'not genuine history'. Nevertheless though the tales of early times are full of fancies, folk memory accurately reported some essential features of the remote past. The *filid* grouped the tales into four main cycles. The Mythological Cycle was followed by the Heroic Cycle, centred on the Ulaid heroes of about the first century AD; the Finn Cycle was concerned with Cormac's wars in the third century, and the Historic Cycle treated of more recent kings. The stories of the last three cycles abound in details of barbarian Ireland, which lasted into the 6th century, and have rightly been termed a 'Window on the Iron Age', for no other western people has preserved such vivid record of the remote past.

The weight of ancient story made the Irish more conscious of an ageless past than any other European people. It constrained the Christian Irish to continue to report the present and developed the forms of record that the Welsh and English later adapted. But it divided monk and layman. The Annalists ignored the story-tellers as often as they could, and the Latin-language Lives of the Saints were severely restricted to incidents factually related, concerning named peoples and places of the saints' own time and region. Though each story is the setting of an imaginative miracle, the Lives are cast in the mould of rational history. But the laity who knew no Latin were provided with the vernacular Irish versions, whose translators borrowed from the wonders of the story-teller without regard to time or place. Yet the quantity of stories kept them continuously alive; the Lives were recopied without interruption, suffering no periods of oblivion and revival like the tales of Welsh saints.

The Irish literary tradition was imprisoned by its own wealth and age. The discipline of the *filid* was prolonged until the Elizabethan conquest and the Cromwellian settlement; the last of the ancient scholars, Duald MacFirbis, after poverty had forced him to sell the last of his books, was murdered in a Sligo tavern in 1670, at the age of 80, by a drunken English gentleman. Learning that was older than the Greeks was ended by a sordid crime. But its discipline had long been oppressive; new literary forms were hard to evolve in a conservative tradition that issued degrees to those who mastered a set syllabus, and had no use for unqualified talent. The 'new writers' of the 8th century had forced their way into the approved canon of Irish literature, but their innovations evoked a keener response in the more receptive minds of the Welsh and of the nations of Europe than at home. The Irish poets were the first to move men deeply by tales of the tenderness of tragic love that overrides all else, but they were confined by fixed forms, traditional themes and a language unknown outside their island. They inspired the poets of the Welsh and English, and passed their stories of romantic love to the French, who permanently implanted them in the literary tradition of Europe. But they could not enrich the future of their home-land with a lasting native literature, renewing itself in successive generations with the vigour and flexibility of Welsh or English letters. The splendour of Irish learning and letters, like the inheritance of Irish art, was centred upon its Latin monasteries, not upon its secular schools or vernacular literature. That literature was not an article of export; its content and idiom were insular, and stories set in Ireland had little interest for foreigners. Its contribution to other lands was its aim and method, the recording of the past and the present and, above all, the gift to the Welsh and the English of the ability to write their own spoken language, in an age when all other literature was still composed in Latin alone.

Humour

One notable by-product of Welsh and Irish Literature was parody and satire. Though a few men wrote masterpieces and others wrote well, most produced dreary texts, pompous and jejune. Their banality provoked quiet mockery. One well worn pious theme, first elaborated in Adomnan's Life of Columba, praises the simple ignorance of children who tried to milk a bull. One author, transcribing such a tale, notes the 'columbine innocence' of Fechin of Fore who

> did not know the difference between a bull and a cow, and went up
> to a bull, and squeezed its genitals like a cow's udder.

The bull not only tolerated the assault, but gave milk. The author drily comments on

> a remarkable and unusual novelty. But that is what is possible in a
> country where honey is commonly produced from stones, and oil
> from the hardest rocks,

for such marvels were commoner in the Lives of the Saints of Ireland than of other lands.

Many authors vaunt the magic of the saint's curse, that kills the impious; and avoid the implication of a divine murderer by making the saint's prayer restore his victim to a penitent life. When the author of the verse Life of Senan met such a tale, he turned it to irreverent doggerel,

> The pious father's prayer
> Produced a sweetly flowing spring
> That the brethren largely used
> And thanked him for as often. . . .

There the holy Finan
The blessed man's disciple . . .
Came as was his wont
To sit beside the well,
Praising life's creator.

There came a peasant girl
And sat herself beside him.
She brought her little boy
To wash him clean. . . .

Most ill the monk regarded
The interruption of his prayer
By the washing of a child,
Polluting holy liquor.

So, moved to anger
For the wronging of the well,
He prayed to God
To sink the child beneath the waves.

Soon the waters' flux
That daily mounted there
At God's command took off the lad
And bore him out to sea.

When the mother saw him
Carried far from shore
Straightaway she sought the bishop
Wailing for her son. . . .

Stern the bishop summoned him
And bade him straightaway
Fetch back the wretched child
Or else be drowned himself.

No sooner said, the holy man
Ran off to brave the danger,
Sparing not his feet,
His holy staff in hand.

Carefully he measured
How deep the waters were
Wishing to wade no deeper
Than his holy middle.

For he was fearful
And had a firm intention
To go no deeper in
Than his staff would show was safe. . . .

> Then, lo, a miracle.
> The sea beneath his feet
> Turned hard as rock
> Although it was most deep. . . .
>
> And there he found the lad
> Not dead, but playing happily. . . .
>
> The credit for the miracle
> The master gave to the disciple,
> The disciple to the master.
>
> Yet in the eyes of each
> Both of them were very humble,
> And seeing what was done
> They honoured one another.

Such elaborate parody is unusual; but light irony is not uncommon. Another convention gives many saints long conversations with angels. One author protested. Transcribing the tireless energy with which the virgin Attracta pestered the Deity to add a minor miracle to a mighty wonder, he made the angel of the Lord warn her solemnly

> The Lord thy God is getting bored with thee.

Sometimes irony preached common sense; the strongest of conventions required saints of eminence to revive many from the dead, but such wonders normally belonged to the remote past. The author of an Irish Life of Adomnan dealt severely with an embarrassing consequence. When the body of the king of the Picts was brought to Iona for burial in 691 Adomnan and his clergy kept vigil by the bier. During the night a limb of the corpse moved, as rigor mortis set in. Movement naturally caused excitement, and raised expectation of a latter-day resurrection. But a 'certain pious man' warned Adomnan

> if you try to raise the dead, your precedent will become a reproach to your successors, who cannot do so.

Adomnan was made to reply

> There is something in what you say. It will be more proper to confine ourselves to blessing the body and soul of the king.

Irish irony was occasionally echoed by the Welsh. A favourite mythological theme is the hero who takes the shape of an animal. In the late Mabinogion tale called *Taliesin*, Ceridwen pursued Gwion Bach, who turned himself into a hare; so she became a greyhound, an otter when he became a fish, a hawk when he flew away as a bird; as he dived into a heap of corn to become a wheat grain, she became a hen and gobbled him up. The pursuit ended, and

> she bore him nine months, and when she was delivered of him, she

found him too beautiful to kill, so she put him in a leather bag and threw him into the sea. And it was the 29th day of April.

Welsh prose authors were of sufficient intellectual calibre to protest against the sterility of a worn-out convention as vigorously as Cervantes' *Don Quixote* protests against the rubbishy late romances of chivalry.

Parody courts disaster when it is so subtle that men do not perceive it; and Welsh parody aborted in catastrophe. The eccentric genius of Geoffrey of Monmouth in the 12th century protested against the arid academics of his day, notably Henry of Huntingdon and William of Malmesbury, and gleefully refuted them with a pretended Welsh book which, he warned his more sober readers, stemmed from Walter of Oxford. He should have been safe enough, for he used the standard texts known to the academic historians, and made fun of them. He repeated the Roman historian's account of the defeat of a third-century British rebel by the Caesar Constantius and his prefect Asclepiodotus; but when he decorated known history by appointing Asclepiodotus to the dukedom of Cornwall, and marrying Constantius to the daughter of Old King Cole, he and the historians knew that he was satirising. When he reproduced Bede's account of the wars of Catwallaun and Penda, he and they knew that he was guying history when he made Catwallaun outlive Penda, that the British might bury him in a bronze horse on the top of Ludgate; any educated man might read Bede for himself.

Geoffrey's wry fancy stirred his many sources into a soup of names. But his jest took himself and his readers captive. Whether he liked it or not, he was taken seriously. His mock solemnity aped the formalism of academic teaching, as bitingly as Sellar and Yeatman's *1066 and All That* in our day; he was as convincingly soaked in his material as Tolkien, author of *Lord of the Rings*. But Geoffrey confused satire with sincerity, putting into his book his own deeply held philosophy. Of Armorican origin, born in Wales, he was a patriotic servant of the English king, convinced that Britain was a family of nations among whom the English were senior; the fiction that made Loegrius of England the elder brother of Albanus and Camber of Scotland and Wales personified his conviction, and was a potent immediate political ideal, acceptable not only to the English but also to propertied Welshmen and Scots, who welcomed an excuse to decline futile national resistance that risked their lands and property.

Geoffrey's convincing fantasy was immediately accepted; it remained the received account of British history for many centuries, the foundation upon which Great Britain was built. It was not seriously challenged until the Renaissance, and was widely believed into the 18th century. Even today a thick dust of Geoffrey's imagination obscures understanding. Since countless names and incidents that Geoffrey annexed occur in other records, it is still quite common to cite Geoffrey as though he might be evidence for some tradition otherwise lost. Yet most of his sources are known; and his riotous plunder of the names they

427

mention regularly and deliberately conflicts with what they say; even if he plundered an unknown source, his use of it was perverse. It ought not to be necessary to warn that no word or line of Geoffrey can legitimately be considered in the study of any historical problem; but the warning unfortunately remains necessary.

Parody can be powerful, even when it is known for what it is. But it is rare. The main body of Irish, Welsh and English literature in the 6th and 7th centuries is sober and straightforward. It was one of the formative influences in the literature of Europe. It stimulated the renewed vigour of Latin, and enriched it with a delight in language and a zest for experiment that classical tradition had long since stifled. But its most important influence was the precedent it set. Because the native languages of the British Isles were written, they became a model and an encouragement to the nations of Europe, who ultimately freed themselves from the exclusive use of Latin letters and took to writing original work in their own tongues. Modern European literature was born in the peculiar conditions of the British Isles in the sixth century, and was nursed by bilingual monks. The short life of Arthurian Britain brought into being a society that needed a modern literature, and knew how to create it.

CHAPTER TWENTY-TWO

THE ECONOMY

Roman Britain

Almost all men lived by the land, and fared better on good lands. But the fall of Rome left lands good and bad peopled by farmers of unlike skills and experience. The fertile lowlands were wasted; from the sandy coasts of Germany the first English brought techniques fitted only for alluvial lands by river banks, and for soils as easy. The wealth of the Severn estuary escaped the wars, but not the ruin of the Roman economy; the Pennine north, the Welsh hills and the Dumnonian moors were less affected, for they were poorer lands, that had never shared in the prosperity of the lowlands, and the north had always obeyed a hungry army. Beyond the Roman frontiers little changed, and in Armorica British immigrants resumed the cultivation of lands untilled for many years, but still recognisably cleared. The sources that described the agriculture of each region are as varied, and are imperfectly assessed; most of them are published but the texts are often indifferently edited, and rarely analysed. The ancient laws of the Welsh, the Irish and the English illuminate much of Britain, but the histories of churchmen, and the land grants of the Irish, Welsh and English are preserved only from a few regions. There is plenty of raw evidence, but until it has been sifted, the links between the several texts are hard to recognise; their undigested statements provoke a turbulence of ideas, whose ordering and assessment must await the labours of the future.

Roman Britain had integrated widely different economies. In the lowlands, towns large and small were set close together, 8 to 12 miles apart, joined to one another and to the surrounding rural population by main and minor roads. The owners of mansions, of substantial farms and of small cottages were all able to buy large quantities of pottery and other commercial products. But the highlands were poorer and more isolated; often a scrap of metal or a couple of pot sherds is the only evidence that a pre-Roman Iron Age farm lasted into and through the Roman period; and many others that lack such scraps may have lasted as long. Small regions differ greatly from each other, but the overall contrast between the two main divisions of Britain is sharp and clear. The peasants of the lowlands were exploited by their lords, but they were fully absorbed into Roman civilisation, customers in its markets; the small farmers in much of the highlands were little affected by Roman economy, but they were integrated into the Roman state by the agencies of government, language and law, that made them Roman citizens.

The last generations of Roman Britain brought important change to the lowlands. The ownership of land was concentrated into the hands of fewer great landowners, including the emperor, many of them absentees; many isolated farms of the early empire were deserted, and in several areas peasants congregated in poorly built villages and hamlets. On absentee estates the mansions rotted, but rents were collected, and unwanted living rooms were sometimes used as storehouses or workshops. Periodical fairs eroded the trade of some towns and many renders were paid in kind. Currency disappeared from much of the countryside, and concentrated in some great ports, like Richborough, in some towns, or parts of towns, and on fairgrounds, where peasants and their masters sold their produce to pay their dues, and spent what cash was left. Beyond these centres distribution proceeded by barter and exchange, and by the management of bailiffs.

The root cause of change was the crushing weight of taxation. Its consequence, the uneven circulation of late money, does not mean that more people lived in areas where money was more plentiful, or that people died or went away where money ceased to circulate. But it does mean that the fibres which bound countrymen to the urban economy were weakening. Farmers whose ancestors had been poor freeholders or tenants became *coloni*, semi-servile bondsmen, squeezed hard to pay their dues to the factor of an alien owner, less able to afford the manufacturers' products. Until the quantities and proportions of late objects on different kinds of sites have been studied more closely, it is not possible to discover how these changes progressed in different areas. But the direction of change was to detach the lowland peasant from Roman civilisation, to approximate him towards the status of the highland cultivator. It also prepared him for the future. His ancestors had been citizens of Roman *civitates*, poor, but none the less citizens. He became the servile dependent of a distant lord. That bond was easily snapped by political crisis. In Europe, the grandson of Ausonius of Bordeaux found it impossible to collect his rents from Macedonia in the Balkans, where Goths were settled as local landlords. After the political separation of Britain from Rome in 410 some Europeans who owned estates in Britain may have continued to receive their rents; but the disasters of the mid fifth century clearly smashed all alien obligations, as well as many of those due to the native magnates who were massacred or emigrated abroad.

In lowland Britain the old landlords were not replaced by new Germanic landowners, as in Macedonia or Gaul, for the English were not yet able to settle most of the territories they raided. In many areas the peasants of Roman Britain were freed from their old tribute. Those who remained on their land during the wars of the later fifth century faced the irregular demands of British war bands and the risk of plundering English forces; when the lowland areas were recovered by the forces of Ambrosius and Arthur, they were exposed to more regular impositions, at first their patriotic contributions to the war effort of their fellow-citizens, the *cives* or *Cumbrogi*, later the tributes of corn that fed the warlords' horses. The changes of the late empire had prepared them to become tributary subjects. The peace of Arthur directly subjected them to the demands of a new government. But in the interval no force had compelled them to grow more than they needed for their families; and a government that had to exact tribute direct from peasants, without the intermediary of landed nobility, cannot have enforced anything like as large a surplus of food production as the empire had enjoyed. The sixth-century economy was agricultural alone, admitting no role for towns; that is why in Gildas' day the towns were 'no longer inhabited as they used to be'.

Arable and Pasture

Arthur and his successors inherited two quite different kinds of agriculture, both established for many centuries. In simple language, the economy of low-land Roman Britain was arable, the economy of the highland west and north pastoral, geared upon cattle; and the economy of the barbarians beyond the frontier, in Ireland and the north, was also pastoral. The words are over-simple. The pastoral, cattle-raising peoples grew some corn, fodder for beasts, bread or porridge for themselves; arable farmers kept cows for milk and butter, and sometimes ate meat, if only on festive occasions. Britain was renowned for one specialised breed, exported to Ireland. But, variations apart, the extremes are the economy of Ireland, where cattle loomed large and corn was secondary, and that of the rich lowlands, where corn mattered more than cows.

An important indication in the balance of the economy lies in the proportions between different kinds of animals. Normally, settled farmers with acres to plough tend to have more sheep or pigs. The quantities of animal bones are not always thoroughly analysed; but the recent report of the excavation of a small chieftain's fortress at Dinas Powys near Cardiff examined bones from the kitchen refuse of the 5th and 6th centuries, and compared them with the figures available from Irish sites of the same period, as well as with three downland Wessex sites, one pre-Roman, one Roman, and one of the Arthurian period. The proportions in the three periods in Wessex are roughly similar to one another. But the regions contrast. In Dinas Powys, in the Vale of Glamorgan, an extension of lowland Britain, cattle bones make one-fifth of the total; in arable Wessex they are about one-third, but in Ireland they are well over three-quarters. In the Wessex chalklands sheep are as numerous as cattle, pigs fewer. In the wooded country of Dinas Powys, pigs constitute nearly two-thirds of the total, sheep barely one-eighth. In Ireland pigs and sheep are both few, and horses are numerous only in Wessex.

Ireland

The texts concur. Cattle obtrude into every Irish story. In the Irish reckoning of value, the unit of the *cumal*, 'slave girl', derived from the raiding days of the 4th century, was equated with three cows, and became the standard unit of price. In Wales, grants ascribed to the 7th and later centuries in the Llancarfan and Llandaff registers normally price swords, horses and other commodities as worth so many cows, usually three or four. Lists of renders emphasise that cattle remained less important than in Ireland. Payments due in the early 9th century to Llandeilo near Carmarthen, extant in the original, specify stated quantities of sheep and of bread and of butter, but not of live cows; those of Wessex, a century earlier, demand 300 loaves, much beer and butter, but only 2 cows or 10 wethers from each 100 hides; Llancarfan and Llandaff grants relating to the 6th, 7th and 8th centuries fix payments in beer and bread, meat and honey. They specify quantity only for the beer, and do not distinguish the kind of meat. But the tributes claimed in the Irish Book of Rights, set down much later, after arable agriculture had greatly extended in Ireland, still require no bread, corn or beer, and cattle still outnumber other animals.

Monastic economy transformed agriculture. Until the fifth century Irish cattle and Wessex corn marked the extreme variations; but the sixth century brought a large extension of agriculture, most marked in Ireland, where arable had hitherto been least in evidence. The chief agent of change was the monastery. Monasteries were many, and some were very large. All were stable communities in need of food; many refused to eat meat on principle, and all required a great deal of corn and many vegetables. They were established in south Wales, where the elements of an arable economy already existed; in Brittany where abandoned Roman estates were not yet wholly overgrown; in Ireland; and on a lesser scale in north Wales and northern Britain, where the cattle economy was not yet adapted to their needs.

The accounts of the first monks are shot through with conscious enthusiasm for pioneering agriculture. The austerity of David, Carthacus, Fintan Munnu and others required their monks to pull their own ploughs, but most houses used animals. All were eager for results. Ciaran of Clonmacnoise experimented with a horse-drawn plough, Aed with a three-ox plough. David's tradition boasted of his enormous yield, despite his lack of oxen, and Illtud's king is made to encourage him to 'till the land until it is rich in harvests', for 'it is land that ought to be cultivated', more fertile than 'the soil of Italy'. The Irish experimented with new fruits, and imported bee-keeping from Britain. In Brittany, Paul Aurelian, Fracan and others took over Roman estates, where their first concern was to beat the bounds and secure legal entitlement, their second to establish a secure water supply; for the saint whose staff tapped the ground to call forth a miraculous spring was archaeologist enough to know that a Roman site must have a well, that probing might discover. Elsewhere, on overgrown land, Maudetus burnt the scrub, and Leonorus felled trees, though he could not move the trunks until a miraculous storm swept them away.

In Britain and Ireland there was less empty land. In north Wales, Beuno secured the grant of particular estates already defined, but found that one of them already had a legal occupant, whom the king had dispossessed without his knowledge. In Ireland Berachus and others acquired land that had formerly belonged to druids, while king Angus of Munster, in the late 5th century, took it for granted that churchmen, if granted property at all, should receive 'good fertile lands near my royal residence'. But many saints deliberately sought solitude, removed from the territories where men ordinarily lived. Samson sought and found isolated lands in Cornwall and Brittany; Irishmen looked for them in or across the Atlantic, and some found them, in Ocean islands and in Iceland. In Ireland itself numerous accounts imply the establishment of monasteries on land not previously cultivated; for the crops of their early years were frequently disturbed by the horses, or sometimes the cattle, that had formerly pastured there.

Several texts minutely list the farmer's tools and furniture. The most striking innovation in Ireland and in Brittany is the water mill, named in many Lives, usually powered by the diversion of a river or the construction of a canal, occasionally worked by the tides; and in Italy the novel skills of Irish water engineers seemed miraculous to Gregory the Great. The baker (*pistor*) is frequently mentioned in all countries, but few stories are told of mills in Britain. Harvesting is as common an occasion for miracles as ploughing; harvested corn needed threshing and drying. Cainnech's monks complained that 'in wet weather we cannot thresh the corn without a building to protect it'. Cainnech's monastery did not then have

> craftsmen and workmen capable of building a shed for the drying
> and threshing of corn,

so he solved the immediate problem by blessing the 'open floor', which thereafter stayed dry without a roof while rain fell around it.

Skill was needed less for the shed itself (*canaba*), than for the kiln within. The Life of Ciaran of Clonmacnoise names the apparatus, *zabulum*, and describes it as

> a wheel made of interwoven brushwood, covered with ears of corn,
> placed over a fire, for drying and threshing in the manner of the
> westerners, that is of the British and Irish.

It differed from the stone and tile flues for drying corn that have been recognised on Roman farms in Britain, and could leave little archaeological trace beyond a burnt patch on the ground, with holes for supporting the posts. But corn kilns, whatever their construction, are in the Roman centuries peculiar to Britain, and have not yet been noticed in the European provinces; they are also frequently named in early medieval Welsh and Irish texts. Many Irish saints had such kilns, and one Irish monastic poem defines the process of corn production as 'ploughing, reaping, scorching'. In both Welsh and Irish law the corn kiln was regarded as essential to any well stocked farm; it is likely to have been brought by monks from Britain to Ireland.

At first, monks aroused hostility in many kings and lords, who lost manpower and revenue. Many kings sought to use the concentrated resources of the monasteries to maintain their men, by billeting or tribute; and very many tales of early monks record grants of exemption secured by the miraculous punishment of wicked kings who demanded secular service. Some rulers were thoroughly hostile to the expanding monks; a few were friendly from the first and gave them land, the more readily because many monastic founders preferred remote and underpopulated regions, of little profit to the kings. But some lords demanded and obtained compensation; Patrick had to pay a price for the individuals he converted and Finnian of Clonard paid an ounce of gold for a site in Leinster. Many Welsh and a few Irish grants detail the expensive gifts that brought permanent exemption from dues and claims from a variety of lay proprietors and rulers.

Enclosures

Monastic agriculture required the enclosure of open lands. Illtud and Paul Aurelian built sea dykes to reclaim coastal tracts; Tyssilio planted hedges in north Wales; Blaan built field walls in Bute; Lasrian of Devenish helped Aed to bring woodland under the plough. But the monks were not the only enclosers. Ireland was full of growing dynasties, and local warlords multiplied in Britain, while kings great and small sought horse pastures. Many Irish saints suffered from the encroachment of royal horses; in Wales Illtud was troubled by a royal *praepositus* who took over his meadows and impounded his cattle to make room for the king's horses.

Most of the stories told of monastic enclosure concern the clearance of waste land for arable farming, but most accounts of early secular enclosure concern the seizure of grazing land for horse pasture; but there are exceptions. Some monasteries were planted in well-populated lands, and sometimes aroused popular resentment. In Brittany Malo was accused of engrossing so much land that the next generation would have nothing to live on, and was expelled by the indignation of the 'godless' population. Beuno in Wales and Berachus in Ireland were among those who faced angry dispossessed owners. Arable farming among laymen was denounced when it enclosed former open grazing lands. Resentment is strongest in the traditions of Brigit of Kildare, who lived and died before male monasteries became numerous, about the late 530s. Her economy is principally concerned with dairy farming, rather than with the growing of crops, and an early Life, by Ultan, vividly expresses popular hostility to lay enclosures. A wealthy nobleman of Macha, Armagh, was

> cursed by everyone in the district, as a farmer who surrounds his lands with hedges, changing all the open straight roads.

On another occasion when Brigit drove in her carriage in Leinster she found a man fencing his land. He refused to let her drive through and told her to go round; her driver disregarded her advice to avoid a quarrel, and tried to force his way through. The landowner resisted and the carriage was overturned, but a speedy death brought to the enclosing farmer his just deserts. Nevertheless cornlands were spreading by the 550s, when the child Lugid fell foul of a secular miller.

Over the next hundred years enclosure greatly increased, and many men hungered. Famine sealed the change. The most detailed account is preserved in the Life of 'Gerald' of Mayo. About 665, shortly before the great plague, the pressure of a starving population constrained the high kings Diarmait and Blathmacc, sons of Aed Slane, to convene clerics and laymen in an assembly of all Ireland at Tara. The kings' edict proposed to allot to each *colonus*, or subject tenant, a minimum holding of 7 to 9 *iugera*, about 10 acres, of good land, with 8 of rough land and 9 of woodland, because

> the population was so great that the whole land did not suffice them
> for agriculture.

The nobility, encouraged by abbot Fechin of Fore, opposed the edict, and prayed to the Lord to send some sickness that might relieve them of

> a part of the burdensome multitude of inferior people, that the rest
> might live more easily . . . since overpopulation was the cause of the
> famine.

Gerald denounced the monstrous proposition, inhuman and immoral, on the ground that

> it is no harder for God to augment the food supply than to increase
> the population.

Fechin's prayer was granted, but Gerald's humanity was justified, for God's anger killed Fechin in the plague, together with the kings of Ireland and many other notables, but Gerald was spared. Plague solved the immediate crisis, and weakened resistance to enclosures, for the reduced population pressed less upon the land, and in the next generation arable agriculture took too firm a hold to be overset thereafter.

Tradition looked back upon the plague and the Tara convention as the turning point in Irish agriculture, dramatically condensing the processes of two centuries into the years of crisis alone. The Life of Flannan of Killaloe explained that until his time, in the early and mid 7th century

> the earth was unsown and no seed was sown.

Another tradition held that

> there was neither mound nor hedge nor stone walls round land in

Ireland, . . . until the time of the sons of Aed Slane, but all was unbroken plain.

These are the tales that later Irishmen set down. The central dispute reported from the convention of Tara is not confined to seventh-century Ireland; it is the enduring argument between those who hold that hunger should be stopped by keeping down the numbers of the population, and those who would change the economy to increase the food supply.

The stories give no detail of who went hungry; but the core of the problem is written into the circumstances of expanding arable agriculture. Those who managed to enclose sufficient land prospered; those who starved were men whose livelihood had depended on grazing the lands now enclosed; and when possessions were few, famine struck easily. Throughout Ireland, the scale of property was small. A law tract, set down a generation or so later, after arable farming was well established, defines the minimum qualification that entitled a man to the rank of noble, *bo-aire*, 'lord of cattle'. But, by the time of the law tract, the cattle lord needed land as well. The lowest grade required 7 *celi*, 'vassals' or dependent labourers, 12 cows, 16 sheep, and land worth 14 *cumal* or 42 cows, with a corn kiln, mill and barn. The possession of a plough, with twice as much land and proportionately more animals, bestowed a more honourable rank; the highest grade, the *aire forgaill*, who commanded a hundred in war, needed no more land, but must have a minimum of 28 dependents, 30 cows and 30 sheep. Twice that mobile property, 40 dependents, with 60 cows and 60 sheep, was the qualification of the lowest grade of king, the king of a *tuath*, or people. The higher grades are distinguished from their inferiors by the ownership of more cattle, and the control of more dependents, but not by any larger acreage. It is therefore probable that the basis of the grading dates back to the centuries before the enclosures, and that the extension of arable farming added to a pre-existing system the need for 14 or 28 *cumals* of land, with the accessory equipment for harvested corn, the kiln, the mill and the barn.

These herds are not large, but they match the dimensions of the smaller excavated *raths*. Commonly a roughly circular enclosed area, about 100 feet in diameter, contained a barn, a few querns, occasionally a kiln, and a house, with a superficial area of between 100 and 200 square feet, enough for the parents and children of a single family; it might accommodate the cattle of the *bo-aire*, when weather or danger constrained him to congregate them within his defences. Ploughs, discovered on about 10% of the sites, are listed as the mark of the higher grades of *bo-aire*; while the very small enclosures, surrounding a single house without a barn, suggest the homes of the dependent *celi*.

When 12 cows made a nobleman, plebeians were poor. Their few cows and a little land were at the mercy of a cattle plague or a poor harvest, and they lacked any communal reserve. Another law tract defined 'the full property of the *tuath*, the legal equal right of men of all degrees'; the common property was limited to defined rights on wood and water, both of them regarded as private property on which the public retained a few minor claims, but only the upland, 'the unenclosed above the rest', remained common. Whatever the *tuath* had owned earlier was gone; enclosure was thorough and complete. Private pasture and private arable fields had replaced 'unbroken plains'.

Tradition outlines a double-sided process. At first, dynasts and local lords enclosed chiefly for cattle and horses, monasteries for arable farming; but later laymen also turned to arable, and by the middle of the 7th century enclosure provoked the insurgent demand for the distribution of the land, the familiar demand that runs through the history of peasant societies from the Hebrews, the Greeks and the Romans to the present day.

The aftermath of the plague consolidated change. Arable enclosure riveted the grip of little local lords in Ireland upon their dependent herdsmen and cultivators. It also opened new possibilities to agriculture abroad. It brought the economy of Ireland closer to the economy that Britain had inherited from the Roman past, and made new ideas easier to exchange and imitate. The difference was chiefly in outlook. In the former provinces of Rome the techniques of arable agriculture were old and conservative. But since arable farming was itself new to the Irish, they were as open to new techniques as to old ways. They made the water mill a commonplace instead of a rarity, pioneered horse-ploughing and other novelties. They were still innovators when they carried the faith and the economy of the monastery to Europe. They came at a time when important new technical possibilities had entered Europe from the east. The sixth-century Avars and the Slavs brought with them the Chinese devices of the metal stirrup and the horse collar. The stirrup in time transformed warfare, and the collar made the horse economic. In antiquity the horse that pulled against a trace exerted hardly more than four times the strength of a man, and cost four times as much as a man to feed; but the collar quadrupled the power of the horse, and more than justified his cost.

The innovations spread slowly and unevenly, for they could not be fully exploited until they were fitted to the heavy horse. The heavy horse was bred in antiquity, but is not known to have been common outside the small territory of Noricum, roughly modern Austria. Its first familiar breeding-ground elsewhere is in Flanders, in or shortly before the 11th century. It was bred because the collar and the stirrup needed it. Little is yet known of who disseminated the new devices, or when and where, between the 6th century and the 11th; but it is likely that the monasteries of Irish and Anglo-Irish origin in Europe were a principal agent in making men familiar with the new possibilities. They developed a concentrated agriculture, much of it in lands hitherto lightly tilled; and were readier than others to seize upon new methods. The monks were the first westerners who made peaceful contact with the Slavs, hitherto sundered from Christendom by the pagan Saxons and Thuringians; and were first able to appreciate the value of the horse collar. Their close contacts with one another enabled new knowledge to travel fast from Bohemia and the Danube to the low countries and France. Direct evidence is wanting, for early monastic records in Europe concentrate upon churchmen and rulers, and have little to say of agricultural practice. What is known is that the monks were better placed than others to observe and make known the new agricultural possibilities.

The Picts

Monasteries transformed the economy of Ireland, and opened new possibilities in Europe. Elsewhere their impact was less dramatic, though often important. Among the Picts evidence fails. Some had slaves; elaborate tombstones and the text of Adomnan betoken a nobility; some property was private, and was bequeathed by inheritance. Roman writers assert that the Picts were wholly unacquainted with tillage, but doubtless generalise from the rougher highlands, for the cultivation of the more fertile regions, ample in the middle ages, is likely to be as old as the Romans, or older. Irish monasteries spread in and after the 7th century, stimulating arable farming, and in time the Irish absorbed the Picts. But the evidence is not yet enough to show how, when and where the economy changed.

The British and the English

Among the northern British monasteries were few, and were soon overtaken by English conquest, before they had time to bring significant change to the older economy. In the shattered lowlands of Britain crops were grown and horses reared to feed the wartime armies and the warbands that succeeded Arthur. But there is as yet hardly any evidence for their economy before the English conquest.

The English themselves brought from Germany a mixed economy, whose balance of corn and cattle fitted well with the economy they found in Roman Britain. At first they were confined to lands easily tilled, but in time they learnt to plough heavier soils; their adaptation and diffusion will be known when care is taken to observe the local geological situation of the sites of successive periods. But their most striking difference from the British is in their homes. Most of the British, like the Irish, lived in isolated homesteads; small towns were numerous, and some peasants gathered into villages in some regions at the end of the empire, but the great majority still lived on isolated farmsteads, commonly rectangular. But the first English, in Britain as in Germany, normally lived in concentrated villages. In the less permeable soils of Britain they changed the architecture of their cottages. Their rural homes in Germany were also rectangular timber buildings, often long and thin, with cattle sheds built onto the living room. Though some such houses are found in Britain, the overwhelming majority lived in short rectangular dug-out houses; a foot or two of soil was removed and piled into a low wall around the edges of the excavation to keep out the water that would not drain away. Groups of such houses were built within the walls of

Canterbury, Dorchester-on-Thames and other Roman towns, and in the open country, often closely adjacent to Roman farms. The graveyards are similarly located, and, until the colonising period of the late 6th and early 7th centuries, the great majority are the burial-grounds of small communities; only a very few sites contain one or two burials in each successive generation, suggesting the burial-place of a single family homestead.

In the colonising period, from the late sixth century onward, many more single burials and many place names suggest a much higher proportion of homestead than of village settlement. But the homestead, like the village, practised a mixed economy, attested by the laws and by the words used for new settlements. It is probable that English farming technique had learnt something from its short fifth-century apprenticeship to the economy of Roman Britain. But there is no reason to suppose that there was significant change in the balance of the economy, the type of crops cultivated, the breeds of cattle raised. Nor had the English the same need of monastic agriculture. Monasteries were proportionately fewer; though many extended the arable acreage, secular colonisation opened up far more empty lands. The impact of monastic economy is more noticeable as a stimulus and example to the lay farmer than as a source of change in his methods.

Among the Welsh, monasteries are relatively few in the north, though some of them were very large. In the south, they were many. Most were quite small, but their number attests a considerable withdrawal of population from their old homes and a noteworthy extension of arable farming, much of it in areas where evidence for earlier cultivation is weak or wanting. The British Lives have more to say than the Irish about estates that paid rent to monasteries. Their stories more often illustrate the breaking of fresh lands to the plough, by existing methods, than a change in the economy, for in several regions, arable farming was already extensive. Throughout, Welsh miracles have more to do with corn and less with animals than the Irish. Few concern the water mill, for the techniques of an established arable economy were less responsive to innovation than in a land where arable farming was itself relatively novel; from the early 7th century onward, it became increasingly easy for dependent peasants to feed the Welsh monasteries. The impact of the monasteries extended the area of cultivation, and change has more to do with social organisation than with farming methods. Wealth increased, and its increase is confirmed by excavation, for the quantities of imports discovered on substantial sites argue that kings and monks were rich enough to pay for them. Their riches were not drawn from monasteries modelled upon the practice of David, whose inmates provided all their needs by their own labour, but from those who were supplied by the labour of *operarii*, dependent cultivators, in the tradition of Cadoc and Illtud, or by the dues furnished from estates instanced in the grants of Llandeilo, Llancarfan and Llandaff. Such dues were evidently already paid in the 6th century, for it is not probable that the tiny monastery of Tintagel, on an isolated rock off the coast, found the means to pay for the imports that excavation has there revealed solely from the acreage that the monks were able to till or pasture themselves. Their meditations are likely to have been sustained by food contributed by lay farmers on the lands above the cliffs, in sufficient quantity to afford a surplus for the purchase of foreign produce.

Craftsmen

Throughout the British Isles the economy was agricultural, and during the 6th and 7th centuries, the quantity of corn produced increased. Much of it went to monasteries and kings, and both were able to maintain specialised craftsmen. Simpler trades required few special skills; monasteries and their churches were normally of wood, save in Cornwall and parts of Wales, where abundant stone had always been cheap and easily available. The *artifex*, the craftsman, protected by his status in the older ordering of barbarian Irish society, was in short supply and high demand. Cainnech could not find a craftsman to make a kiln; Brendan had to go to Connacht to find a man who could build a timber boat; the father of Ciaran of Clonmacnoise was a carriage-wright, free to migrate from one lord to another, all of whom were eager to receive him; Findbarr was also the son of a smith, of considerable personal independence.

But from the beginning monasteries as well as kings kept their own craftsmen. Brendan of Clonfert maintained goldsmiths. Mo-Choemog's father was Ita's smith, 'skilled in wood and stone'. Expanding agriculture created a demand for the *artifex* who could build a mill, and several houses produced their own engineers. Irish carriages and carriage horses were prized, and Samson's biographer makes a boast of those that the saint brought back with him from Ireland. But the principal effort of the monastic artisan was directed to the production of things needed by the monastery that were elsewhere unobtainable, church furniture, books and bookbindings, bells, croziers and the like. Tradition celebrates Dagaeus as the founder of the Irish ecclesiastical art, in enthusiastic detail, but it also especially honours Columba of Iona as the inspirer or organiser of Irish calligraphy, of the dissemination of Gospel Books, and as the protector of traditional learning within the new Christian society. The outstanding achievements of Irish art, the Books of Durrow, Lindisfarne and Kells, are all products of Columban houses; the exquisite pillow stones of Lindisfarne, and the great stone crosses of northern England, also derive from the Columban inspiration, adapted by pupils.

Among the British, the technology of the Roman engineer and builder died with urban civilisation. The English brought with them skilled jewellers and potters, whose products were at first used in quantity in every village; in the 7th century, the craftsmen of Kent took hold of Frankish decorative tradition and transformed it into the short-lived splendour of Kentish ornament, that ranks among the noblest achievements of the jeweller's craft in any age in any country. But its splendour confined it to the rich, and as the craftsmen found wealthy patrons, so the tradition of fine ornament made for simple villagers faded away. It did not long outlive the pagan religion. Thenceforth pottery and ornament are rare in farm and village; where they survived, in towns and among the well-to-do, they soon lost their vitality. The arts and skills of Christian England are not those of the potter and the jeweller, but of the church, of its literature and its art. There the craftsman prospered, for in the lay society of Rome, and of the German barbarians, the craftsman was a humble servant, but the craftsmen of the church inherited something of the high honour accorded to the artisan in the tradition of Ireland.

Exchange and Trade

Some foreign trade persisted at all times, from the Roman empire to the late middle ages. But often there was little of it, and that little reached only to the surface of society. Wine came to Britain and to Ireland. In Muirchu's account King Loegaire drank wine at Tara in the 430s; whether he did or not, Muirchu in the 7th century thought it normal that he should. 'Merchants who came with Gallic wine' visited Clonmacnoise, but their visit was isolated and long-remembered; and Muirchu also regarded the 'wonderful foreign bronze vessel' that Daire gave to Patrick as a rarity. But though wine and foreign bronzes were rare, traffic of some sort was less unusual. Columba learnt of a disastrous eruption in Italy from the crew of a Gallic vessel that put in to a Kintyre harbour. Columban was deported a few years later from Nantes on a 'ship engaged in the Irish trade'. Early in the 5th century Patrick had embarked 200 miles from Sliabh Mis in Antrim, scarcely nearer than Wexford or Cork. As well as direct voyages to Europe there was plenty of traffic through Wales and Cornwall; the commonest landfalls in Britain were Porth Mawr, Whitesands Bay, in Pembrokeshire, and Padstow, and the main port of embarkation for Europe was Fowey. Little is said of the manner of travel, save for those who crossed on miraculous leaves or stones, but most voyaged like Finnian of Llancarfan 'with merchants, but with a different purpose, he seeking to purchase the kingdom of heaven, they to gain worldly lucre', in a journey that brought him to St. David's by Porth Mawr.

What was traded is less clear than the fact of trade. The pottery imports are of two main kinds. Mediterranean vessels, including a fair proportion of wine jars, are common in Cornwall, Somerset and south Wales, and are also found on some southern Irish sites; Gaulish vessels are found on the same sites, and also in Meath, Ulster and south-west Scotland. The Irish distributions may prove misleading when other sites elsewhere are excavated in greater numbers, but the present pattern is clear. The mediterranean trade is evidenced from the other end by a single passage in the Life of an Egyptian saint of the early 7th century, John the Almsgiver; a vessel sailed to Alexandria from Britain with a cargo of tin, doubtless from Cornwall. The products of Irish monastic craftsmen circulated among foreign monasteries and were rewarded with corresponding ecclesiastical gifts, but they had less value in secular society; in the one recorded transaction, about 800, a layman sold the Book of Teilo, or Chad, to the monastery for no more than a 'best horse'. Irish brooches are occasionally found in Britain, but a lead pattern, prepared for the casting of an Irish brooch-maker's mould, found at Dinas Powys, near Cardiff, suggests that the craftsman exported himself rather than his product. Similarly, the splendid scroll escutcheons attached to hanging bowls that are often found in rich late pagan English graves are of Irish workmanship; but it is likely that their makers worked in Britain.

The mediterranean trade brought wine, perhaps in larger quantities than later Irishmen knew, and carried back metals; it was essentially trade with the Severn estuary, a very little of which spilled over into Munster. The Gaulish trade is another matter. It brought domestic pottery, jugs, plates and bowls, and doubtless other perishable goods whose nature is guesswork. It may have taken away cloaks, dogs, horses and the like. Its currency was precious metal. The merchants who sailed to Pembrokeshire sought 'lucre', and 'lucre' was known and feared in monasteries; abbess Ita so abhorred it that she washed her hands if she touched silver; but she evidently sometimes had to touch it, and Finnian of Clonard had to pay for land in gold. Some of the metal currency is identifiable; some silver ingots found in Britain, Ireland and Germany are dated to the early 5th century by their maker's name, and unstamped rings or bars of gold and silver that carry no date doubtless circulated then and later. Men traded; but the volume of trade was small enough to manage without coinage.

Internal trade is less in evidence. The monks of Ireland prevented Ruadan's attempts to market a new drink, and the economy of monks and laymen was self-sufficing in Ireland and Wales, its import chiefly restricted to foreign luxuries. Among the English, specialist jewellers and potters worked within local limits before the conquest, while the movement of their products after the conquest is more likely to be the consequence of the movement of their owners than of their makers. Roads fell out of use. Burials cut into the metalling of the Watling Street, at Cestersover in Warwickshire and elsewhere, are proof enough that roads were out of use and grass-grown. A road was a *herepaeth*, an 'army path', and early settlements are commonly discreetly set back from roads, for the passage of an army threatened the farmer's livestock and his daughters. The roads did not revive for centuries; the Roman towns along the Icknield Way at its junctions with the northward roads from London, at Dunstable, Baldock and Royston, reverted to woodland until all three were refounded in the 12th century, when new towns were planted on their sites, as traffic along the road resumed, and charters were granted for fairs. In the 6th and 7th centuries churchmen, kings, armies, and a few well-to-do notables travelled, but there is little sign of the exchange of goods.

What trade there was was suspect. At the end of the 7th century, the laws of the West Saxons forbade trade without witnesses, and fined the merchant who could not prove that his goods were not stolen, while Kentish law insisted that purchases in London must be registered with the king's officer and required that 'traders and other strangers who cross the border' must have a sponsor responsible for their good conduct. Later laws confined trade to towns. The merchant was by definition a suspected thief, a foreigner of ill repute, rare and unwelcome. Trade there was. But it was largely in foreign hands, limited in kind and in scope, and to a few places, to London above all. It was an incidental phenomenon on the margins of the economy, irrelevant to the lives of nine-tenths of the population.

Throughout the British Isles, tribute mattered more than trade. Native traders are rare in the records of the Irish, the Welsh, or the English, for the exchange of commodities was more the business of kings and lords than of merchants. In Ireland, the 'Book of Rights' sets down an elaborate, and perhaps ideal list of tributes exacted by the greater Irish kings, and of gifts they dispensed. The kings received large quantities of animals, and some clothing. They distributed weapons, armour, horses, horns, ornaments, and occasionally a few animals and a little clothing. Though the figures are late and perhaps unreal, the principle is amply attested in the Lives, the Annals and the stories. The payment of tribute was secured by the retention of hostages, and was enforced by war when it was withheld. British kings followed the Irish example; Maelgwn and others levied cattle to maintain their military companions; the poems praise northern kings, like Owain, who 'hoarded' wealth exacted from his subjects or looted from his enemies 'like a miser', and 'gave it freely' to his retainers. Penda of Mercia held Oswy's son as a hostage, exacted tribute from subject Northumbria and distributed it to his British and English allies. The British king who collected and distributed more tribute and booty than others commonly earned the epithet *Hael*, 'open-handed' or 'generous'. The process by which animals taken in tribute were turned into weapons and ornaments involved either using the food rent to maintain craftsmen, or exchanging cattle for the smith's products.

Only the English minted money. It priced fines. It served kings and abbots for the payment of rents, and for the purchase of great men's needs; it circulated within towns. Close examination of what coins have been found where may help to show how far and when it began to link lesser men. Present evidence suggests that trade between towns, and outside towns and fairs, was slight before the 9th and 10th centuries, not considerable until the 12th. Most men lived upon the produce of their lands, and paid a tax or tribute to lords and kings. The principal commodities that circulated internally, salt, iron, fish and others were paid as annual tribute to the lords, who most commonly paid two-thirds of their price to the king if and when they sold them. The earliest articles of export were slaves, usually prisoners of war, though the stronger kings forbade and often curtailed the export of men. By the 8th century, cloth, wool and cheese were shipped to Gaul, though they were principally sold by lords who had received them in tribute, chiefly in exchange for silks, wine, precious stones and metals and other luxuries. A little commercial production prospered in a few towns, mainly through craftsmen whose raw materials came through the lords' tribute. Before the Scandinavian disturbances, the principal source of raw material was tribute rather than purchase and the craftsman and distributor were bound to the lord from whom they received the raw material. Trade, the buying and selling of commodities, was still a relatively insignificant element in the exchange of goods.

CHAPTER TWENTY-THREE

WELSH, IRISH AND NORTHERN SOCIETY

The Family

Throughout the British Isles, the unit of society was the single family of parents and their children, living in a family house. All other associations of people, social or political, were no more than groups of such families, differently organised for different purposes. Welsh law made intimate provision for a secure family, with personal equality for both parents, and care for the upbringing and rights of children. It dealt with the ordinary contingencies of private life in pragmatic detail, with respect for the feelings and dignity of the individual. The law defined the signs of a well inhabited land as 'little children; dogs; and cocks'. Obligations were incurred by actual relationships, not only by their legal registration. A man who slept three nights or more with a girl must give her three oxen if he deserted her; cohabitation ranked as marriage after 7 years. A child 'begotten in brake and bush' must be wholly maintained by the father. The boy came of age at 14, the girl at 12; she then 'possesses her own property, and need not remain at her father's table, unless she so wishes.'

On marriage the girl received an *agweddi*, dowry, from her father, and also a *cowyll*, marriage gift, from her husband. Occasions of dispute were foreseen. The girl's kin might choose to certify her a virgin bride if they wished; if they did so falsely, the husband might shame her by slitting her shift in the presence of the bridal guests, provided that before consummation, he jumped out of bed 'immediately on his discovery; but if he stays in bed through the night, he is deemed to have accepted her as a virgin'. The father must provide for the children's upbringing until they came of age; thereafter he might not chastise them. In Irish law, where 'fosterage', the education of the children away from home, is more prominent than in Wales, both parents had equal responsibility for the children's education.

If a couple divorced within seven years, the woman took only her dowry and marriage gift, whether she were the innocent or guilty party. If she went off with another man, he must compensate the husband. After seven years, the whole property of the homestead was equally divided on divorce. The meaning of equality was not left to the embittered couple to dispute, but laid down in exact detail. The wife took one-third of the children, the husband two-thirds, including the oldest and the youngest. If the wife was pregnant, the husband must pay for the child till he came of age. A detailed schedule apportioned every object likely to be found on a farmstead, the general principle being that the tools of agriculture and stock raising went to the man, dairy farming and the household gear to the woman.

The grounds for divorce were 'leprosy', meaning all incurable illness, bad breath, and impotence. Adultery was not included. Adultery was punished by the payment of *wyneb-werth*, *faciei pretium* in Latin, payment for loss of face by the guilty husband to his wife, or the guilty wife to her husband; and the adulterer must also pay a fine to the husband. Wife beating by the husband, or shrewish scolding by the wife, were normally punishable by a fine, payable to the injured party; but were permitted in the case of adultery, though if the husband beat up an adulterous wife he forfeited his 'face payment'. The wife was also exempt from normal penalties for assault if she attacked her husband's mistress. But if the husband committed adultery three times, the wife who did not leave him received no more 'face money'.

Kissing or cuddling another man's wife was punishable by a fine to the husband, except on festival occasions. Illegitimate children were accepted into the *cenedl*, kindred, if acknowledged by the father, or if paternity was proven; children of untraceable fathers belonged to their mother's kin. The laws provided full defence against accusations; 'leprosy' must be proved incurable by a doctor's certificate; a charge of impotence might be rebutted by a public demonstration in a form prescribed in uninhibited detail; charges against women were examined by elder women, denied by a formidable oath, or tested before witnesses, the trials and tests being conducted by the *penncenedl*, chief of kindred.

Irish law had similar grounds for divorce, with numerous additions of detail. Impotence and infertility were distinguished; the taking of a monastic vow and long absence were added; some texts add chattering to strangers about prowess in bed. In both Wales and Ireland the church contested the marriage laws, but with little success. The text termed *Hibernensis*, which commonly offered a judge a choice of rulings, cited Deuteronomy (24,1), 'if she find no favour in his eyes ... let him write her a bill of divorcement', but it also added from the Gospel (Matthew 5,31–32) 'a man shall not put away his wife, save for the cause of adultery'. It then cited from Isidore

> What if she be barren, deformed, a hag; fetid, violent, cross; an evil liver, luxurious and gluttonous, cursing or swearing? Do you keep her or reject her? Whether you like it or not, you must keep her as you took her.

In Britain one text observed that its provisions on the inheritance of illegitimate children were counter to 'Church Law', which prescribed that the patrimony should go only to the 'father's eldest son by his married wife'; but it replied that 'the law of Howel ... decides that the father's sin, or his illegal act, is not to be brought against the son's patrimony'.

These were the practical regulations of a small community where everyone knew his neighbours. Family quarrels were brought to open court as soon as they erupted into violence in word or deed, and the pressure of public opinion, under the guidance of the *penncenedl*, was brought to bear to sober the pair. But when a marriage had irrevocably broken down, the troublesome division of the home was automatically regulated, and the law ensured that the children were protected.

Welsh law treated the family as an association of responsible individuals, not as an institution. The law protected the privacy, the dignity and the freedom of man and wife, and of sons and daughters who had reached puberty. Each was legally independent, of equal rights and status. Their personal relationships were their own affair; the law intervened only to protect children and to prevent violence. Safeguards for bastards, and for adolescents against their parents, contrast with the provisions of most legal codes. The law and custom of most of Europe and Asia interferes in family relationships and encourages outsiders to impose taboos upon them. Roman law forbade adultery and enhanced the father's authority, though without savage penalties. Brutal repression of women remains a chief means of perpetuating peasant poverty in many Asian societies, while the persecution and slaughter of unchaste girls and soured old women was sanctioned in the name of honour and virtue among many Germanic peoples, and constituted one of the principal barbarian contributions to the doctrines of the medieval Christian church.

Kindred

In Welsh and Irish law, the kindred had two main functions. It regulated the inheritance of men who died without sons, and it ensured the payment of damages to the victims of violence. Its terminology varied. In Wales, the *cenedl* protected freeborn subjects; but the Irish *cinel* is most prominent as a ruler's kindred, and variations of the word *fine* described family groupings.

Welsh and Irish legislation on violence was mainly concerned with compensation to the victim and his dependents. It contrasts with the moral outlook of the laws of Rome and of most modern states, whose chief concern is punishment, theoretically justified on the grounds that fear of the law will deter the criminal, and that if vengeance is not exacted by society it will be exacted privately by the victim's friends and relatives. The law of terror commonly kills, maims or imprisons the wrongdoer, and places emphasis on his motives, inflicting lesser penalties on those who acted in momentary anger or by accident. Welsh and Irish codes were more concerned with the consequences of the offence than with the offender's motive and with preventing violence rather than with punishment. They imposed damages rather than fines; the scale began with small payments for an insult or a blow of the fist, and rose through the loss of limbs and physical ability to the loss of life. Since the offender might lack the means to pay the damages himself, his relatives must make good the deficit, the nearer relatives contributing the larger share. Each individual in the community was therefore given a powerful incentive to restrain a relative who was temperamentally prone to violence, and to do so early, before violence passed beyond rowdiness.

Inheritance

Welsh and Irish law compelled men to bequeath their most essential property to their family and kin. In Wales, the youngest son took the family house, with a few acres of land, on the assumption that his elder brothers were more likely to have married and moved into their own houses. He also took the cauldron, the axe and the coulter, with the harp. The youngest son divided the rest of the land into equal portions, and the brothers chose in turn, the eldest first. There is no mention of cattle in the division between brothers, or between husband and wife on divorce; for cattle were personal property and were also currency. The laws carefully distinguished the *tir gwelyauc*, family land, divided by inheritance, from *tir cyvriv*, usually Englished as 'register land', the property of the *tref*, or township, that might be granted to the dead man's son, but could not be inherited.

Most men had sons, and when they did the inheritance laws worked simply. Complications arose when there were no sons. Claims of kinsmen were harder to accommodate, both in law and in practice. In Ireland and Wales inheritance passed only from father to son, never directly from brother to brother or from uncle to nephew. A childless man's land passed back into the inheritance of his father or grandfather, even when they were dead, and through them to their heirs. Irish law retained a series of terms for *fine*, family, with differing rights. In the prime of life a man's *Geil Fine* comprised his father, his sons, his brothers and their sons, a three-generation family containing all his father's male descendants. His *Derb Fine* added his grandfather's other descendants, his uncles and his cousins and their sons, a four-generation family. The *Iar Fine* comprised five generations, descending from his great-grandfather, the *Ind Fine* six generations from his great-great-grandfather.

In practice, most important rights fell to his *Derb Fine* of four generations, both in inheritance and in the mutual respect and self-help which society expected of a family. The wider groups of remoter cousins retained marginal rights in certain contingencies, and owed small shares of the compensations due from the kin. The *Derb Fine* was the normal word used in the law books for a man's immediate relatives; at least from the 10th century onward, succession to political sovereignty was, in theory at least, confined to the king's *Derb Fine*, whose members were *Rigdomna*, royal heirs. A man might claim a throne that his great-grandfather or nearer relative had held, but could not claim succession from his great-great-grandfather. The custom is likely to have established itself piecemeal over a long period, earlier among some dynasties than others, before it was formally and generally recognised; but it is in practice reported among the Ui Neill from the fifth century onward.

Welsh law also confined effective inheritance to the four-generation family, the equivalent of the Irish *Derb Fine*. By the later middle ages it had acquired a general name, *gwely*, 'bed', but the laws spell out what they mean in detail without using a generic term. The land of the childless is divided three times, between brothers, between cousins, and between second cousins, who constitute the members of a four-generation family. Thereafter, 'there is no division'.

These laws concerned a time when the kindred was no longer the political unit; the Welsh *tref* and the Irish *tuath* and *baile* included many different unrelated kindreds, and men related to the fourth or ninth degree might farm lands in different communities. The laws regulated inheritance of land, houses and gear rather than of cattle, and therefore mattered more where arable agriculture was more extensive. They persisted in an age when the bulk of the free population was dispersed in separate family homesteads, and the kindred of four generations or more no longer lived together, farming lands that lay in one block. But it is likely that they had their origin in an earlier age, when the kindred lived together, with all its land in walking distance of its home. Societies so organised still exist in Asia, in parts of the Balkans, and elsewhere; they may have existed in parts of Ireland and in Britain into the Roman period. Such extended families are the likely builders of the 'native villages' of Roman Britain, that consisted of a few houses clustered together, as at Chysauster in Cornwall or Ewe Close in Westmorland; or of the large round houses, 30 foot or more in diameter, known in the earlier generations of the Iron Age of southern Britain. But from at least the sixth century onward, though the kindred retained important rights and responsibilities, it was no longer the main basis of political society.

Community: the Irish.
Class Difference

Families and kindreds, with their inheritance laws, each lived within a particular political society. Society contained a number of recognised divisions, of different origins, which the lawyers endeavoured to arrange into an orderly structure, and distinguished by technical terms.

The oldest division of Irish society was between the *nemed*, 'sacred persons', and the *celi*, 'plebeians', who became vassals dependent upon chiefs. The concept is pre-Christian, for the term *nemed*, meaning 'holy' in all the Celtic languages, was intimately associated with pagan religion and subsisted in Christian times only when it could not be avoided.

By the time of the oldest lawbooks both classes were divided into *soer* and *doer*, 'free' and 'unfree'. The freemen of the sacred class, *soernemed*, included kings and chiefs; the learned professions, the *filid*; churchmen, the *feni*, military officers, who were equated with the *airig*, nobility, graded by their wealth in cattle, and later in land; and the rise of the kings added a number of royal officials. The 'sacred unfree', *doernemed*, were primarily the craftsmen, builders and metal-workers, doctors and lawyers, and included the humbled *drui*. The dependent plebeians were divided into freemen, *soercheli*, who owed military service and annual tribute and must contribute to a king's ransom, and the unfree *doercheli*, who paid rent, provided maintenance for royal officers and owed menial services. The *celi* were all owners of cattle and of land, but the *doercheli* might not leave his land, nor be evicted, so long as he retained his cattle.

Below these landowners stood the landless, classified in the law books according to their supposed origin. The *fuidir* was a free stranger from another *tuath*, or political state; he was the equivalent of the Greek *metic*, the Latin *advena*. The *senleithi*, 'old refugees', were descendants of prisoners and hired fighting men; the *bothach*, cottager, was a native without property. Below them all were the slaves, male and female, *mug* and *cumal*, rarely encountered outside the law books, save as the personal servants of chiefs and kings.

The terminology echoes successive layers of forgotten conquest and migration, for even the word *doer* has the root meaning of 'stranger', 'foreigner'. The classification of the status of persons was cut across by the classification of peoples. The word *tuath* denotes people in the most general sense, as varied as the Greek *ethnos*, more varied than the Latin *civitas*. The Israelites were the *Tuath De*, the *civitas Dei*, people of God. Time hardened the meaning, until *tuath* normally denoted a tiny state, often subject to a greater neighbour. The Ireland of the 1st century AD, as described by Ptolemy, comprised fifteen political states; Irish names record other still older peoples, usually called by their distinctive names, Lugne, Galenga and the like, or known by the appellation *Fir*, 'men of', the *Fir Domnann* and others. In a pastoral society enclosed within an island, groups of such older peoples wandered widely to different districts, sometimes losing their identity, sometimes imposing their name. When a people lived long in a defined territory the word *tuath* denoted both the people and the territory.

By the time of the early Christian writers Ptolemy's fifteen states had divided into something over a hundred, whose schematic hierarchy grouped them into five provinces, though several large kingdoms, like Ossory or Airgialla, were at best nominally and intermittently subject to provincial kings. Almost all were subject to dynastic chiefs, who awarded lordship and lands to their nearer relatives. A law of the 7th or 8th century prescribes distinctive dress for different classes, yellow or black or white for subjects, grey, brown and red for nobles; purple and blue for kings. Later texts limit the number of colours that each class might wear, rising from one for slaves to two for subjects and six for the learned *filid*, seven for the king.

The spread of dynastic kingship divided the Irish states into three categories, the *Soer Tuatha*, free states; the subject states, *Aithech Tuatha*; and the intermediate *For Tuatha*, autonomous but tributary. Most, though not all, of the free states were known by the name of their dynasty, while *tuath* was commoner among the subject states. The principal origin of the difference lay in conquest; the *tuath* whose kings had subjected weaker neighbours was free, the subject neighbours unfree.

The Irish: Village and Hundred

Kings and chiefs needed armies and a stable mechanism to raise them. As among most Indo–European peoples, the unit of military organisation was the hundred. Later texts schematise its developed form. The higher grades of *aire*, 'nobles of property', were qualified to command a hundred, a *cet*, in war; the standard concept of a large military formation was the *tricha cet*, 'thirty hundreds'. But the *tuatha* were of varying size. Each comprised a number of *baile*, the origin of the common Irish place name element 'Bally-'. In its civil function the word meant 'enclosed farmstead', or 'town', almost the precise equivalent of the English *-tun*. In its military aspect it is alternatively described as the *baile biataigh*, 'supply *baile*', its duty to supply a hundred men, a *cet*. Though schematised, the terminology is deeply embedded in Irish stories and in the notices of the Annals. It lasted as long as Irish independence. The muster of the last native army, destroyed at Kinsale in 1601, enjoined the 'constable of each hundred' to levy 84 men, but to receive and distribute the pay of a full hundred.

The actual organisation that underlies the scheme is preserved in a late 7th-century text of the Irish colonists in British Dal Riada, the *Miniugid Senchusa Fir n-Alban*, the 'Explanation of the History of the Men of Britain'. It divides the Dal Riada Scots under their three dynastic *Cinel*, and subdivides each *Cinel* into groups, some with territorial names, some with the names of small chiefs. Each group comprises a number of houses, *tech*, reckoned in multiples of 5 and 10, 20 and 30 being the commonest numbers; and it gives the total land and sea muster for each *Cinel*. The average demand is for about 3 men from every two houses for the land muster, 2 men from every three houses for the sea muster. These are the houses of individual families. The larger groupings of 60 or 100 houses correspond to the future *baile*, the smaller groupings of 20 to 30 houses to a half or third of a *baile*. The harsh geography of Argyle, dividing its people among islands and headlands of unequal size, prevented any simple schematic equalisation of areas; the term 'Bally-' did not extend to the place names of the Argyle Irish, and was probably not developed when the *Senchus* was written. But the easier geography of mainland Ireland made such simplification easier.

The power of the people was greatly less among the Irish than among the Welsh or the English. The assembly of the local *tuath* did not control its lands; local political authority was vested in its king, who was himself the tributary of a greater king, and formed the lowest grade in a hierarchy of despots; jurisdiction was the business of professional lawmen, rather than of local courts. The popular assemblies that tradition remembers are those of large regions or of the whole country, called together at fairs and conventions. Such meetings were necessarily restricted to delegates and representatives, and met under the presidency of kings, their debates dominated by the nobility, their decisions regulated by professional custodians of the law. It was only on rare occasions, like the great famine of the 660s, that desperation gave the plebeians courage to voice their independent initiative.

In Ireland the institution of the monastery was widely and rapidly welcomed by the subjects of the dynasts. The monks themselves were divided between those who welcomed a strong high king, and those who saw him as the arch tyrant, and proclaimed the power of the church as the alternative to all secular authority. They prevailed, and broke the power of the monarchy. But they were not able to unseat the regional and local kings and lords; the monasteries remained islands of independence, a refuge and a shield against the excess of tyranny, but they were not the authors or patrons of an alternative social order. At the convention of Drumceat, the church blessed the ancient learned class and in time fused with it; and it thereby opened the doors of learning more widely to men of humble birth.

The extreme subjection of the Irish peasant gave the monasteries their first inmates, and maintained for centuries a continuing supply of fresh recruits and a steady flow of learned emigrants abroad. It also conditioned the nature of Irish lordship. The Irish lord cared little for the ownership of land or the enjoyment of its revenue, in the manner that Rome had taught to Britain. Like the patrician of Rome, his power and his prosperity rested on the number and the status of his dependent clients; he was a lord of men rather than a lord of land. These ancient notions of submission to authority enfeebled Ireland for centuries. The lord who exacted submission from his own clients readily acknowledged himself the client of a greater lord; so that when the Norman and the English conqueror asserted his superiority by force, he was more easily accepted as a still greater lord, entitled to the obedience of his clients. Ireland submitted, for peasants who had never ruled themselves knew not how to organise effective resistance when their lords failed them. Medieval Ireland found no plebeian national leader; and until after 1916, English rule rarely faced a challenge more serious than local or regional risings, conspiracy or parliamentary protest; half a century of independence has not yet wholly eliminated the old habits that were formed in remote antiquity and hardened in early Christian Ireland, of grudging submission occasionally goaded into sporadic violence.

The North

The nations of the north slowly combined into the kingdom of Scotland. The dynasty of the Dal Riada Irish acquired the Pictish throne in the 9th century, and subsequently annexed the English of the Forth and the British of the Clyde; in time its authority prevailed beyond the Great Glen, and in the 15th century it subdued the western and northern Isles. Its records deal with rulers, nobles and churchmen, and have little to say of the early society of their subjects. As yet, the archaeological evidence is too little and too loosely dated to make good the silence of the written record.

The Irish dynasty brought with it the society of its homeland. The church was Irish, and disseminated Irish notions; their impact was strongest among notables, and in the lands where lords and wars were most frequent, but little of the pace and detail of change can be traced. Almost nothing is known of the society of the Picts, save that the inheritance of land and property as well as of political sovereignty passed through the woman; and that there were lords and great men who could afford to purchase slaves and to erect elaborate stone monuments.

In the sparsely populated lands beyond the Great Glen the brochs and duns are the memorials of unremembered peoples, whose military might had faded before the fall of Rome. The earliest coherent accounts of their way of life were set down by the 18th and 19th century travellers to the islands. There, very small independent communities of 4, 6 or 12 families then met annually to decide what lands to crop and to divide them by lot; the land was unfenced and the cattle were herded by day, pounded by night. The numbers that might graze the land were limited; excess cattle must be kept on the croft, or grazed by renting the rights or the land of a neighbour. Though earlier evidence fails, there is no reason to suppose significant change in their society over very many centuries. They were unharassed by king or landlord, without need of armies or commanders, chiefs or rulers, long isolated by geographical and political frontiers. Their institutions, or lack of them, fit the peaceful economy of some prehistoric peoples, whose excavated homes show no signs of kings, wealth or violence; but they do not fit the military vigour of the Argyle Scots or of the peoples of the Pictish lowland.

The Clan

Little is known of the early peoples of the future Scotland, but much is fancied. The understanding of what little evidence there is has long been bedevilled by the romantic myth of a 'clan society'. Its pretended antiquity is altogether bogus. 'Clan' is a modern word with a modern meaning, albeit foggy and changeable. In the circumspect language of the 19th century it meant

> a tribe . . . regarded as having a common ancestor;

but in the looser popular idiom of the 20th century Oxford dictionary it became

> Scotch highlanders with common ancestor; tribe.

The definition is confusing, for though 'tribe' is identified with 'clan', 'tribe' is itself defined as a 'group of barbarous clans'.

The dictionaries are accurate, for their business is to report current usage, not to correct its muddles. The meaning of 'clan' is shrouded, for it is simultaneously a subdivision of a 'tribe', and the 'tribe' itself. The word is misty, because the term 'tribe', to which it is related, is even vaguer. It is nowadays commonly used to lump together peoples little influenced by European technology, and often distorts enquiry into their separate customs.

The uncertainties are chiefly caused by confusing the modern meanings of these words with their origin and evolution. The *tribus* was an administrative division of the Roman people. The Latin Bible used the Latin word to describe the twelve stocks of the ancient Israelites; and the English Bible transliterated *tribus* into 'tribe'. The Old Testament Israelites practised a simple economy, rare in renaissance Europe, and European explorers therefore applied the familiar biblical term to newly discovered peoples whose way of life was simple. In consequence, it has acquired racial and patronising overtones, stigmatising the peoples to whom it is applied as 'backward', or even 'barbarous'.

The modern notion of a 'clan', a population supposedly descended from a common ancestor, was brought into frequent English usage by the romantic writers of the 18th century, and popularised by the novels of Sir Walter Scott. Generations of imperial administrators thereafter used biblical tribes and Scott's clans as shorthand labels for the societies of distant continents; the carefree use of such labels inspired belief in an abstract 'tribal society' and 'clan system', whose imaginary institutions were assumed to have been shared by the ancestors of the modern Scots, and many other peoples. Various attempts to define these words failed, for it is not possible to classify real institutions in the language of romantic fiction; and many anthropologists now avoid the words. They linger however among historians. The Macedonians of Alexander the Great are commonly termed 'clansmen' because they also inhabited a hilly homeland and felt its impact; the word 'tribe' is still often applied both to the migrating nations of the Germans and also to the sophisticated Roman *civitates* which they attacked, though no ancient writers described either by any word that corresponds to English 'tribe' or 'clan'; and these words abound in most short accounts of early Ireland and Scotland.

Many peoples trace their origin to a legendary common ancestor. The Hebrews and the Christians descend all mankind from one individual. But many other nations do not, and among them are the Irish and the Scots, whose myths record few traditions of a common national ancestor, except in some medieval tales that imitate Christian idiom. The word 'clan' seems ancient only because it derives from an Irish word that had a precise but different meaning. *Clanna*, like its Welsh equivalent, *plant*, means 'children', and by extension 'descendants'. It was one of many words used to distinguish the descendants of a ruler from the rest of his subjects, and in this sense meant 'royal family' or 'dynasty'. It was a late comer among these numerous equivalent terms, and is rarely used of a dynasty whose founder was held to have lived earlier than the 9th century; but in later medieval Scotland it became the commonest of such words. It outlived the Irish language, for successive foreign conquerors used it to induce their subjects to accept their rule.

The corporate *clanna*, or dynasty, is first reported in Scotland in the 12th century, in Buchan, in the fertile lowland territory of the northern Picts. The founder of the *clanna* Morgan was held to have lived some three centuries earlier. His name was British in origin, but had long been adopted through marriage into the royal family of the Argyle Scots; his dynasty were *mormaers*, Irish rulers imposed upon the native population, and the latest of them assumed the prouder title of Kings of Moray.

The power of the dynasty of Morgan died with its last great king, Macbeth. He was overthrown by English invaders, who installed the heirs of the exiled southern dynasty of Albany. They brought with them English and Norman barons, to rule men of Irish speech. The coming of the English overlaid the old antagonisms between Pict and Irish, and the new lords found an Irish pedigree useful. Their genealogists traced the Campbells to the Bronze Age Kings of Ireland by way of King Arthur; the Earls of Lennox were represented as descendants of the Kings of Munster by the assertion that a 12th century Norman was the son of 6th century Irishman, and Albany was peopled with his supposed descendants by the alteration of a single letter in an ancient text. These early *clanna* were limited to lowlanders, or to lowland rulers imposed upon the fringes of the highlands; and they still sharply distinguished members of the ruling dynasty from their subjects. In 14th-century Fife, membership of the ruling *Clanna* MacDuff was still rigidly restricted to nine generations in descent from an acknowledged ruler. The restriction shut out plebeians, and denied them the right to wear the multi-coloured clothing proper to nobility.

By the end of the 14th century, the prestige of the Irish past had dwindled in the lowlands, and lowland *clanna* passed from record. But at the same time, lowland authority began to be asserted powerfully in the Irish-speaking highlands. Hitherto, resentments were little enflamed, and a 14th-century lowland gentleman could still describe the 'Highlanders and peoples of the Islands' with distant tolerance as

> savage and rude, independent, ease-loving, of a docile and warm
> disposition, comely in person but unsightly in dress, hostile to the
> Anglic people and language ... They are however easily made to
> submit if properly governed.

The 'Anglic people' were the lowlanders of Scotland, whose speech was English. 'Proper government' entailed obedience to a co-operative local lord and his dynasty, still termed in Irish his *clanna*. The first highland *clanna* are recorded in 1396, and the earliest known chief of a highland *clanna* bore the English name of Johnson. Little lords multiplied, many of them of local birth and Irish speech. The sovereign authority of the 'Anglic' lowland government was strengthened if the highland chiefs fought each other in savage feuds, and if each dynasty engulfed its population. The end result was described by a shrewd 18th-century observer.

> The lands are set by the landlord during pleasure, or on a short tack,
> to people ... of a superior station ... These are generally the sons,
> brothers, cousins or nearest relations of the landlord or chief. This
> land ... they, their children and grandchildren possess at an easy
> rent, until a nearer descendant be ... preferred. As the pro-
> pinquity removes, they ... degenerate to be of the common
> people. As this hath been an ancient custom, most of the farmers and
> cottars are of the same name and clan as the proprietor.

Over a period of four centuries the 'common people' of each valley assumed the 'name and clan' of their rulers. In a small enclosed population it was not easy to disprove a man's claim to noble rank and clothing by descent through nine generations, from a ruler dead for three hundred years; nor was there incentive to challenge such claims, for 'as propinquity removed' it was more decent to dispossess a distant cousin in favour of a near relative than a stranger who owed no family allegiance. When the dynastic *clanna* was extended to admit the whole population, its founder was necessarily accepted as their common ancestor. The modern clan was born.

The clan owes its origin to a peculiar combination of Scottish geography and Irish customary law. Peoples and regions elsewhere take their name from an individual who ruled long ago, but no one pretends that the whole population of Lorraine or Tirconnel are descendants of Lothaire or Connel; and few Lorrainers remember ancestors older than their grandfathers. But Irish and Welsh custom had always devolved rights and obligations upon a nine generation family; and the population of many highland valleys was small enough to be credibly accommodated within a nine generation family, isolated enough to make marriage outside the community a rarity.

In a more tranquil age the highland clan might have remained a short lived local institution, confined to the mountains and to the age that created it. But the convulsions of the 16th and 17th centuries enlisted neighbouring valleys on opposing sides in greater wars, and loosed them upon each other and upon lowland supporters of the opposite party. Repeated raids taught the lowlanders to fear and abhor highland savagery; but fears faded when William III fortified the Great Glen, and the Act of Union inclined many lowlanders to sympathy with highland dislike of English rule. Fashionable ladies whose mothers shuddered at the sight of highland dress began to wear highland ornament. In 1745, the romantic failure of the Young Pretender, clad in a 'Royal Stewart tartan' that would have startled his royal ancestors, made heroes of the highlanders, so soon as they were safely defeated. The English government banned the tartan from the highland hills, but when the ban was lifted the tartan spread to lowland streets. The magnificently blended colours evolved by the weavers of the valleys delighted elegant urban taste, and Scott's novels endowed the clansmen of the past with a generous nobility.

The pageantry of pipe and tartan has become the symbol of modern Scotland, rooted in the highlands, but no longer confined within them. Nineteenth century lowland gentlemen discovered that they too were clansmen, and devised their own tartans and their own ancestors. The modern clan is a recent institution. An institution is none the worse for being modern; but when a modern institution asserts a sham antiquity, it degrades those whom it pretends to ennoble. The ceremonies of the Scottish clan are far removed from the trivial modern romances of the rest of Britain, King Arthur's Tintagel among the English, or the latter day Druids of the Welsh; for the innate good taste of the highlanders has invested the clan and its observances with a dignity that makes them a worthy symbol of a modern nation.

The clan is embedded in modern society. But neither clan nor tribe have any legitimate place in an account of early Ireland or Scotland. They need explanation, because they still frequently corrupt such accounts, even though scholars intimate with the evidence have stigmatised their irrelevance for more than half a century. Eoin MacNeill is judged by the most learned of his successors to have 'done more than any other to place the history of pre-Norman Ireland on the basis of sound historical criticism'; and, as leader of the Irish Volunteers, he is also numbered among the creators of modern Ireland. In 1921 he summarised the evidence in words too little heeded:

> the only technical meaning that *clann* has in Irish is that of 'children'. All this solemn classification of family, sept, clan or . . . tribe is so much rubbish, . . . rubbish . . . imposed by the careless, the presuming and the ignorant.

The judgement is as valid for Scotland as for Ireland. The evidence for Scotland was assembled and surveyed by W.F. Skene more than a hundred years ago, and interpreted in the light of mid Victorian assumptions. No study of early Scotland on a comparable scale has since appeared; until it does, fancy prevails, and the nation is robbed of its history. Reality is a surer foundation for national sentiment than make-believe; and reality discredits sweetened romance, but honours the men and women who created a single and confident nation out of numerous discordant peoples with unlike customs, beliefs and institutions.

Community: the Welsh
Class Difference

Welsh and Irish society were not alike, for in Britain four centuries of Roman government had absorbed the notables and modified their relations to the poor. The society of early Wales is most fully described in their laws. Welsh law is difficult to interpret, since the only texts preserved are late and have therefore been unduly disregarded. They have not yet received sufficient historical study, and their enactments are sometimes uncritically dismissed as late invention. But a few commonsense rule-of-thumb principles pinpoint the main stages in their evolution. They contain little medieval English law, for the Edwardian conquest tended to impose English law, to abrogate Welsh law rather than alter it. Values expressed in English pence cannot be earlier than the 10th century, when English money began to circulate freely, and may be later; but they commonly translate values previously expressed in cattle. Some sections transcribed from West-Saxon law are unlikely to be earlier. But the dating of older sections rests primarily on comparison with legal practice outside Wales. Institutions that are also found in Cumberland, in Brittany, or among the Welsh of Wessex are likely to have existed before the 6th century, when English conquest sundered these regions from one another; what is paralleled in Irish law, and not found elsewhere, is likely to date back to an earlier age, before the Roman conquest separated Britain from Ireland.

The social divisions of early Wales are akin to those of the late Roman empire, that distinguished the *ingenuus*, the free-born native citizen, from the bond *colonus*, and the slave, *servus*. But changing late Roman economy altered the meaning of words used for bondman and slave; Latin *servus* in law denoted the marketable human property, whom the modern English language calls slave, in contrast to the serf, who is bound to the soil, but cannot be sold apart from his land. But in practice the *servus* so often remained on his land that the word gave birth to the English term 'serf'. The process was so far advanced in Wales that Welsh Latin writers commonly preferred the clarity of the alternative Latin word *mancipium*, a 'purchased or captured slave'. There were plenty of men of servile legal status, but marketable slaves were rare.

Welsh laws distinguished three categories of native Cymro, the free, the bond, and the slave, as in Roman law. Free men included the *boneddig*, free-born, whether he owned land or no; the *priodaur*, who owned land; and the noble *uchelwr*, upper man, who owned much land. Below them were the *taeog*, a cultivator bound to the soil, termed *rusticus* or *servus* in Latin, and the *caeth*, slave, commonly called *mancipium* in Latin. The language of the Saints' Lives uses similar terms; *liberi* were free men in general and included *possessores* and *domini*, owners of the land and masters of men, and *nobiles*, nobles; below them were bond rent-paying *rustici* and *servi* and slave *mancipia*. These provisions echo the central distinction of later Roman law, between *honestiores* and *humiliores*, 'worthier' and 'humbler' citizens.

These Roman categories date back in Wales to the 6th century. Somewhere about 560, Gildas warned that David's radicalism 'preferred serfs above their masters, the commons above their kings' (*servos dominis, vulgus regibus*). The parents of Samson were *nobiles* and landowners; when they took monastic vows, they 'gave alms to the poor, relaxed their claims upon their debtors, lightened the tribute of their serfs' (*tributa servis suis levigantes*); the near-contemporary author got his information, at one remove, from Samson's mother. Hervé in Brittany encountered the chief of a *plebs* who was chasing runaway rustics; both Roman and Welsh law are clear that the rustic who escaped might find plenty of other lords who were ready to receive strangers on their lands. On Ramsey Island by St. Davids, the hermit Justinian was killed by his *servi*. In 7th-century Wessex the Welshman's kin might be free or unfree. The distinction was plainly inherited from the independent British of the 6th century.

Large landowners are frequently named. Illtud's monastery was his 'earthly inheritance'; it contained the ruins of a mansion. Paul Aurelian's father was a nobleman and landowner, and his sister had trouble with 'wicked co-heirs' near Exeter. Both these texts rest on 6th-century originals. Tatheus was entertained by a rich man near Chepstow, who still heated his bath on Saturdays in the manner of his Roman forbears. Lesser freemen are also common; many saints were entertained by small farmers who lived in a *tuguriolum*, a cottage; by men of modest means who owned a few cows; or by the swineherds of wealthier men. Land was measured in the laws by the *erw*, acre, but in the Llandaff texts its value was assessed in units of so many cows, or by its arable yield, reckoned by the *uncia* and the *modius*.

The earlier texts of Brittany emphasise the gulf between the free classes and the rustics. Malo lost and regained his cloak; when he learned that a cottager had used it as a blanket he refused to wear it, 'thinking a garment that had lain upon rustics unworthy of him'. Winwaloe fed the poor and his 'usual custom' was to offer them 'the hope of eternal reward and the solace of prayer'; but 'the high master did not deign to call them brothers', though he accepted 'lesser brethren' as labourers in his monastery, as did Illtud, and Cassiodorus in Italy. These are the poor whom Roman usage called *rustici* in their social status, *coloni* in their economic condition. Medieval Welsh law used different words for men of the same status and condition.

The Welsh: Village and Hundred

The 6th-century emigrants to Brittany were organised into *plebes*, composed of a number of *tribus*, each of which contained a number of *domus*, houses. The names were borrowed from Jerome's account of the monks of Egypt, but they were used of secular as well as monastic organisation. The three words were translated as *Plou*, *tref* and *ker*; all are common in place names, and are often followed by a personal name. In Wales, *plwyf* meant a parish, but is rare in place names; *tref* is as common in local names, while *caer* was normally reserved for substantial fortifications, except in parts of Dumnonia, and the usual word for a house is *ty*, or its variants. In north Wales a number of *tref* were commonly termed a *maenol*, in the south a *mainaur*; though the schematism that assigned 64 houses to each *tref* and 4 *tref* to each *maenol* is late, the word *mainaur* was already established by the 8th century.

The native inhabitants of the *tref* were free, bond or slave. But the laws have much to say of the *aillt*, glossed as *estron*, stranger. He was normally a Cymro, from another part of Wales, a refugee or a landless freeman who sought to better himself elsewhere. The strangers also included the *alltud*, defined as 'from overseas, from another country, speaking a different language', among them shipwrecked sailors. The law prescribed that the stranger, like the rustic *taeog*, must have a lord. The reasons repeated in the texts echoed laws older than themselves. Strangers must be prevented from plotting; the foreigner must not acquire Cymric land; nugatory marriages and illegitimate children must be avoided. The last reason had troubled 5th-century Rome. In 451 Valentinian III tackled the troubles of *coloni originarii*, native rustics, or tied tenants, disturbed by *advenae*, strangers, 'often poor . . . who accepted food and clothing, thereby escaping the squalor of indigence', by 'pretending to undertake labour and duties', but who, thinking nothing of the misery they caused, chose women belonging to the estate, and, when they had had enough of them, went off, unmindful of their former state, ignoring their cohabitation and their lovely sons, with no law to stop them.

Valentinian enacted that the stranger must register on a particular estate, and might not thereafter desert his home or his wife. The Welsh law re-enacted Valentinian's.

The stranger is prominent in the law books, for the unusual is commonly more difficult for lawyers to describe, and needs more words. But the stranger played a large part in the economy, especially in unfree *tref*; for the *tref* was of two kinds, *rhydd*, free, and *taeog*, unfree. The land of the free *tref* was divided by the free man's law, but in the unfree *tref* it was assigned by the *arglwyd*, the lord, though it commonly went to the dead man's heirs, since the laws prescribe fees paid for the son's succession to his father's land. The land of the unfree *tref* was *tir cyvriv*, 'register land'; the modern Welsh *cyfrif* means 'counting' or 'reckoning', its derivative *cyfrifeb* a 'return', a 'census' or 'statistics', what is entered in a written record; *tir cyvriv* is land registered in a document or book. The laws measure land by area, by the *erw*, 'acre'; but the Llandaff documents measure by capacity, by the *modius*, or bushel, and *uncia*, a 'twelfth', perhaps of the *iugum* of Roman Britain.

Taxation of free and unfree land differed. Booked land paid *cyllid*, rent or tax, in Latin *vectigal*, to lord or king, but was exempt from the food tribute, *gwestva*. The king exacted *gwestva* from free *uchelwr*, nobles; Roman law had called it *pastus*, and it was held to have been originally levied when the king was on progress, dispensing justice. Taxes were differently collected. The twice yearly *cylch*, or 'circuit', of royal officers called *cais*, collected the unfree tax, but not the nobleman's food tribute. The Saints' Lives record the visits of these officers to each *pagus*, the equivalent of *tref* in the sixth century, and describe them by their late Roman name of *exactores*. Sometimes they demanded payment in the valuable ancient breed of white cattle with red ears; but in the laws these special cattle are demanded only as compensation for insult or injury to the king, his *saraad*.

The extent of unfree land is not known. Medieval schematism reckoned it at about one-third of all Welsh land; though the figures are unreal, the proportions are closer to reality, but they do not show how and when the amount of servile land grew. The free and unfree *tref* were envisaged as physically different. The houses on the free man's heritable land, partitioned among his sons, are treated as scattered separate farmsteads, but the unfree *tref* is regarded as a compact village. The laws on fire prevention enact that its bath must be built at a specified distance from the nearest house, that its smithy must be roofed with tiles or sods, not thatch; and require that accusations of arson must be cleared by the oath of 50 men, half of them *Gwyr Nod*, in Latin *viri noti*, respectable persons, or 'men of note', an oath that is normal for the bond *taeog*, not for the free man. These physical distinctions are recognisable on excavated sites. The compact hill-top village of Tre'r Ceiri in Caernarvonshire corresponds to the inflammable *taeog tref* of the laws; the chieftain's residence of Dinas Powys by Cardiff was a fit home for a lord, *arglwyd*; and the known numerous farmsteads of varying sizes suit the landowners and nobles, *priodorion* and *uchelwr*, of varying degrees.

The laws were written down for the benefit of kings and have most to say of the servile *tref*, which lay directly in his power; there he settled his strangers, who did not acquire free Cymro status until after nine generations of marriage with native women and therefore tended to increase in numbers. Their rents were earmarked for the king's dogs, horses and progress, and over them he placed his lord, who received part of their revenues. Less is said of the free *tref*, save that it was a unit of taxation, with fixed bounds. There is no sign that it had its own assembly or council, or any administrative or judicial function; but its notables met the king at regular times and places in the assembly of the *cantref*, the unit of a hundred *tref*, which constituted a principal court for civil and criminal offences; and might also censure a king and compel him to right an individual deemed to have been unjustly wronged.

The laws assign the political administration of the free Cymro not to the residential *tref*, but to the *cenedl*, the kindred of related families. It was a nine-generation group, whose functions included the defence of the free *bonheddig* against the encroachments of the king and the *taeog*. Its head, the *penncenedl*, in Latin *caput gentis*, was elected. Under his guidance it undertook a wide range of civil and criminal jurisdiction. In particular, though *saraad*, compensation for injury, was borne by the four-generation *gwely*, the more expensive *galanas*, compensation for manslaughter, was spread among the *cenedl*, with exact practical provisions to meet the difficulty of finding out who belonged to the eighth and ninth degrees of kinship. Some texts give the *penncenedl* a war leader and other assistants, but all agree that he must be a noble *uchelwr*, and emphatically repeat that no lord or royal official might be chosen.

The *cenedl* is rarely named outside the laws, and there is therefore no guide to its effective reality. But its name and form are closely paralleled by the earliest form of Scottish *clanna*, whose earlier names had included *cinel*. The functions differed, for the *clanna* organised a dynasty, while the *cenedl* organised freemen independently of kings. The similarities imply an ancient institution that the Welsh and Irish put to different uses; among the Welsh, the name may be later than the institution, for the earliest original texts, dated to about 800 or earlier, knew a kinship group called *luidt*, not recorded later; it may have been the ancestor of the *cenedl*.

Land Tenure

Welsh law mixed Roman and native precedent. Roman law classified men by status and domicile, native law by kinship. The dynasties that succeeded Arthur added the new claims of kings, and the spread of monasteries brought new problems, at first hard to resolve, that centred upon the tenure and inheritance of land. The claims of king and church conflicted with the rights of kin. The new problems are illustrated in the Life of Wenefred. Early in the 7th century, Teuyth of Tegeingl, Flintshire, was the *possessor* of three *villae*. He had no sons and decided to grant a *villa*, *tref*, to St. Beuno. He asked king Cadfan to 'fulfil for him his intentions about his patrimony'. Cadfan, whom his tombstone honours as the 'most learned of kings', replied

> The decision is neither mine nor yours; for we ought not to harm your interest or my need by separating land from the community of the province. But I will make you a free grant of whichever *villa* you choose, if you will be content to leave me the others.

The text is late and much corrupted; but what it reports is a problem of the 7th century, when monks were relatively new in north Wales, and the mechanics of how to grant them lands still needed careful thought. By the time the Life was written the problem had been solved for centuries.

The words and clauses are expressed in awkward Latin, but the problem and solution are clearly defined. Seen solely from the standpoint of Roman law and its modern heirs, in terms of the simple polarised abstractions 'private property' and 'communal property', the transaction bristles with apparent contradictions. Teuyth was a *possessor* who could not alienate; the decision was not his or the king's, but he and the king decided. They alienated part of Teuyth's 'possessions' from the 'community', but what Teuyth retained was the king's.

Seen in the language of early Welsh law these statements are more easily intelligible. Teuyth was lord of a *maenol*, comprising three unfree *tref*. The land was *tir cyvriv*, the documented property of the *tref*, not legally inherited, paying *cyllid*, tax, to Teuyth and to the king. Its transfer from the community to the individual involved other interests besides the loss of revenue to king and lord, for the nearer relations of Teuyth's *gwely* were his heirs, and his larger *cenedl* also had claims upon his inheritance. These interests were appeased or overridden by the cession of one *tref*; the others remained the king's, for the principal renders were his. The grant to the monk entailed further complication. Later law enacted that when the king authorised the construction of a church in a servile *tref*, its inhabitants were freed; they ceased to pay servile tax, their land ceased to be registered communal property, and passed by family inheritance. The later law generalised claims that monks had advanced from the beginning in respect of individual estates, and may have been secured by Beuno.

King Cadfan's learning found the problems difficult in the early 7th century, chiefly because of the claims of kin. The residual claims of distant heirs mattered most in times of expanding population, when good land was short. Exact detail is recorded in 14th-century surveys. Then, in one district, the heirs of four landowners numbered more than 200 persons after 150 years, and their holdings were drastically partitioned. One of the four ancestors had held five whole *tref* and fragments of others, together equivalent to a sixth. Some heirs had divided their inheritance, but others jointly farmed undivided lands. The undivided holding had become the property of the ancestor's *gwely*, his four-generation family; its separate divided portions were termed *gavell*, and fines had confiscated tiny portions, as exact as five eighths or seven sixty-fourths of a gavell, that became the king's property. He might either assign them to his unfree cultivators, or allot them to free *bonheddig*, provided that they paid servile tax. Though each man knew his own acres, the revenue officers faced a mathematical nightmare.

The result was not only the subdivision of large estates into small holdings. The wealth and status of families changed. The proprietor of six *tref* had been a great landlord. The descendant who held fragments of a few *gavell* was a poor peasant. The principles of the law operated, but their operation was far more complex than the simple legal contrast between a *tref* that was entirely free, and another that was unfree. Two parts of the holding of one *gwely* were held on servile *taeog* tenure, paying servile tax, but the rest was held in free tenure; and one *gwely* might hold several *tref*, differently partitioned among its members, so that beside the free and unfree *tref* there were others that were part free, part unfree.

The survey is late, but it illuminates an older system. It shows what happened when the birth rate was high. Holdings then fragmented. But in times of falling population they consolidated. Over centuries of fluctuating population inheritance by kin divorced land-holding from territorial political organisation. But the chief gainer was the king; his lands were enlarged by fines, and he also acquired the 'extinct *erw*', the acres of a free man who left no heir in his four-generation *gwely*; and death without heirs was commoner when population contracted. Crown lands grew, and when population rose the freeman's demand for more acres sharpened, strengthening his need of his *cenedl*, and inciting him to bring a suit of *dadenhudd*, 'recovery of patrimony'.

The claim of patrimony threatened church lands, for the church did not die and did not partition its estates. The legal problem was real, for a free man was entitled to inheritance by ancient custom, that no king or lord had power to override in native law. The church therefore asserted the tenures of late Roman law, *ius perpetuum*, everlasting right, or *ius ecclesiasticum*, church right, against *ius hereditarium*, the claims of kin. But when two legal systems conflicted, force was the arbiter between opposing rights. Commonly, an individual's grant of land, ratified by the king, sufficed to deter the claims of his heirs to recover the land in law; but not infrequently a great-grandson might disregard a grant made a century before, sometimes with no greater violence than withholding rents claimed by the church; and many charters are re-grants of old donations ignored by later landowners.

But prudence dictated that all possible steps should be taken to satisfy the claims of heirs, and to make a suit for recovery of patrimony legally invalid. The most sensible way was to compensate the heirs in advance. The medieval charter

463

memoranda of the Books of Llancarfan and Llandaff altered much of the wording of the grants they transcribed to suit the needs of their own day, but they often retained elaborate details of the gifts made to redeem the rights of all the interests involved; their transcripts illustrate the efforts of early 7th-century Welsh lawyers to fight their way through to safe legal forms.

The Llancarfan texts give most detail. Guorcinnim bought an estate from the king 'into his own inheritance', for a sword worth 25 cows. The king freed servile land and made it the 'perpetual inheritance' of Guorcinnim; but it was still subject to the law of kin, so Guorcinnim gave another gift to Mesioc, 'whom it concerned by hereditary right', and then assigned the estate to the monastery of Cadoc 'in perpetual possession'. But Cadoc's heirs also had claims upon his monastic lands, for his immediate successors were lay abbots chosen from his kin; so Guorcinnim also gave gifts to the son and grandson of the lay abbot. In addition he compensated the son and grandson of the king, and also Guengarth, styled *procurator*, who had previously levied services and dues upon the estate. The whole transaction was termed an *emptio*, 'purchase'.

A little later Guengarth himself was given an estate by the king. He gave its rents to the church, and gave 'his guilded sword Hipiclaur, worth 70 cows' to the abbot, who then gave it to the king, in exchange for confirmation, for the remission of all secular dues and for an assurance that the estate should never be subjected to any lord but Guengarth and his heirs. On another occasion the king himself gave a sword and a cloak to the abbot, who used them to buy an estate; he then held it in *ius perpetuum* from two laymen, evidently joint-heirs, who themselves gave two cows to the lord, to free it from royal dues, and 'held a charter on the hand of the abbot', who beat the bounds in token of 'private possession', *propriae possessionis*. Another landowner gave an estate that was his 'by hereditary right' to the abbot, in 'perpetual right'; he also 'bought' it from another man, 'to whom it had devolved', evidently a kinsman and heir. Another estate belonged jointly to two brothers and a sister, together with two parts of a second property, and was granted by the king, who himself 'held a charter on the hand of the abbot'; the abbot then gave the king a horse, which he passed on to a royal officer.

The texts that report these details are late, but their matter is not. Most of the later grants, in the Llandaff book, are content to record that a man gave an estate, transferring it from 'hereditary right' to 'perpetual right', for the procedures were then standardised and recognised. They hardened early, for late 8th-century grants preserved in the original in the Book of Teilo, or Chad, found no such detailed explanation necessary.

Similar problems beset the grant of land to Irish monasteries. The earliest records date from the late 7th century, and the scribe who copied them into the Book of Armagh a little over a hundred years later found them difficult to understand. In the fullest of them, two persons, the virgin Cummen and Brethan, bought Oughteragh in Leitrim from property bequeathed to Cummen and two other virgins. The estate was the half of her own inheritance. The value of the personal mobile property due to her was paid in animals and old plate, which she presumably passed on to her co-heirs. She then wove a cloak and gave it to the chief of the ruling dynasty; he gave her a horse, which she gave to 'Colman of the Britons', who sold it for a *cumal* of silver; and the *cumal* went to the price of the estate. Not everything is clear in the difficult language; but the substance is that the donor bought out the rights of her kin and of the king. Colman was probably the former bishop of the Northumbrians, the date about 665 or soon after. The Tigernach Annals 750 entry seems to rest on a confusion.

Kin were not always bought out in Ireland. In another text in the same collection Feth made a formal oath to the monks and nobility that there should be no kin over the monastery of Drumlease in Leitrim save his own, and that the abbot should be chosen from his kin so long as there was a qualified candidate. These practices remained normal. For more than a hundred years the successors of Columba at Iona were chosen from his kin, and many other abbots were kinsmen of the founder of their house. Very many houses also remained in secular law the property of the founder's kin, whose head was an *erenarch*, 'lay proprietor'; the normal word for the religious abbots of the greater houses was *comarb*, 'joint heir', jointly with the lay heir.

The institution of the lay abbot is not reported in Wales after the early 7th century, and the kinsmen of abbots are less in evidence throughout. But in Ireland the *erenarch* took firm root. Early in the 9th century the notice of Foirtchernn's foundation of Trim, in the middle of the 5th century, is followed by a list of eight religious abbots who succeeded him, and also of eight generations of 'secular heirs', *erenarchs*, who descended from his brother. But, as in Wales, procedures were standardised, and in the 9th century it was sufficient to record that the kin, *genus*, of Binean's mother 'gave him the inheritance' on which he built a church.

Irish and Welsh society shared a remote common past. But the Welsh had also experienced four hundred years of Roman rule, which differentiated them from the Irish, even though their monasteries transmitted some of that experience to Ireland. Their lawyers had to improvise, but their solutions endured at home and became one of the influences that bore upon the formative years of the English. The men who faced and solved the problems that Arthur's successors passed to the British and Irish contributed to the common culture of medieval Britain.

CHAPTER TWENTY-FOUR

ENGLISH SOCIETY

Local Difference

Early English society is more difficult to comprehend than Welsh or Irish. It was more varied and changed more quickly. Much more is known about it, but large sections of the evidence are still unsifted. Its simplest outlines are clearer. At the beginning of the seventh century the English conquerors had no common custom and no fixed social order. The conventions of the Welsh and the Irish had hardened over many centuries, but English society was new, unformed, and full of local variation; and the speed and extent of recent conquest brought violent upheaval. From the seventh century onward lawyers struggled to impose uniformity, but found that words were more easily standardised than the things they represented. Uniformity of custom could not be achieved by the pen of the administrator, for diversity was deep seated. The chief difference was that which separated the old kingdoms from those that had acquired vast lands in need of colonisation, the Northumbrians, the West Saxons and the Mercians. But within this general distinction, the needs and outlook of each kingdom, and of regions within kingdoms, differed greatly.

The English brought their national monarchy to Britain in the late fifth century. But partition long prevented it from uniting the English in Britain. Each monarchy had its own tradition. Kent alone was ruled by a long established monarchy. Monarchy was old among the East Angles, but the dynasty was new. The East and South Saxon kings were too weak to assert lasting independence against their greater neighbours, and Lindsey was long buffeted between the Northumbrians and Mercians. In Northumbria repeated military success endowed the kings with enormous personal prestige, but the affection inspired by the sincerity of Irish monks gave churchmen power to curb the kings. The numerous small peoples of the midlands were still loosely adjusted to the growing power of the Mercian monarchs, and the five West Saxon kingdoms admitted the suzerainty of an overking only when they must.

Within each kingdom the proportions of great men and small varied, and variation caused different relations between them; in addition, the proportions and relations between the English and the native British, or Welsh, were as diversified. All these differences were accentuated in the newly subdued lands, that invited settlement by young men of energy, particularly in the west, beyond the furthest frontiers of their forefathers. There men risked destruction by native rebellion, or by invasion from the still unconquered Welsh kingdoms, but those who secured their lands became lords of native subjects, more than the possessors of lands that they must cultivate by their own labour.

The Sources

The main witness to the evolution of English society in the 5th and 6th centuries is the mass of material interred in pagan graves; thereafter, evidence comes chiefly from place names, supplemented by laws, charters and other texts. The different kinds of evidence are dissimilar. The 7th-century law codes of Kent and Wessex survive as they were written, and report the lawyer's view of their society. Charters are preserved from several regions of the south and midlands, but their rich reserves of information have as yet scarcely begun to be explored. The texts are available only in imperfect modern editions, inadequately indexed, whose shortcomings hamper their study; a few texts survive unaltered, and a very few are wholly the invention of later ages, but most have been altered in the copying to suit later interest. The alterations are sometimes trivial, sometimes extensive, but it has not yet been possible to distinguish systematically between the original content and later additions, and the charters are therefore still often herded into the oversimple categories of 'forged' or 'genuine', though few of them are properly described by either term. The study of place names suffers from a different handicap; the greater part of their evidence cannot be assessed until the survey is complete, but nearly a third of the counties are not yet published. These several sources also overlap in time. The earliest Kentish law-code was drawn up at the beginning of the 7th century, the earliest West Saxon code at the end of the century. With few exceptions the charters do not begin until the 670s, but much of the place name evidence concerns earlier generations, and some of it reaches back into the 6th century, when pagan cemetery burial was still normal.

Graves

The pagan burials illustrate the beginnings of social difference. Most of the 5th-century cemeteries were the graveyards of communities, and most of the graves were of equal wealth; the women were buried with a pair of simple brooches, the men with spear and shield. Swords, and emblems of female wealth and authority increased during the 6th century, and were matched by greater numbers of poorly furnished burials. Contrast is more marked after the conquest. A majority of the latest burials were the tombs of individuals or of families, often wealthy. Prominent barrows were erected over the remains of the local kings of the West Saxons; early in the 7th century the Mercian barrows in the uplands beyond the Trent sometimes contained costly armour, and in the south the dazzling royal tombs of Taplow, Broomfield and Sutton Hoo witness the sudden emergence of splendid kingship. Many lesser men were also buried richly, for the institution of monarchy required the support of a nobility, graded by differing degrees of wealth and power.

Place names

The evidence of place names confirms and continues the evolution traced by the graves. Many kinds of names carry their date with them. No place, save sometimes a region or a large town, could acquire an English name before its first English settlers arrived, and their arrival is dated by the graves, by the Saxon Chronicle, Bede, and other texts who report either the first arrival of the English in particular districts, or the existence of particular names at specific dates. It is rarely possible to know when a name form altogether passed from use, for isolated instances lingered long; but it is frequently observed that some forms are common in older areas, rare in regions settled later, while others are rare in old areas, common in lands first settled after the conquest. It is hardly ever possible to date the name of a particular place, for when a name form was established in a district, it often remained long in use; but the texts and graves frequently indicate when and where particular types of name came into widespread use.

Communities

Only a fraction of the evidence can yet be studied, but understanding has been greatly helped by the publication of volumes analysing the meaning and distribution of the main elements used in forming names, and by recent thorough study of the element *-ing*. Interpretation of its various forms demands nice attention to Old English spelling and grammar and usage, but the basic meaning

---

Map 30

	single sites	frequent
Names in *-ingas*	I	|||
Names in *-ingaham*	O	=
Names in *-inga-*	■	///

Sites outside the areas of frequency are marked individually

.._.._. Boundary of counties examined

━━━ Approximate limit of 6th century
pagan burials within the area   *(cf. Map 21, p.297)*

MAP 30 ENGLISH COLONISATION: PLACE NAMES I

The South and the Midlands, names in *-inga(s)*

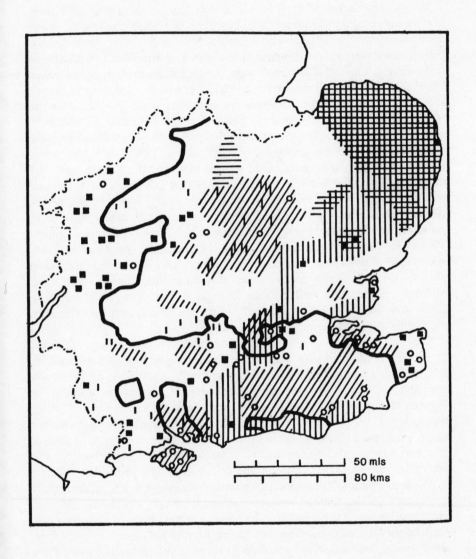

50 mls

80 kms

is clear. It is a word ending, not unlike the modern *-ine* or *-ite*, but more widely employed, meaning a place or people who belong in some sense to the word that precedes it; the *Haestingas*, who named Hastings, were Haesta's people, and Tyningham means the home of the people who lived by the river Tyne.

Maps 30 and 36 show where these names were mainly used in England. Names in *-ingaham* abound in East Anglia, and extend to the Middle Angles and to Kent in smaller numbers. Elsewhere they are common only among sixth-century English emigrants to Gaul, in Artois and western Flanders (Map 19A, p. 288); in south-eastern England a few exist upon the immediate margins of the pagan burial areas, but they are very rare in districts that were first colonised in the 7th and later centuries. Names in *-ingas* are somewhat more widespread in the districts of the 5th and 6th-century English, but they are also rare in 7th-century areas. But they do not mark the names of the earliest English. Though they are common in the older areas, very few of them are close enough to known cemeteries to have been the names of the villages that used those cemeteries; and many among the few burial grounds that lie within half a mile of villages so named are cemeteries of mid or late 6th-century origin. Most of these names surround cemeteries or groups of cemeteries at a distance of several miles, or lie between them. Map 31, showing part of Bedfordshire, is typical of many localities. Though it is in theory possible that many old names have been lost, and that many cemeteries have not been discovered, the evidence of what is known is too plain to disregard. These are the names of offshoots from the first villages, of colonists who moved a little distance from home. Names of this type plainly began to be used in or before the middle of the 6th century, but were rare after the middle of the 7th century.

These are the names of independent communities. Names in *-inga-* followed by another word, commonly *denn*, swine pasture, or *hyrst*, wooded upland, or *fold*, enclosed grazing, describe later dependent settlements. Their distribution is altogether different. They are rare in the older areas, except in the districts between reserves in which the English were confined during the years of British supremacy. There the English came in the late 6th century; and these dependent names continued in common use in the western lands between Avon and Severn, that were first peopled by the English between the end of pagan burial in the early 7th century and the granting of the first charters, fifty years later.

The commonest of the community names, *-tun*, cannot yet be studied, for it is frequent in the counties not yet published, and its significance depends chiefly on the words that precede it. Its basic meaning, 'fence', is perpetuated by the modern German word *Zaun*. In Old English it usually means a fenced area, sometimes agricultural, as in *gaerstun*, grass enclosure, and is used for a house in a couple of exceptional passages. But its ordinary meaning in the 7th century and later, when places were receiving their names, was 'village', a collection of houses, compact or scattered, forming a single political unit. In place names it has no other meaning. It is regularly translated in Latin by the word *villa*, that was

MAP 31 ENGLISH COLONISATION: PLACE NAMES 2

Central Bedfordshire, names in -*inga*(*s*)

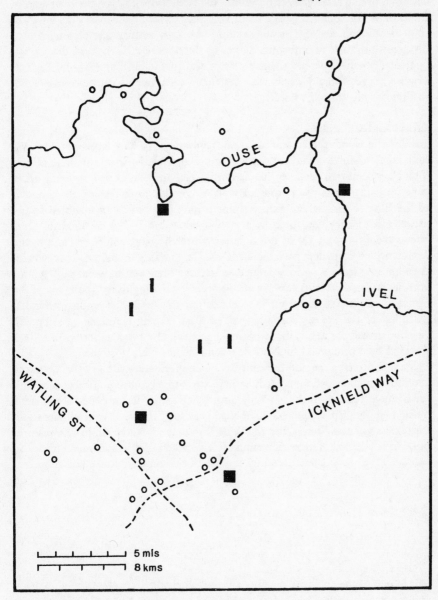

■   Main early pagan cemeteries

O   Other pagan English burial grounds

I   Place names in -*ingas*

also used to translate the Welsh *tref*. But in place names it 'was not so common in the earliest Old English period', and is 'associated with secondary colonisation from established centres.' It was not until the 12th century that men needed to distinguish the size of unfortified places by different words; then the diminutive *villagium* began to denote smaller places, and to establish the word village in English usage; the old words were restricted to larger places, becoming 'ville' in French and 'town' in English.

Individual Colonists

Besides the words for communities and collections of houses, words denoting individual holdings of varying size and importance were used for naming places. The Northumbrian *-botl*, as in Harbottle, had the specialised meaning of 'a superior hall, a mansion, a castle'. The word is early, for in Europe it is confined to the Elbe regions where Saxons from Britain are said to have settled in the earlier 6th century, and there it is now spelled *-büttl;* but in English place names (Maps 35 and 36) its use is restricted to the Northumbrians, and to the Mercians, whose dialect gave the form *-bold* or *-bald*, as in Bolton or Newbald. A commoner word is *-worth*, defined as an 'individual and personal possession'; with its regional variants *-worthy* and *-wardine*, it distinguished the home of the ordinary substantial freeman, the *ceorl*, from the *-cote*, the 'cottage, humble dwelling' of the poorer peasant. Besides these descriptive names, the ending *-ingtun*, usually preceded by a personal name, most often describes a village founded by a prominent individual, accompanied by his dependents.

Map 32 displays the numbers of places named *-worth*, *-cote* and *-ingtun* in the counties that have been surveyed, and of *-worth* in all counties. These names are relatively infrequent in the old kingdoms. They are most numerous in the lands opened to English settlement in the 7th century, in the Weald of Kent and Sussex, in western Mercia and the West Riding, and, above all, in Devonshire; but they were no longer in common use when English names spread in

---

Map 32

Place names in *-worth* etc.   []

        -cote   ▧

        -ingtun   ▉

The length of the columns, measured against the scale on the left, indicates the numbers of each type of name in each county. In the counties shaded comparable information is accessible only for *-worth*.

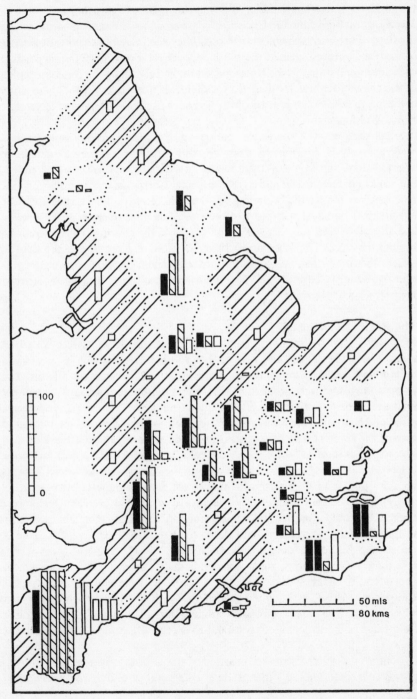

Cumberland and Westmorland, and are also relatively rare in north-western Mercia, in Staffordshire and Cheshire. In general, they are most plentiful where the *-ingas* and *-ingaham* names are fewest. They confirm and extend the evidence of the pagan graves, that in the old kingdoms most men lived in independent communities, but that in the lands opened to the English by the conquest, much of the colonisation was conducted by individuals, great and small. There many of the humbler *-cote* names are likely to have been used of the homes of dependent native Welshmen.

Small scale maps of the whole country or large areas can only show general tendencies. It is possible to examine some districts in greater detail. In Warwickshire, the river Avon still marked a frontier when pagan burial ended; the English did not master and settle the former Cornovian territories beyond the river until well after the beginning of the 7th century. There the *-cotes* are equally distributed on both sides of the river, but three quarters of the *-ingtuns* and all the *-worths*, together with nine-tenths of the clearings called *-leah*, lie beyond the river. The 6th-century English plainly did not live in the kind of society that used these names, but in a world of villages; but many of the 7th-century colonists beyond the river followed local lords, or lived in separate homesteads and clearings.

The Regions Colonised

Preliminary studies also indicate something of the complexity of Kentish settlement. There, the English took over an intact Roman society, with its great landlords and its native custom of dividing peasant inheritance between all sons. The towns and villages were grouped in nine 'lathes' with their own jurisdiction, not unlike the *cantref* of Wales; each was named from a royal centre, that had been a place of importance since the 5th century, with a large early cemetery, and in each of the seven coastal lathes had been a Roman town. In each the king had his own lands, farmed by his servile dependents, as in Wales; and to each lathe belonged a detached portion of the central Weald, usually not adjacent to its borders. But, as in Wales, land holdings were more complicated than political divisions. In the Downs and the coastlands, large estates were many; they were termed *land*, and were usually named from an individual, sometimes British, or from a family, comparable with the *gwely*, like *Welkechildeland*, the estate of the *childe*, children or descendants, of Welke. Many or most of these estates had their swine pastures, their woodland, their enclosed grazing and other dependencies in the Weald. Sussex was similarly organised into nine 'rapes', equivalent to lathes, with numerous *lands* and their Wealden dependencies; but when Sussex names are more closely studied, their distribution is likely to differ from those of Kent, for more roads and rivers run from the Weald through the Downs.

Kentish and South Saxon colonisation of the Weald, shown on Map 33, was plainly not pioneered by independent communities and hardy individuals, penetrating into the forest at random, but was planned and organised by kings and lords. The freeman's *worth* seldom reaches beyond the fringes of the Weald, and the humble *-cote* is rare, though somewhat commoner in the more loosely organised territories of Surrey, but *-inga*, *-ingtun* and the estate names spread throughout the Weald, to face each other across the modern county boundaries. Other regions show a different kind of colonisation. In Hertfordshire and Middlesex (Map 34), *-ingtun* and estate names are rare; *-worth* and *-cote* reach into the London clays from the pagan settlement districts by the Thames and the Icknield Way, but they do not meet; the first settlers in the difficult soils between them used other forms of name, many of them perhaps at a later date.

Northern regional difference is marked; *-worths* are many in the southernmost Pennines, and also in Durham and on Tyneside, but there are hardly any in between, from the East Riding to Cumberland; there the *-ingtuns* reach into the eastern Pennines, and the *-botl* strongholds guard the passes and the coasts. The blend of different kinds of settlements established lasting local customs, whose consequences may be detected only in the local history of each area. They will be better understood when a far wider range of place names can be studied and compared.

These are preliminary indications, that serious local study will clarify and correct. They suggest three main stages in the expansion of the English, the first delineated by the pagan cemeteries of the 5th and 6th centuries, the second in the nearer regions opened to settlement in the later 6th and early 7th centuries, and the third indicating the extensive colonisation of the 7th century. The community names are commonest within the 6th-century frontiers and just beyond their borders; but in the 7th century most colonisation was undertaken by lords who led their followers. The exceptions are the dangerous borders where enemies might be expected in arms. There, large concentrations of lesser freemen defended their own lands. Their *worths* are most numerous in Devon, where they are four times as many as in a dozen eastern counties put together; in Gloucestershire; and on the frontiers between the Mercians and the Northumbrians. Though new villages continued to be founded and named for centuries, it is probable that the great majority of the districts rich in colonising names had already been settled before the end of the 8th century, and that the derivative names became more usual thereafter.

The three stages of English expansion are the century and a half of war and partition, when the pagan English survived beside and among stronger Christian British neighbours; the age of conquest and conversion; and the age of colonisation. Cemeteries are the main evidence for the first stage of war and partition; place names are the chief witness of where the conquerors and early colonists settled.

MAP 33 ENGLISH COLONISATION: PLACE NAMES 4

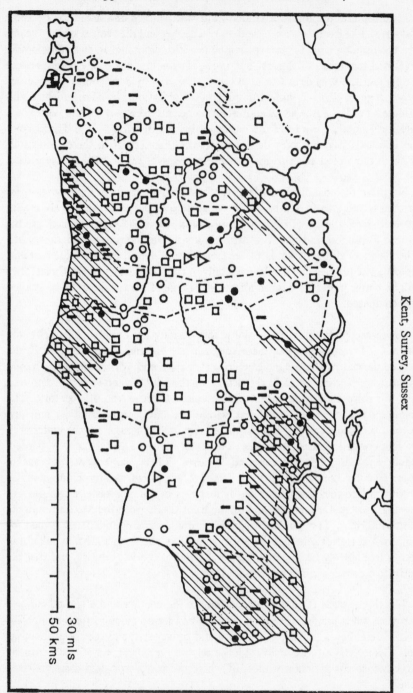

Kent, Surrey, Sussex

30 mls
50 kms

MAP 34 ENGLISH COLONISATION: PLACE NAMES 5

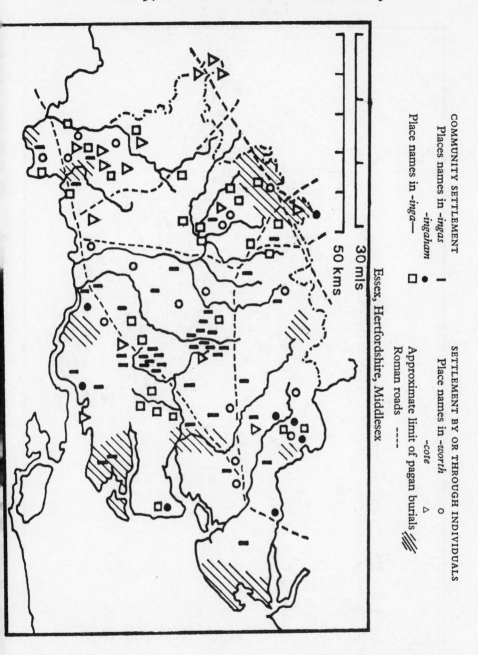

COMUNITY SETTLEMENT
Places names in -ingas
        -ingaham
Place names in -inga—

SETTLEMENT BY OR THROUGH INDIVIDUALS
Place names in -worth
        -cote

Approximate limit of pagan burials
Roman roads

Essex, Hertfordshire, Middlesex

30 mls

50 Kms

MAP 35 ENGLISH COLONISATION: PLACE NAMES 6
The North and West

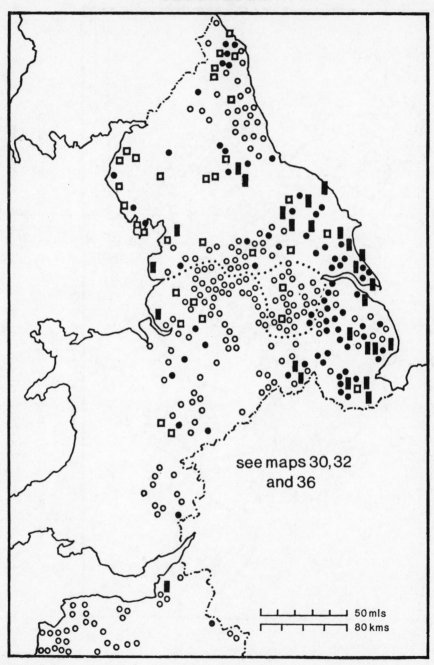

see maps 30, 32
and 36

50 mls
80 kms

Symbols, see p. 479

MAP 36 ENGLISH COLONISATION: PLACE NAMES 7

-botl and variants in the South

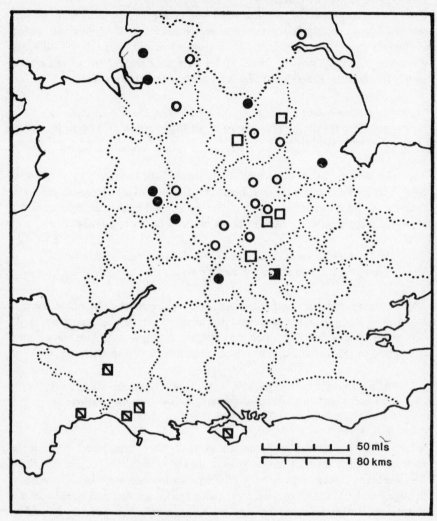

NORTHUMBRIAN: *-botl* ■; Newbottle □
MERCIAN: *-bold, -bald* ●; Newbold, Newbald O
WEST SAXON: *-buddle* and variants ◩
The dotted lines represent modern county boundaries

Map 35

COMMUNITY SETTLEMENT: Place names in *-ingas* ■; in *-ingaham* ●
SETTLEMENT BY OR THROUGH INDIVIDUALS: Place names in *-worth,* etc. o; in
    -botl and variants □
Approximate frontiers of Mercia and Elmet ···· Limit of area surveyed —·—·—

The Organisation of Colonies

The 7th-century laws of Wessex show something of how colonisation was organised and controlled. It was not a haphazard affair of adventurous young men who moved their families and belongings when and where they liked. Care was taken to see that existing communities were not damaged by sudden erratic withdrawal of their manpower. The laws provide that when a man

> intends to depart (*faran wille*), he who has 20 hides shall show 12 hides cultivated; he who has 10 hides shall show 6 cultivated, he who has 3 shall show $1\frac{1}{2}$.

The man with 20 hides was a powerful magnate, the man with 3 a substantial *ceorl*. The laws envisaged the likelihood that freemen of all degrees might leave their lands, and required that the lands be left in good heart, tilled by cultivators who would continue to supply the king's needs. The laws also enact that

> if a nobleman (*gesithcundmon*) depart, he may take with him his reeve, his smith, and his children's tutor.

The limitation matters more than the permitted retinue. The noble colonist might not depopulate his homeland by taking with him a large part of its dependent cultivators. If he took dependents, he must find them among men authorised to follow him. Unauthorised emigration was forbidden.

> If a man departs from his lord without permission and steals away into another shire, and is discovered, he shall return to where he was, and pay his lord 60 shillings.

Law codes cannot show whether the offences they forbid were frequent or rare, nor whether the laws were regularly obeyed or regularly broken. But these laws were enacted at a time when West Saxon colonists were arriving in Devonshire in large numbers, and were devised to check tendencies that had already shown themselves. Other laws concern the colonists' new homes. Those that relate to the *worth* of the *ceorl* were enacted for all Wessex; but the circumstances they envisage are likely to have been commonest among the *worths* that were multiplying on the western frontiers when the laws were enacted. They provide that

> a *ceorl*'s *worth* shall be fenced in summer and in winter. If not, and a neighbour's beast strays through the gap he has left, he shall have no claim on the beast; he shall chase it out and accept the damage.
> If *ceorls* have a grass enclosure, or other apportioned land to fence, and some have fenced their part and some have not, and (cattle

get in) and eat their common arable or grass, those responsible for
the gap shall offer compensation for the damage done to the others,
who have enclosed their part. They shall demand from the (owners
of the) cattle whatever reparation is proper.

But if a beast breaks through the *hegas* and wanders within,
since its owner cannot or will not control it, he who finds it on his
arable shall take it and kill it. The owner shall have its hide and
flesh, and accept the loss of the rest.

The *worth* is a self-contained individual farm; its fences, hedges or banks must
be permanent. But, in addition to their separate *worths*, the *ceorls* may also have
enclosed grass, a *gaerstun*, or other 'apportioned', *gedal*, land, in common. They
must hedge or fence it, to keep cattle out; if the cattle get in, everyone's crop is
damaged.

The *gaerstun* contains grass that cattle are not supposed to eat. The grass is
therefore intended for hay, winter fodder. The enclosure may also be used for
other crops, though the law primarily envisages hay fields. Within the enclosure
there is no division. The 'arable or grass' is common. When an animal gets in it
can eat the lot; if the enclosure were subdivided into individual portions, each
separately fenced, then animals could only get at the unfenced portions, and those
who had put up their barriers would suffer no damage and require no law to
secure their compensation.

The part, *dael*, which each man must fence can therefore only be his portion
of the bank or hedge which surrounds the whole enclosure. In calling the land
'*gedal land*', divided or apportioned land, the law does not mean that it is to be
subdivided; it means that it has already been doled out by allotment. Provision
is made for a rough beast that forces its way through a hedge or fence that is
judged strong enough to keep out normal animals. The procedure is normal
sensible farming practice, among colonists in new lands. Each has his own farm,
but they pool their resources for their winter fodder and may grow in common
other crops as well as grass. The law prescribed that the *ceorl's* own fence must
be permanent; and plainly supposed that the fence of the land they farmed in
common should be as well protected. The 'fences' to be built were not temporary
affairs; they might be hedges, or might be the steep banks of Devon fields. The
law chiefly concerned land that was being enclosed by the English for the first
time.

These are laws that compelled the free *ceorl* to respect each other's interests
and common good. They presuppose communities where the English lived
together. But when the great nobleman with his reeve conducted parties of
lesser men who had obtained permission to leave, such regulations were more
easily enforced by him, and many such parties did not live alone by themselves in
their new homes. Very many of the 5th- and 6th-century settlers were located
in or beside Roman towns and villages, mansions and farms, originally billeted
upon their owners; and many of the earliest colonising settlements, marked by

481

the small cemeteries and single graves common in the latest age of pagan burial, had also been established immediately beside British farmsteads. Often, the reason why the Roman British farmhouse was abandoned, and reverted to ploughland or pasture instead of continuing in use, was that an English farm or village had already been established nearby, its people working the same or adjacent acres, until the heirs of the native farmstead intermarried with the English, or moved into their village; their fusion is occasionally noticed by British burials in an English graveyard, sometimes marked by native hob-nailed boots, where the soil preserves their traces, on the feet of buried bodies.

There are many local variants. In parts of the West Riding, of central Wessex and elsewhere, places called Walton or the like and places with British names cluster together, with a few early English names among them. But in other areas a few English mastered many Welsh. One Sussex charter suggests a probable instance. At Heberden, now abandoned in Madehurst, north of Arundel, king Nunna in 725 granted to the bishop twenty tax-paying *tributarii* at 'Huga's hills and the *denn*', the pasture land, commonly for pigs. The district had not been English for much longer than a century; Huga had been dead for some time, since his heirs had disappeared and the land was now royal; he may well have been the original settler. The bounds are given, from Lavington Dyke to the Stane Street, stretching north to the Billingas of Billingshurst; they adjoin cleared land still unoccupied, termed 'No Man's Land'. They border on, and perhaps include, the arable land of the huge Roman mansion of Bignor. Huga doubtless brought his reeve, and perhaps some English dependents, but it is likely that many of the *tributarii* were the descendants of the peasants who had tilled the estates of the Roman magnate. They, and doubtless many of the inhabitants of a *cote*, a *botl* or an -*ingtun*, were conquered natives to be treated as the English Saxons treated the 'natives' whom they had conquered in Thuringia in the 530s. The Saxons there received the conquered territory, but

> because they were too few to occupy it all, they assigned part
> to dependent cultivators, subject to tribute, but held the rest
> themselves.

It may be that the Welsh of Bignor were obliged to guard and pasture English pigs, and that they were in time assimilated, for Huga's hills and the *denn* later merged into a single village, named Heberden. But whatever the speech of Heberden, conquered Welshmen and Englishmen with little land both became *tributarii* in English law.

Only a fraction of the evidence can yet be assessed. As far as it goes, it points to some regional characteristics. Institutions and ideas inherited from Roman landlords affected the English most deeply in Kent. Compact communities were most numerous in the old kingdoms inhabited by the English throughout the 6th century; separate farmsteads, great lords and subject Welshmen were most numerous in the lands colonised in and after the late 6th century. But the mixture varied. Men who lived in compact villages most easily preserved the tradition that all men's voices must be heard on matters of common interest; but colonists who came from such villages carried long established village attitudes with them to their new homes, and adapted them to a new environment when they were numerous. Lordship and patronage are most obvious in the colonial lands; but kings bred aristocracy, and imposed lords upon villages in the old kingdoms as well. The quality of lordship varied. The loyalties that men accorded to a great captain who had led them to a distant home and there protected them were not the same as those accorded to a lord imposed by a king over villagers who tilled ancestral lands. The attitudes of cottagers, Welsh and English, and of two hundred shilling *ceorls* were not identical. The nature of lordship therefore depended on the degree of obedience and the kind of rights and privileges that each local custom recognised as proper.

Time smoothed many differences, but it also hardened others. The disasters of the 9th and 10th centuries broke up old conventions, and subjected English society to the unchecked violence of brutal landlords and power happy magnates, whose mutual hatreds exposed England to conquest by the Normans. The ample evidence of late Saxon poems and of recorded individual instances depicts the misery of exploited peasants in the West Saxon period, but it has little direct relevance to the conditions of the age of colonisation and of the Mercian empire. The documents of this earlier age suggest an unusual blend of aristocratic privilege and of social equality, both of them prominent and widespread from the 6th century onward. Beyond this easy generalisation, their interaction can only be discerned by local and regional studies.

The Family

As among other peoples, the family was the basis of English social and political organisation. Their terminology differed slightly. The Dal Riada Scots organised their fighting force by houses, and assumed that each house had land; Welsh law grouped men by houses, and expected each house to have a minimum of 5 acres of land. But English usage listed family landholdings, and assumed that a house went with each holding, for the earliest English free men's homes were grouped in compact villages, that were more sensibly estimated by the extent of their land than by the number of their buildings. Seventh and perhaps sixth century documents, used by Bede, grouped and counted populations by such holdings, termed *hides*, and commonly equate one tax-payer with one hide. Like the Welsh and Irish, the English were a nation of two-generation families. Their excavated homes, grouped in villages or singly sited, are too small to accommodate more than parents and their children; such was the family of the great noble, who might take his children's nurse when he emigrated, and so also was the family of the *ceorl*.

The numbers and the economy of the Welsh and English family were much alike. But the English shared with almost all Germanic peoples a common attitude to marriage, divorce and children that differed radically from Welsh and Irish concepts. Custom harshly punished unchaste women, but condoned unchastity in men. It excluded and stigmatised the bastard, unless his father vigorously asserted paternity. The laws have little to say of marriage, divorce or adultery, for these are the concern of the customary popular courts and of the church; most of what the royal laws say concerns compensations to the cuckold and to the master of seduced servile girls. But Alfred's laws expressly authorised a man to kill the lover of his wife or sister without punishment, where Welsh law offered the alternative of a blow in anger or a 'face payment'. National attitudes harden and endure, and Alfred's outlook is not far removed from the lenient sympathy that some modern judges showed to the violence of returning wartime soldiers, outraged by the infidelity of lonely wives. The essential difference is that Welsh law rigidly asserted the equal rights of men, women, and adult children, while early English law upheld the superior authority of the husband, the father and the brother.

Kindred

As among the Welsh and Irish, the kindred legislation of the English mainly concerned the inheritance of the minority of men who left no sons, and compensation to the victims of violence. But the English legislators faced quite different practical problems. Most Welshmen lived and died near to the homes of their fathers and grandfathers, their cousins and second cousins; the rights and duties of the kin worked easily in communities that stayed together, where a man's second or third cousin might readily be identified. The bonds of kinship also retained their hold among most of the Germanic peoples of Europe, for the greater part of them moved to their new homes as coherent nations, or as large sections of such nations, so that in practice a great part of a man's kin moved with him. But repeated migration weakened the kindreds of the English. In the fifth century men of quite different continental origins shared the same cemetery, with most of their kinsmen left at home, or settled elsewhere in Britain. But the mass migration of the Angles at the end of the century was clearly able to maintain its ancient kin, and in the old kingdoms kinship had time to grow again by the end of the sixth century. But after the conquest, the colonists of Northumbria, Wessex and Mercia broke their kin connections a second time. Some doubtless moved with their relatives, but many were younger sons and landless men, given permission to move, who at first were not related to their neighbours in their new homes.

The main age of colonisation was the seventh century, but movement did not thereafter cease. Many laws seek to prohibit the unauthorised movement of men, but their wording and their frequency proclaim that considerable movement was permitted, and that much illicit migration continued. The disasters of the Scandinavian invasions, in and after the 9th century, clearly increased its volume.

There were at all times many Englishmen whose relatives could not be traced within the shire, or even the kingdom, in which they lived. English law therefore has no defined terms that correspond to Welsh and Irish *fine, cinel, cenedl, gwely;* it cannot particularise beyond the portmanteau term *maegas,* relatives in general.

The weakness of English kinship entailed important consequences. The laws of violence prescribed compensation for injury, as in other codes. Welsh law assumed that the offender's kin would in fact pay the sums due, and devised elaborate procedures to discover who was or was not distantly related to the offender. West Saxon law treated its Welshmen in the same way; the kinsmen must pay, if the criminal had a free kindred (*gif he maegburg haebbe freo*); only if he had not was he handed over to his enemies. But no such provision was made for the English offender. The law assumed that he would pay himself; his relatives are mentioned only rarely, and then were obliged to pay only a proportion of the sums due, if they could be found; if the offender did not pay he was exposed to *faehdhe,* 'enmity', and might legitimately be killed by his victim's relatives, who did not thereby make themselves liable to legal counter-violence from his relatives. A man's relations might ransom him; but they need not do so.

Enmity might satisfy revenge, but it earned no compensation. Other compulsions were necessary. The codes of Kent and Wessex devolved considerable responsibility on the lord. In Kent, he was called the *dryhten,* the personal superior, in Wessex the *hlaford,* the 'loaf-keeper'. Every poor man had his immediate lord, but even the *gesithcund* nobleman, master of numerous dependents, free and unfree, had over him his *hlaford,* who received dues and undertook to answer for him. The lords did not undertake to pay from their own pockets the fines and compensation due from their dependents; yet many men were too poor to pay a *wergild,* a man's worth; and means had to be found to meet the needs of the victim's kin. Wessex law therefore devised the *gyld.* The 'guild' was essentially an association of men who between them undertook to provide the *wergild* of a member; the earliest of references, in Ine's laws, assumed that the most natural association was between relatives; but membership could not be confined to relatives, and not all relatives were compelled to associate. In default of relatives, the most natural association was among residents and, later, among persons of the same trade in towns, whose groupings were the ancestors of the medieval trade guilds.

Inheritance

The inheritance laws of the continental Germanic codes were not repeated in the legislation of Kent and Wessex; among the English they primarily concerned local customary law rather than the king's law. Local custom varied, and was also modified by experience learnt in Britain. The Germanic codes were mostly set down in writing between the 7th and the 9th centuries, and they too vary. Sons inherited equally among the Salic and Ripuarian Franks, the Scandinavians and the Lombards; the Lombards and some of the Franks assumed that brothers might live together, jointly sharing their father's inheritance without division, provided that one at least must stay at home when others go to war. The exceptions were the English of Thuringia, who speak of a single son as heir, and the Frisians, who envisaged a single heir. In default of children inheritance passed to the mother's kin as well as the father's among the Franks and the Frisians, the Saxons and the Norse; the vague Lombardic *parentes* perhaps also denoted the kin of both parents. Exceptionally, the Thuringian English confined inheritance to the father's kin. The childless inheritance was shared among a four-generation family by the Frisians, among five generations by the Franks and the Thuringian English, seven by the Lombards.

A long history plainly underlies these considerable variations. It left no clear-cut distinction between a prevailing Germanic custom and a prevailing Celtic custom. The Irish, the Welsh and the continental English agreed with one another, and differ from the rest, in their emphasis on paternal kinship. The English and the Frisians differed from the Welsh and from the rest of the Germans in avoiding divided inheritance. But the most striking difference was that between the continental Saxons and the continental Angles. The Saxon law explicitly enacted that 'in default of sons, the whole inheritance passes to the daughters', but the corresponding Anglian law asserted 'to the daughter the movables; but the land to the nearest male paternal relative'. In Britain, West Saxon law allotted to the mother's kin a share in the payment and receipt of *wergild;* but in time the Anglian custom of the inheritance of political power and of landed property by the nearest paternal male relative prevailed throughout most of England.

Community:
Class Difference

Welsh customary law spells out its social classification. English customary law, *folc riht*, was never written down. Unlike Welsh law, original 7th-century texts survive from Kent and Wessex and fragments of later laws from other kingdoms are also known. These texts treat of the various classes of society, but do not describe or relate them to one another. Their terminology suggests a structure that was in origin not greatly different from the Welsh. The general term of *frigman*, 'free man', excluded the servile *theow* and the slave, *esne*. The Welsh of Wessex and the *laet* of Kent were graded into three classes like the Welsh of Wales, but the value of each class was rated lower than that of the corresponding English grade. As among the Welsh, the English distinguish two superior categories of free men, the land-owning *ceorl*, who in Kent at least was master of dependent 'loaf-eaters'; and the noble, called *eorl* in Kent, *gesith* among the West Saxons.

Wergild

These words denoted birth and status, and they gave rise to adjectives and categories, the nobility, *eorlcund* and *gesithcund*, 'noble kind'; and *cierlisc*, commoner. The laws imposed fines and obligations and admitted compensations, that were expressed in terms of currency or of land. The English, unlike the Welsh, minted money. The standard unit was the shilling; originally it was perhaps a valuation of cows, like the Irish *cumal*, but in long-established Kent, where the word may have been used of Roman coins before the English minted their own, its 7th-century value was twice as much as in Wessex; the *wergild* or *leod* of a Kentish *eorl* required 300 shillings, of a West Saxon *gesith* 600 shillings; but in both kingdoms the noble was worth three *ceorl*.

The Hide

The worth of men was measured in money after money was minted. The differences it measured were older, and rested on the extent of a man's land. Land was measured by its actual capacity, calculated by its extent, its fertility, and of the man power that tilled it; and was first measured by kings in need of men and money. The early English kings, like the Welsh and Irish, numbered and taxed their subjects by families. As the Dal Riada Scots listed the numbers of houses in each region, so Bede normally described the extent of kingdoms, districts and estates as the 'land of so many families'.

The Old English version of Bede translated the Latin *familia* by English *hide*. The language of the charters was similar. Where the Latin text granted twenty *tributarii*, tax-payers, the English version granted hides, save in Kent, whose lawyers preferred to grant 'ploughs', *aratra*. The notion of the hide, measuring the capacity of land, is alien to modern thinking, that prefers the less accurate measurement of crude acres, without regard to their quality or population. Later lawyers tried to equate the hide with a fixed number of acres, often favouring the figure of 120, but with indifferent success. The English hide calculated practical value, like the Welsh *uncia* and the late Roman *iugum*, and may well have originated in whatever form of *iugum* was standard in the taxation of late Roman Britain.

The hide, the land of a household and a taxpayer, became the standard English unit of land measurement. Like most standards, it became notional. But circumstances severely limited the extent to which it could depart from its original meaning. Governments counted hides and families for two purposes, raising men for the army and raising dues from the cultivators. The military assessment was the most severely limited; no estate could send more men to the army than its actual population. Taxation might bear heavily, demanding more than the cultivators could reasonably afford, particularly when population fell and revenue officers demanded the old dues; but in a subsistence economy, when men produced only for themselves with little surplus for the market, the excess that overtaxation could actually extract was not great. It was easier to undertax land than overtax it; great landlords might be assessed at fewer hides than they actually possessed. Yet, though there are plenty of individual vagaries, no convincing evidence yet observed suggests that there was any wide overall discrepancy between the actual and assessed capacity of the land, or any difference at all in the earlier 7th century. Difference was social rather than fiscal. Long before Bede's time, and before the 7th century laws were drafted, some men possessed many hides, while many poor men had no land at all, or much less than a full hide. 'Possession' bestowed the right to receive the cultivators' dues; and the possession of much land gave rank and standing that could be classified in shillings.

Military nobility: in Wessex

The noblemen and landowners were graded in the laws by shillings and hides. The development of the monarchy created higher ranks of nobility. Among the Welsh of Wessex the king's messenger and five-hide man were distinguished above the rest. English landowners were rated at three, ten and twenty hides, their worth or *wergild* fixed at 200, 600 and 1,200 shillings; and they were therefore classified as *twyhynde, syxhynde* and *twelfhynde*. These three classes were also named the *ceorl*, the noblemen 'without land', and the *gesithcundes monnes landhaebbendes*, noblemen with land. The title of 'landed nobleman' does not imply that other 'landless' nobles were paupers, literally without any land at all. The title describes holders of a special kind of land. Its status is explained by the law of compensation for *burgbryc*, 'breach, or violation, of a stronghold'. The landed nobleman was the lowest of the categories who owned a *burg*, ranking after the king and the bishop, the *ealdorman* and the thane. He differed from the 'landless noble' because he owned a *burg*; and other *burgs* belonged only to important officers of the king and the church. His land clearly went with his *burg*, and recompensed an obligation to the king. Another law defines the nature of the obligation. If a 'landed nobleman' neglected military service, he forfeited his land; other *gesithcund* nobles were fined, but forfeited no land. All nobles possessed inherited land; the greater noble whom the laws called 'landed' received additional land, granted for specific military service, which the king reclaimed if he failed to discharge his obligation. In the source of his land, though not the nature of his service, he was the equivalent of the Welsh *arglwyd*, the lord installed by the king on his 'documented land'.

Such royal land, revocable when service ended, and not inherited, was plainly only possible when kings disposed of ample lordless lands, when the English kingdoms were young and still expanding. It had doubtless been the original source of noblemen's estates in the old kingdoms in the pagan period; but the pressures of an aristocracy commonly constrain monarchs to renew a grant in favour of an old retainer's son, that in a few generations becomes in practice hereditary. The Roman and European *comes*, or count, and the English *gesith* had originally been royal companions, rewarded with land because they served the king in arms; but the succession of their sons and grandsons turned their titles to hereditary rank, too deeply rooted in national custom for kings to cancel, without the excuse of open treason.

In Northumbria

Such revocable military tenures are not again recorded among the southern
English. But Bede describes similar lords of royal land in Northumbria. There
nobleman and peasant were sharply differentiated. By 679 rustic Deirans served
in the army's supply train, but their speech was far removed from their lords',
doubtless distinguished by the influence of British idiom and pronunciation; so
that a noble prisoner who tried to disguise himself as a rustic was immediately
detected by his Mercian captors as soon as he opened his mouth. Deira was a
land of peasant villages, some long settled, some new, but in the early 7th
century there cannot have been many young Bernicians who could not make
themselves masters of men if they had the will and the personality, for they were
few in a very large British territory, recently conquered. The kings needed lords
to place over their subjects. Bede records how they found them. Benedict
Biscop was 'born of a noble English family', in the time of Edwin. His father
plainly owned lands that he stood to inherit, but in his early twenties he became a
minister, or thane, of Oswy, about 650, and the king gave him 'landed possessions adequate to his rank'. Biscop gave them up when he entered religious life
at the age of 25, rejecting 'earthly service with its perishable donative'. Bede
deliberately selected an old-fashioned word, rare in the Latin of his day, that
meant the gifts that Roman emperors gave to their troops, donatives.

Allocations of land with military obligations continued into the early 8th
century, and the grants were made by written charter. By Bede's time they had
become a scandal. In a letter to Egbert, that he dated on the 5th of November
734, he complained of fraudulent grants authorised by

> a senseless pen . . . the lying pen of corrupt clerks.

Bede is chiefly concerned with the corruption of monasteries, but he saw the
proper purpose of charters as twofold, monastic and secular. Lands were
properly granted either

> that a regular life may be observed towards God

or that they be owned by

> the soldiers or military companions of the secular powers, who
> defend our nation against the barbarians.

His complaint is that since king Aldfrith's death, thirty years before, almost
every reeve and thane and noble has bought such charters so that now

> there is absolutely nowhere where the son of nobles or of retired
> soldiers may acquire possessions.

Therefore the young men who ought to be fighting for their country could not
do so; they stayed unmarried, and either emigrated abroad or led dissipated

lives, seducing nuns. The fraudulent grants owed their authority entirely to 'royal edicts' and to the 'improper decisions of kings'. Egbert was therefore urged to induce the reigning 'religious king' to

> scrutinise the bad Acts and Documents of former kings, and pick out those which are useful to God, or to the laity.

The system had worked well throughout the 7th century and was still justified in the 8th, if its corruption could be cured. Some noblemen were granted lordships with military commitments, and relinquished them when they entered the church or otherwise ceased to discharge their commitment; some commoners spent their active lives as professional royal soldiers until they were too old to fight. Bede describes them as *emeriti*, the technical Roman army term for discharged veterans, and, like Roman *emeriti*, they were entitled to a grant of land on discharge. The corruption was especially rampant among grants nominally intended for monasteries, since a commitment to live a religious life in private could be disregarded with less flagrant publicity than a commitment to serve in the army; but it impinged upon military charters, because it left them no land to grant. Time had eroded the system, for grants of land in successive generations could function smoothly only when ample lordless land remained.

In the rest of England

The Northumbrian armies were static, guarding their borders and restraining their Welsh subjects, and assembled only occasionally for massive foreign expeditions, which altogether ended with Egferth's death in 685. But West Saxon kings were involved in continuous smaller wars, internally and on several distant frontiers. The welfare of king or kingdom was not served by requiring every land holder in Devonshire to serve in every campaign in Sussex or Kent; national security needed most of them at home to guarantee local defence. The 'landed nobles' provided a specialised force, more easily mobilised under the king's personal command; many of them were doubtless young men, nobly born, like Benedict in Northumbria, the senior among them called 'thanes'. The king's retainers also included humbler free men; before the conquest the English had long been accustomed to the warbands of the British, and early West Saxon stories praise in their own kings' military companions the same ruthless devotion of the professional soldier that the Welsh poets had honoured in the time of Urien and Cynddylan. The compact kingdom of Kent had less need of such mobile forces, and there the available land and lordships had been granted long before the early 7th century. Then Frankish terms were still in use; the king summoned his *leode*, and the great lord was a *grafio*. But later, when English words replaced them, there is no obvious sign of an equivalent of the 'landed noble'. The few fragments of the laws of the Mercians, whose armies also fought principally in occasional powerful expeditions, also observe only one class of nobles, the *twelfhynde*, rated at six times the *coerl*'s worth. East Anglian and East

Saxon needs are likely to have resembled those of Kent and Mercia, but no text survives to show their social categories.

The social order of the several English kingdoms differed greatly. In the old kingdoms difference had evolved over centuries; in the colonial lands some men lived under the tight and immediate control of their lords, others more freely; some were masters of the local native population, others were their neighbours, equal in all but legal worth. But the English nobility differed in one important particular from the Welsh. In Wales, most men had held their land by inheritance from ancestors time out of mind; but the greater part of the English had won their lands by recent conquest. All lands acquired since the English conquest were held by grant of the king, or by his confirmation of tenure; and so were all lands in the dominions of the Kentish and Anglian monarchies, that had been acquired since the dynasties were established in the 5th century. Old grants of heritable land could not normally be revoked, but new royal grants continued to make men great, and more closely related the landowner and the royal officer; they linked a man's hereditary status with his material wealth, for in time they expressly enabled a man who had acquired the land that befitted a higher rank to attain that rank.

Villages

Before the conquest most of the earliest English lived in compact village communities. Their insecurity reinforced the traditions of their homeland. But after the conquest many pioneers enclosed substantial individual farmsteads, and others obeyed those who conducted their migration. But compact or scattered, free or subject, each political community formed a -*tun*, or village, a basic unit of society already normal by the 7th century. Wider concerns grouped the -*tuns* into larger areas, whose common council was composed of representatives of each constituent -*tun*.

The Hundred

Monarchy and lordship were grafted on to older institutions. The beginnings of English administration, law and justice were rooted in the old kingdoms, whence colonists came, and where kings continued to reside. The royal law codes were founded upon these older laws and took them for granted; the aim of royal law was to assert royal and ecclesiastical rights, and to standardise local practice. They therefore refer only occasionally to the principal institution of everyday English administration, the *folc gemot*, called in Latin *populare concilium*, 'public assembly'. In Alfred's laws the assembly heard legal cases, in which one man brought an accusation against another, and was responsible for licensing traders and registering the number of persons each might take with him. It was a judicial and administrative body, meeting in the presence of the king's reeve and under the protection of the *ealdorman*, whose supervision is likely to have smoothed out local differences. It was already ancient by 800, when Coenwulf of Mercia liberated Harrow from

> exaction of all payments, works and services due to the Treasury, or to the Public Assembly . . . save that it must give account for three Public Services, namely the building of bridges and of strongholds and the supply of 5 men when a campaign is necessary.

It was a district assembly, already long established and taken for granted in the late 7th century. Ine's laws rule that

> if a man wishes to deny on oath a charge of homicide, there shall be in the Hundred a king's oath of 30 hides, whether he be noble or commoner.

In later times, the English Hundreds were grouped into large shires, and many changed their boundaries and their names. But traces of their antiquity remain. Earlier usage, formed long before the creation of the large modern counties, described the hundred itself as a 'shire', literally a division, of a kingdom. A number of Hundreds are named from pagan barrows or burial-grounds, and some long continued to meet there; such sites cannot have been first chosen after Christianity had made bishops the advisers of kings and peoples; they remained in use when they had already been meeting-places in the 6th century or the early 7th. Such meeting places were familiar to the continental English; one, at Thorsberg in Angel, marked by a monument in the midst of a large cemetery, was an important regional centre, possibly the national centre.

The Hundred was the first fundamental form of English government. It is one of the earliest and most widespread institutions of the European peoples, known to the early Romans, the early Germans, the Welsh and the Irish. Its purpose was commonly to provide a hundred fighting men, in simple societies where it was originally normal for one man from each family to serve in the army. It remained the natural form of English organisation, so that when the lawless violence of the 10th century constrained the Londoners, *eorlisc* and *ceorlisc* together, to organise the fellowship or 'gildship' of the city, they did so by grouping the citizens into Hundreds, *hyndena*, each of 100 men under a *hyndenman*, subdivided into groups of ten. In any developed society the Hundred becomes a notional term, but its starting-point is the equation that a hundred fighting men in principle correspond to a hundred families, and to the hundred patches of land that support each family.

The Hundreds were grouped early into larger units. The text that is unhappily labelled 'The Tribal Hidage' is a late corrupt copy of ancient administrative lists of the Mercian kingdom and its subject states. It includes within the kingdom the Isle of Wight, entered separately from Wessex and Sussex, which Wulfhere annexed in 661 and straightway gave to Sussex; the kingdom also includes

Elmet, which is not known to have been in Mercian hands after the frontier was fixed on the Trent in 679; it was not acquainted with the name of Surrey, which came into use in the 670s. The list was evidently drawn up in 661, or immediately after; other later dates have sometimes been asserted, but not evidenced. It records an older list, drawn up 'when Mercia was first so named', in the late 6th century. The Mercian Hundreds are grouped into twenty small regions, each containing 12 Hundreds, or fractions thereof, 9, 6 or 3, and six larger districts of 70 Hundreds, two of them subdivided. Each territory is named, from its people, or from its terrain. Outside Mercia, only the totals of the kingdoms are given. The East and South Saxons are rated at 70 Hundreds, Kent at 150, the East Angles at 300, the West Saxons at 1000. The figures are deliberately reduced to manageable round numbers, for the total of the original Mercia is slightly adjusted to give an even 300 Hundreds; and the partial total is mistakenly added in to the grand total at the end, which adds up to 212,000 hides. It includes the Welsh within the English kingdoms, for the Cornovian *Wrocensaetna* of Wroxeter and Lichfield are entered, five or six years after the English annexed them, at 70 hundreds, long before they received substantial English settlement; and the former British kingdom of Elmet is also listed by its British name.

The text describes the planned organisation of a newly formed English kingdom, and its reorganisation when Wulfhere permanently reasserted the Mercian empire over the southern English. It has not yet been studied by a philologist familiar with the names of early English places, districts and peoples, and much of the detail remains obscure; but the total numbers of hides in each kingdom is roughly proportionate to the population listed for the same territory in the 11th-century Domesday Book, and the absolute figures do not differ widely, for the equivalent Domesday counties list about 250,000 persons.

The Mercian kingdom was from its first beginnings a federation of small peoples, who were organised in groupings of Hundreds; from them and through them it drew its revenues and its armies. Other kingdoms were similarly organised, though in Kent and Sussex the lathes and rapes inherited a stronger influence from the administrative practice of Roman Britain and of Europe. Later Hundreds were often larger, but they and their assemblies remained the principal administrative and judicial institution of early England, with the unseen workings of the village meeting behind them. The day to day importance of the Hundred was the greater because its proceedings were oral, not recorded in writing, so that little can be learnt of how it functioned, save by inference from casual notices in later documents, and from a multitude of chance references to its ancient meeting places in pagan times or in the earliest Christian centuries.

The later Hundreds normally met monthly, their chief business to ensure that every man had the protection of *folc riht*, public law, and that cases were heard with expedition by men who knew the litigants and the circumstances of their cases. It is not probable that the business and the form of the meetings reported in the 10th century differed greatly from those of the 7th century; but it is evident that in practice their internal political working differed greatly from one Hundred to another, from the 7th century onward. In all political assemblies men who are wealthy or powerfully connected carry greater weight than their fellows; among the English, the pagan graves and the place names of colonising settlements indicate that from the 6th century onward some communities were dominated by a single individual, while others contained a limited number of well-to-do families and some consisted of numerous *ceorls* with little social difference between them.

There is little sign of important change during the long Mercian peace; for the well documented transfer of revenues by charter grant, bequest or sale did not directly impinge upon the composition of the Hundred. But the continuing wars of the West Saxon and Scandinavian kings ruptured traditional ways, impoverished many men and brought wealth and power to a few. The pressures of local lords and the power of lawless violence increased within most Hundreds. But the Hundred itself retained and perhaps increased its importance; in the districts where they settled thickly the Danes named it the *wapentake*, the basis of their weapons and of their armed forces. In the 10th and 11th centuries the Hundreds were grouped into the larger units, called shires or counties, intermediate between them and the national government, whose boundaries have endured to the present day, with trifling local adjustments, and have defied repeated tidy minded efforts to abolish or rearrange their time honoured identities. But the Hundred remained the basic unit of English administration throughout the middle ages.

The Hundred proved a tough and resilient institution. Its substance long outlived its form, the principle that local affairs were the business of men of note in each locality. The Norman kings relied upon its sworn jury to verify and assert the facts of land tenure and ancient custom, and thereby to curb the licence of over-mighty magnates. It withstood the brisk efficiency of their Angevin and Plantagenet successors, who sought to impose upon the diversity of the English countryside the bureaucratic uniformity of their European dominions. Their success was limited. When local institutions had been weakened by the violence of great lords, the kings were suffered to withdraw the cognisance and profits of a wide range of legal cases from the traditional speedy justice of local courts, and to import the Roman institution of the professional judge, ignorant of local circumstances and person, assisted by a small number of picked assessors; for men acquiesced in the high cost and inordinate delays of professional lawmen when local justice was overwhelmed by the sword. But the apparatus of centralised administration did not endure. The sheriff and his bailiff proved as corrupt and incompetent as royal officers in other lands. English society rejected them, and reverted to its long established tradition of entrusting local administration to men of local substance. From the close of the middle ages the vestry and the bench of justices regulated the internal affairs of the county and its subdivisions; the officers of the central government did not regain detailed control of local affairs until the later 19th century. From the 7th century to the 19th, local lords and gentry increasingly overrode humbler men; but English society held to its tradition that each small community should properly decide its own affairs, under the presidency of a strong national government; and looked unkindly upon over-large concentrations of political or economic power.

Land Tenure: Charters

The community and its assembly were exceptionally strong in early England because the grip of ancient kin custom was weaker than in other lands. Accidental combinations of custom jostled each other in each kingdom, hundred, district and village; and soon hardened into local ancestral precedents whose just operation could be understood, interpreted and decided only by local inhabitants. Lawyers and royal officers sought uniformity, but found it easier to standardise their words than the institutions and tenures the words described. Their endeavours are illustrated by the early English charters. The texts are poorly published, and have therefore been incompletely studied. The names, the titles and the status of persons, the boundaries, population and history of estates, the circumstances of the grants and the uses to which they were put have not yet been systematically investigated; and Bede's emphatic statements about their use and abuse in his day have often been undervalued. The content of the charters has therefore received less attention than their form. Historians familiar with later medieval law have enquired whether they are 'conveyances' of 'ownership', or merely of rights and powers, though the lawyers of the 7th and 8th centuries had little interest in these distinctions. Words and phrases borrowed from the jargon of 'Roman' or 'Germanic' law have been noted, though it has often been assumed that the customs of different German nations closely resembled each other and English law, or that the usages of Roman law were uniform in the kingdoms of 7th-century Europe. The borrowings prove the obvious, that early English administrators plundered every possible convention to find words to fit their peculiar institutions; but their contradictory usages have sometimes prompted the over easy inference that the same words mean the same things in different texts.

Written charters are preserved from the 7th century onward. They usually authorised their recipients to build a monastery on the land allotted, and to receive the payments that the cultivators had formerly owed to the king, with the exception of the three public services. As in the Welsh grants, the king often gave land to a layman, who then gave it to the church. The surviving copies often conflate the two grants, but sometimes preserve only one of the pair, giving the superficial impression of a purely secular grant. Grants of land to laymen who undertook specific military commitments were older than the written charters of the church. None survive in writing from the early centuries, and they are directly evidenced only among the West Saxons and Northumbrians, who had ample new lands to settle in the 7th century. Such grants are not preserved, for they commonly allotted land for life, or for so long as the specified service was actually performed; though repeated renewal to the sons and grandsons often made them in practice hereditary, their wording bestowed no legal hereditary claim and gave later ages no motive to preserve or copy them. Moreover laymen lacked the clerical staff to file and keep them; and before Christianity brought literacy they were necessarily unwritten, oral statements made before witnesses. Yet though they were unwritten and of little legal value to the future, they provided the first archaic model for the charters of the church. Kings had long granted land in return for a military obligation; Christian kings also granted land in return for the religious obligation of building or maintaining a monastery.

Grants to the church needed documents, and prudence preserved them. The lands and cultivators granted had belonged either to the king or to private persons; and both had heirs who might impugn their ancestors' grant. Moreover, individual churchmen, abbeys and cathedrals disputed the possession of the lands and revenues of dead hermits. At first, different kings and churchmen in search of safeguards borrowed from many different precedents. The earliest Kentish clerks learned from the northern Franks, and Augustine's monks brought Roman forms; Northumbrians and Mercians learnt from Ireland; Wilfred and his companions were instructed in Lyon, in central Gaul; Benedict Biscop carried the practice of Italy and Gaul to Northumbria; archbishop Theodore was trained in the conventions of the eastern Roman empire as well as of Italy; the western Mercians were open to the influence of their Welsh allies. In the later seventh century the energy of Aldhelm began the synthesis of these many precedents. He was the English pupil of an Irish teacher, he lived in a land full of Welshmen and was widely read in European literature; he served both Theodore of Canterbury, who successfully united the English church, and the Mercian kings who forged the cohesion of the southern English nation. The precedents were many, customs varied. At first, numerous local obstacles confronted the single aim of guaranteeing secure tenure to the church.

Monastic Tenure

The earliest records express the eager enthusiasm of recent converts. King Osric of the Hwicce, of Worcestershire and Gloucestershire, began his reign about 670, when Theodore was beginning to press for the establishment of bishops' sees in each kingdom. The Synod of Hertford endorsed his proposals in 672. Four years later, in founding the monastery of Bath, Osric explained that

> when, after baptism, the evangelical and apostolic dogmata were
> explained, and all the ridiculous . . . idols destroyed, . . . we de-
> cided to found an episcopal see, in accordance with the decrees of
> the Synod.

But when the abbeys of Gloucester and Pershore were founded three years later, in 679, Aethelred of Mercia was forewarned of difficulties to come, and observed that

> disputes often arise between and among many clergy . . . and faithful laymen about landed possessions. . . . Therefore I, king Aethelred . . . will give a portion of land, that is 300 *tributarii* at Gloucester, and 300 *cassati* at Pershore, to my two ministers in the province of the Hwicce, Osric and his brother Oswald, in the *vicarium*, so that Osric may receive the *oba* (estate) of Gloucester, and Oswald may have Pershore. Afterwards, I . . . was asked by . . . Osric for permission . . . to found a monastic *locus* (site) and life in that city; . . . and he bought the city with a golden *sule* (measure), in which were 30,000 (pence?), with its land, with full power over everything, into his perpetual inheritance, to possess and to have, and after him to give to whatever hand he wishes in his own kin.

The text, though not the narrative thereto appended, is substantially original. Its eccentric Latin and cumbrous argument wrestle with problems that lawyers of the next century had smoothed into order. It uses two old German words not elsewhere preserved in English, *oba* and *sule*. It also uses the common British word *locus*, site, for monastery, and the British administrative term *vicarium*, for the more usual continental *vicariatus*, the territory or jurisdiction of a *vicarius comes* or *vice comes*, the subordinate ruler. The word is elsewhere recorded only in Brittany, where it is normal, typically instanced in the charters of Landevennec, as when

> Budic *comes* . . . gave . . . from his own inheritance . . . Caer Bullauc in the *vicarium* of Demett.

The word was doubtless also current in 7th-century Wales, though no 7th-century texts survive to witness it.

The grant served practical policy as well as the piety of converts. Gloucester was the key to the control and separation of Wales and Dumnonia, and in the 670s not many of its 300 *tributarii* are likely to have been English in speech or sympathy. The foundation of a substantial monastery was a surer way to win the city than the installation of a garrison. The need was there, but in the 670s men had not yet learnt how monasteries could legally be endowed with land. The wording was devised for the purpose. Some of it is taken from Roman and continental German usage. But Aethelred also learnt from his Welsh neighbours; the Hwicce and the Mercians themselves were too recently baptised to have had direct experience of the disputes of clergy and laymen over the inheritance of estates, but the monasteries of south Wales had encountered such difficulties for more than a century. The substance of the grant imitates the procedures outlined in the Llancarfan texts, that are dated to half a century earlier; the king sold the land to his *minister*, 'under-king', equivalent to the *praefectus* of the

Welsh texts, in exchange for valuable gifts. It then passed into the minister's personal inheritance, and his kin acquired rights upon it. But a different precedent is brought in to avoid the multiple claims of distant heirs that disturbed Welsh monasteries. The grant reproduced the succession practice of the Irish monarchy, whereby one among several qualified heirs within the kin might acquire the undivided inheritance. Chosen by Osric himself, he succeeded to the position of the Irish *erenach*, 'lay proprietor', as Foirtchernn's Trim descended to the heirs of his brother.

The innovation was important. English inheritance was as firmly entailed upon kin as Welsh. The difference was that the Welsh had one common custom, but the English had many different customs; some observed Anglian descent, undivided inheritance by the nearest paternal relative, some accepted the Saxon practice of a daughter's inheritance, and other variants abounded. The monarchy of the Hwicce themselves was shared among sons, but the Mercian kingship passed by Anglian custom to a single heir. Diversity gave the lawyers greater headaches than in Wales, and prevented the adoption of a single solution; but it also prevented collective resistance to change, and in time helped kings and churchmen to subdue the claims of kin altogether.

Aldhelm and Church Right

Time was needed. A few years after the Gloucester grant Aldhelm gave its principles an important twist. The South Saxon king and his West Saxon overlord granted Pagham to bishop Wilfred, with the confirmation of the superior king, Aethelred of Mercia. Aldhelm, writing 'at the instance of archbishop Theodore', added a clause, not contained in the body of the text, 'as the command of the king and the elders decreed'. It runs

> on their authority it is established that the mastery of this . . .
> property is vested in the blessed Wilfred for life, and that on his
> death he should bequeath it in eternal possession to whomsoever
> he will by the law of inheritance.

Again, the bulk of the text has been much adapted by later copyists, but the addition is unequivocally Aldhelm's, in his own idiom, and is followed by a gay verse of his composition. Inheritance still passed by kinship law, as at Gloucester, but the founder who shall choose the heir is the churchman himself, not a lay proprietor; 'inheritance law' is used with deliberate vagueness, and is balanced by the equally vague Roman term of 'eternal possession'. As Aldhelm well knew, the terms conflicted; 'inheritance law', *ius hereditarium*, was the customary term of the Welsh grants for secular inheritance by kin, used in contrast to 'church right', *ius ecclesiasticum*, which was equated with the Roman concept of *ius perpetuum*, 'everlasting right', because the church did not die and had no heirs. The way was prepared to make 'church right' the usual form, and to override 'hereditary right'.

Bookland

The king might grant royal documented land belonging to the kingdom, or else his personal land, inherited from his own kin, on which his heirs had claims; he frequently states explicitly which he grants. Land inherited by the king by *folc riht* from his relations is often named; but when Nunna granted *tributarii* at Heberden in 725, the Latin charter is endorsed in English.

> This is the land book by which king Nunna booked, to bishop Edbert, at Huga's Hills, 20 hides.

His 'booked' or documented land was royal land, not his personal inheritance. But future kings might revoke such grants, and heirs could challenge grants that violated the claims of kin. Nunna, like many other kings, threatened a curse, or anathema, against 'any of my successors' who cancelled the grant. But not every king's successor was frightened by a curse. One of Aethelred's monastic grants was speedily revoked, in about 700. An under-king of the Hwicce claimed the land as the heir of Aethelred's queen, asserting that it was hers, not his, to give away; and won his claim. Such suits for the recovery of inheritance were a commonplace of Welsh law, termed *dadenhudd*, in Latin *actio possessoria*; similar suits, called *hereditaria proclamatio*, 'assertion of kin', long threatened English church estates. As late as the 11th century, a few years before the Norman conquest, the bishop of Worcester complained that

> Toki . . . left me land, by right of hereditary succession . . . in his will, because of our friendship. But his only son Aki, a powerful *minister* of the king, wished to set aside his father's will, and claimed the land by right of kinship succession, with the king's backing. . . . But, on receipt of 8 marks of purest gold, he restored it to me, free of suit for assertion of kin by himself and all his kin.

Grants continued to be made, bestowing church right; they ran the risk not only of challenge by kin, but of the abuses that angered Bede. The abuse was heightened by Aldhelm's formula of granting the recipient the right to bequeath the land to whichever of his kin he chose; and Bede complained that in his day Northumbrian charters caused

> an ever graver scandal, when straightforward laymen . . . buy themselves estates on the pretext of building monasteries . . . and in addition get them assigned in hereditary right by royal edicts, and then secure confirmation of these letters of privilege . . . by the signature of bishops, abbots and secular authorities.

Some southern English charters instance similar grants. About the 680s, Aethelred and the Hwicce king gave land at Withington to a woman and her daughter 'to build a monastery in church right'. The mother willed it to her daughter and grand-daughter, but in the grand-daughter's infancy it was entrusted to her mother, who refused to hand it over when the child grew up, alleging that the charter was lost. A church council restored the land to the grand-daughter, who became a regular abbess, 50 years after the original grant. Her mother and grandmother did not observe the 'regular discipline' that Bede required in a celibate monastery, and resembled the Northumbrian magnates who 'bought themselves a monastery and lived there with their wives'.

But what seemed an abuse to Bede became in time the principal form of English land tenure, the means by which it escaped from stultifying restrictions of kin. Bede's indignation at 'luxury and gluttony', where the name of monastery should mean 'chastity and continence', suggests orgies in a bawdy house, but his factual detail describes the purchase of estates by mature married couples; his objection is that secular estates are called monasteries and eat up the land. They were so called because there was no other way in which men who prospered could buy land. By church right, they acquired royal land, documented or booked by the king, burdened with no claims of other men's kin, and added it to their own inheritance. They were at first also bound to bequeath the land to those whom folk right prescribed as their heirs; but the devices of Theodore and Aldhelm enabled men who held by church right to choose which kinsman should inherit, in disregard of whatever inheritance custom bound their family.

Soon the restriction of choice to an heir within kin was removed. The recipient was permitted to sell the land, or bequeath it to whom he would. The source of such rights was the king's royal booked land, and 'bookland' came to mean land that could be sold or bequeathed without regard to kinship; so a 9th-century king explained that with the consent of his bishops and magnates, he booked estates to himself, 'in order that I may leave them after my death to whoever I wish in perpetuity'. The king's right to book his own estates enabled him to grant his inherited land. Ine of Wessex gave lands

> which I possess by paternal inheritance, and hold in perpetual lordship,

and at the end of the 8th century Beortric of Wessex assigned

> land that is mine by right, that my predecessors and my relatives bequeathed to me to possess by hereditary right ... to ... Hemele ... to possess eternally, to have, to hold or to exchange, and to leave after him to whomsoever he will.

The quantities of available land were increased by exchange and transfer; a 9th-century Kentish king exchanged land that, like Beortric's, was his 'by right', for a subject's land. What he granted became 'bookland', what he received became his 'folk land', replacing what he relinquished.

Estates that became bookland were an extension of church right, and carried with them its important privileges, including exemption from normal taxation. The earliest Mercian grants had made no specific mention of taxation, but Aldhelm's weighty influence soon obliged kings to spell out a precise renunciation of their claims upon the cultivators' dues, in a clear formula that hardened into an inescapable standard clause. The urgent needs of government quickly obliged the church to accept one important qualification of Aldhelm's exemption clause, the discharge of the three public services of the maintenance of the army, fortifications and bridges; but otherwise immunity from normal dues was permanently extended to church right and booked land. Bookland was tax free; but its greater importance was that, in contrast with folk land and loan land, it was held in full private possession, free of claims by the kin of its former owner or of its new owner, unless expressly so bound. A law of Alfred defines the entail.

> If a man has inherited Bookland from his relatives, he may not leave
> it out of his kindred, if there are witnesses or documents to show
> that he was forbidden to do so by those who first acquired it, or
> those who gave it to him.

But if there were no such witnesses or deeds, he was free to leave it out of kin. As in Wales, booked land was free from normal taxes, and free from the claims of heirs.

Folkland

Yet folk right was still powerful; much land was not booked and not free from kin. The distinction was rigorously maintained. A 9th-century *ealdorman* left most of his bookland to his wife and daughter and asked the king to let his son, apparently illegitimate, inherit his folk land; unless the king admitted the son as legitimate heir, the folk land necessarily passed to his nearest legitimate paternal male relative. Folk land lasted long; its disputes were settled, not in the king's courts, but in the *folc gemot*, the public assembly, guided, but not ruled, by the king's reeve. Its function was emphasised in the 10th century. When king Edward the Elder enjoined his reeves to pronounce 'right judgment' in dealing with 'written law', but to 'interpret' public law, he expressly provided that disputes about folk land, but not about book land, should be heard in the reeve's presence, in the public court. The old claims of kin outlived the Norman conquest, and 12th-century London still found it necessary to rule that

> if a citizen of London wishes to sell land because of poverty,
> neither his sons nor his relatives can prevent him.

Some Londoners still maintained that a man's kin had rights upon his land, that prevented him from selling it. The 12th-century ruling extinguished the lingering claim of folk land. Bookland prevailed among men of substance. It emerged from church right. It enabled the powerful to sell, exchange or bequeath their property at will. It also avoided the growth of military tenures, that had been normal in Wessex, Northumbria, and perhaps also Mercia in the 7th century; and when the Norman conquerors sought to impose them, the maturity of the

English freehold prevented them from striking deep, and in time reduced them to an additional form of taxation, thereby shielding England from many of the worst excesses of European military lordship.

The Cultivators

Tenure by bookland was the privilege of greater men. What it granted was not acreage, but the right to receive the rents and dues of those who worked the acres, and to sell or bequeath those rights. No humble cultivator received such charters. The language of the grants distinguishes cultivators by three main terms. *Tributarius* is the Roman lawyers' word for a tax-paying provincial, and translates the English word *gafolgelda*, tax-payer, equivalent to the *boneddig*, the simple free man of Welsh law. The *cassatus* was also a Roman legal term, meaning a dependent established in his *casa* or cottage by his lord; it translates the English *cottar*, the occupier of a *cote*, and is equivalent to the Welsh *taeog*. The third class were the *manentes*, who 'stay' where they are, the dependent population of a *mansio*, a single undivided property; they doubtless included the population of villages named -*ingtun* or -*botl*, and of other places subject to a lord. The *manentes* are also likely to have included the bulk of the Welsh who lived in the 7th-century English kingdoms, with a status not unlike that of the *aillt*, the stranger, in Wales, or of the Latin *coloni originarii*, ancestral cultivators, who had once been free, in contrast to the *cassati* installed by their lord.

The terms are at first used with precision, though a grant that adds together *tributarii*, *cassati* and *manentes* often also used *tributarii* as the general word to describe the grand total; for from the point of view of the lord and the king all the cultivators were liable for tribute, tax or rent. The earliest texts grant persons, *tributarii*, except in Kent, whose documents from the beginning grant *aratra*, ploughs. But from the later 7th century more and more charters grant 'land estimated at (or of) so many *tributarii*', and later texts sometimes confuse the three categories. Their changing usage, and its local variations, cannot be determined until closer study is possible.

The tenures of these small-scale cultivators continued to be governed by kin inheritance, that eroded only slowly under the influence of the lord's bookland; at the end of the 11th century the Domesday Book entries in some counties baldly record many poorer peasants in phrases like '15 men have half a hide' between them. A few charters use similar words. They describe inheritance shared among kin. It lasted longest among the poorest; for though there is relatively little sign of lands divided into fragments, as among the Welsh, there is ample evidence of men who jointly farmed a joint inheritance. Undivided inheritance became usual. The king's concern for a stable nobility, and the influence of his reeve over the development of public law, helped Anglian primogeniture to oust other complex rules of kinship, with all their local variations. The free testamentary inheritance of bookland powerfully aided primogeniture, for most men who have a free choice prefer to leave their land to a son, but to have freedom to provide for daughters and younger sons, and to entail an inheritance if they doubt their heirs. Long custom bred a general opinion that expected men to leave the bulk of their estates to their eldest son, and enforced strict primogeniture upon the succession to rank and title. In contrast with France and many other European lands, the English nobility were able to conserve estates, and lesser men who prospered might grow to the status of gentry.

The Survival of the English

English society was loosely knit. Its numerous intermediate gradations avoided polarisation between the extremes of over-mighty nobles and servile cultivators, crushed, and powerless to voice their resentment. In the most general terms, it owed its cohesion to the simple fact that Britain is an island. Until the coming of the Scandinavians and the Normans, the English were free to choose the foreign customs that influenced their development, and to determine the manner in which those influences should operate. Their early training accustomed them to easy change, and constant contact with foreigners, readily accepted within their island, enabled change to continue by gradual adaptation, without sudden upheaval.

The comfortable England of Bede and Offa was shattered by the invasions of the 9th, 10th and 11th centuries. Damage was most severe at the top of society. The autocracy of Offa had seemed in his lifetime an unassailable sovereignty. But the sharp mind of Alcuin discerned its weakness; in destroying the ancient dynasties of the regional kings, the imperial power had destroyed its own support. Even before the full shock of the invasions, Offa's monarchy was in ruins, and the disappearance of the lesser kings left the English leaderless. Despite their handicap, they rallied behind the new Wessex monarchy. But in the long run, they failed. Not even the victories of Alfred and Athelstan were able to replace the vanished strength of royal government; the power of the monarchy had crumbled before the Norman host landed, and its disintegration made their conquest possible.

The conquerors eliminated the ancient nobility of England. But they could not eliminate the population, and could not suppress or replace the institutions of local decision. Customary tenures survived. The foreigners who were rewarded with the lands of the conquered also inherited their status and tenure; and in spite of the efforts of lawyers and churchmen to impose military fiefs, old tenures persisted. Though land lay in the king's gift in law, his actual power to grant and to revoke rarely reached beyond the mightier lords, whose mutual violence floated upon the top of society. The status of the peasant sunk to the level of the exploited serf, but the old tenures inherited from early England maintained an independent class of small and modest landholders. The yeoman and the franklin, the gentry and the squire were numerous enough and sufficiently secure to retain control of their own localities, and were thereby enabled to grant or withhold the revenues of the central government.

The power of the English Commons owes little but its form to the king's council, the *witan* of 'wise men' and magnates. Its roots lie in land tenure rather than in institutions. It has been less respected in periods when it has submitted to the control of magnates, powerful interests, or professional politicians; but public support has made it all-powerful when it has demonstrably represented the dominant interest and views of the localities that make up the nation. The national assemblies and estates of other nations withered in the middle ages. The English parliament survived because it became the organ of lesser local lords and of their urban equivalents, whose interests repeatedly aligned them with the peasant against the demands of king and baron. It was able to speak for lesser lords because they had asserted effective control of the localities, the shires, the hundreds and the parishes, and had restrained the power of the king's officials and of the nobleman's factor. Their existence and their collective strength ultimately derived from the tenures and the institutions of early England, that proved able to survive Scandinavian and European conquest.

Local tenures and local institutions trained English society to respect governments that coordinate, and to discipline governments that rule by command. From pagan and Mercian times onward, custom has expected that men of suitable standing should be heard before decision is reached; society has frequently disagreed about which men should be heard when, but when it has reached agreement, governments that ignored agreed opinion have been denied obedience and revenue. These attitudes have maintained the flexibility of English society, and secured an easier movement of men and ideas, a speedier and smoother social change than was possible in most of Europe. They were first formed by the piecemeal migrations of the early English, and by their need to absorb the alien natives in the lands they had conquered. The English mastered the fairer part of Britain, and emerged as the most powerful of the successor states within the territory of Arthur's empire. Though they were stronger, they could neither exterminate their neighbours nor drown their identity.

Early experience obliged the English simultaneously to create an unusually powerful central government, and to maintain an unusual degree of regional and local variety and independence. Later experience induced men of all classes and regions to respect the central government so long as it behaved sensibly and retained authority; and also compelled successive rulers to observe the restraints that custom set upon that authority. The English were unable to conquer and annex Wales and Scotland; they were forced to be content with the status of elder brother, their primacy admitted only when they themselves acknowledged its limits. Kings who asserted a loose suzerainty over the 'empire of Britain' also learnt to rule the several regions of the English as loosely, to refrain from annexation, from savage butchery or unbearable extortions after military victory. Time and effort shaped a tradition of firm leadership and light rule. The tradition was often flouted, and as often reasserted, when attempts at autocracy failed. But from its troubled origins and repeated buffetings, the conventions of

English government inherited a resilience that is not easily repressed. English society early learnt and practised the simple truism that the whole is no more than the sum of its parts, and is as strong as the links that bind them together.

CHAPTER TWENTY-FIVE

ARTHUR AND THE FUTURE

The age of Arthur ended Roman Britain, and created the nations of modern Britain. His short empire crowned the efforts of the fifth-century British to retain their island; its dismemberment compelled the peoples of the sixth century to define their identity. His victory briefly demonstrated that Britain was and could be a single political state; his failure obliged the separate nations to tolerate each other's existence, to fight for supremacy over their neighbours, but no longer for their extermination, and to accept the autonomy of regions and districts within each nation. In name he was the last Roman emperor; but he ruled as the first medieval king.

Many permanent institutions, customs and conventions that still influence modern political behaviour begin their history in the Arthurian age. Though the institutions have been transformed, and the ideas hardened and broadened, it is in this age that they were first formed. They were the response of the peoples of Britain to the awful catastrophe of fallen Rome, the sharpest and most sudden break in the history of Europe. Old conventions were everywhere blown into forgetfulness, and men devised new bonds to hold together the shattered fragments of their society. But the transformation of Europe was confined within narrower bounds than in Britain. When once the imperial government disintegrated and admitted independent barbarian nations in arms, without destruction of the Roman economy, the fusion of Roman and German was inescapable; the outcome of political and social initiative could only decide which Germans should rule where, and determine the nature and degree of fusion in each region.

But in Britain, no inevitable necessity compelled events to turn out as they did. When the old order was smashed, and not yet replaced, the issue of each crisis affected all succeeding time. Options were wide open, as they never had been before, and never were to be again. If individual leaders had taken different decisions, Britain might have become Pictland, or Vandalland; if the government of Vortigern had decided to deploy its English federates against the Irish, instead of against the Picts, then the English would have been settled in Snowdonia and Cornwall, not in eastern Britain. If the British had not rallied to the partisan forces of Ambrosius, Britain might have passed under the control of a miscellaneous Germanic soldiery, as mixed as Odovacer's in Italy, and have dissolved like Italy into tiny hostile states, disunited for fifteen centuries. But if the Roman aristocracy of Britain had joined Ambrosius instead of emigrating, they might have won the war before their society was destroyed, and permanently upheld in Britain a western state as Roman as the empire of the east, ruled from a London as imperial as Constantinople.

It is futile to explore the possibilities of what did not happen. But they need to be displayed, for the rigid complacency of historical determinism easily assumes that what actually happened was bound to have happened sooner or later, and easily credits events to the wisdom of individual leaders who perceived the necessities of their age, or to the folly of those who did not. Yet historical events are not determined by the will and understanding of great men alone. They are brought about by the sum of the manifold individual decisions taken by all the men and women concerned, great and small, separately and collectively, to fight or to flee, to obey or to disobey, to bestir themselves or to rest quiet. The quality that distinguishes a leader above his fellows is his ability to arouse sentiments that inspire effective decision, to realise men's hopes.

In settled ages men's aspirations and beliefs are limited by the ideas that they have inherited. Original thinkers may modify and extend their inheritance, but they cannot transform a society whose assumptions are taken for granted by the majority of their fellow-men. When the customary conventions of Roman Britain were suddenly and violently destroyed, all the old controls were overthrown. No later age was free to choose between so wide a range of possibilities. Even the invading Northmen were compelled to accept decisions already taken; from the 9th century to the 13th, five centuries of attempts to impose their languages and institutions yielded to the solid persistence of England, Wales and Scotland, and left native speech and custom modified, but intact. The decisions taken by the men and women of the fifth and sixth centuries moulded the whole future history of the British Isles, and fixed limits that succeeding ages were not able to overstep; if they had taken other decisions, the history of their descendants and the possibilities open to them would have been utterly different.

The debt that modern men owe to the energy of their remote ancestors is easily hidden behind foggy language. The term 'Dark Ages' is not the innocent invention of conscientious academics, stumped for the want of a clearer term. It has always been used to impose a viewpoint and to suppress evidence. It once comprehended all the 'Gothic' centuries of European history between the Romans and the Age of Enlightenment, and condemned them as inferior. The invention of the term 'Middle Ages' rescued several centuries from obscurity and contempt; but 'Dark Age' remained the designation of European society between the Romans and the Crusaders until the words Merovingian and Carolingian replaced it. It was thenceforth confined to Britain.

The term always confused, for it conveyed a two-fold meaning; it implied that the age was dark because men were ignorant, illiterate and brutish, authors of a dismal regression from the elegant splendour of Rome; and was also dark because it was little known. Most aristocratic societies have looked back with nostalgia upon the stable empire of Rome, when the lower orders were content to keep their station more obediently than in later times, and have looked gloomily upon the sequel; their viewpoint was challenged by a different outlook, that defined the 'Dark Age' as a time of 'less light for more people', as the period that initiated the struggles for human liberation that underlie modern ideas of equality and social justice. But 'darkness' remained a reproach, conveying a political judgement, as surely as the later variant, 'sub-Roman', that equally maligns the Romans and their successors.

These verbal controversies belong to the past. Nowadays the term is chiefly restricted to the notion that we cannot see clearly what happened. Yet darkness lies in the eye of the beholder; though much is not yet understood, and much can never be known, yet most darkness is the fault of modern vision. There is no lack of evidence, but there is still a lack of systematic study; and the use of a misleading term itself has dimmed understanding, for it hides the connections between events and people. The convention that normally and properly guides historical enquiry allots neutral distinctive names to defined periods, so that these connections may be recognised; the term Victorian links Swinburne with Gladstone and railway trains, Marx and Verdi, as the term Elizabethan relates Shakespeare and madrigals to American colonists and the Spanish Armada. But the want of sensible terms prevents even specialists from observing the connections between different events in Britain in the centuries after the fall of Rome, and hides their significance.

Yet the decisive events that separate coherent periods in early British history are well known, as self-evident as those that justify terms like Roman or Renaissance; periods, like persons, are not easily understood or described until they are identified. The term 'Roman Britain' conveys a clear meaning, even to those who know little about it. It ended in the middle of the fifth century; though the imperial government ceased to rule Britain in 410, yet the Roman civilisation of Britain and its political institutions lasted a generation longer, into the 450s, until about the time of Arthur's birth.

The end of Roman Britain was immediately followed by the age of Arthur. It includes his own lifetime, and the rule of his successors until the English conquest, half a century after his death. It constitutes a self-contained period, whose important achievement bore heavily on the future, and is thoroughly misunderstood if it is viewed as a vague 'transition' between Rome and the Middle Ages. Thereafter, the periods of English dominance are clearly marked. The Age of Conquest and Conversion reached from the 570s into the 640s, and included the short-lived military supremacy of the Northumbrians. Thenceforth, until modern times, defined periods are clearly marked by the names of the principal ruling dynasties. The Mercian period began with the victories of Penda in the 640s; interrupted only for three years, from 655 to 658, it continued for a century and a half, until Mercian supremacy was challenged and replaced by the sovereignty of the West Saxon dynasty, early in the 9th century. These periods might conveniently be subdivided; yet they are clear and significant stages in the evolution of Britain and England, separated by events that contemporaries recognised as decisive turning-points; and the dynastic names of the Mercian and West Saxon periods are as valid as those of the Norman, Angevin and Plantagenet periods that followed them.

The age of Arthur is the beginning of modern British history. For that reason, it cannot escape controversy. Men are always moved by their beliefs about the past, and the historians who mould those beliefs naturally emphasise aspects and periods that are in their view important. Views vary, for many historians share the outlook of established authority, and some reject it. Recent prejudice has preferred to avoid the origins of British history, and to pretend that modern society is rooted in the despotism of the Normans; as that pretence becomes increasingly untenable, medieval history is less studied, and attention concentrates upon the authoritarian rule of the Tudors and their successors. These attitudes are recent and temporary. Earlier generations lacked the formidable equipment of modern scholarship, but they judged honestly. The instinct of the middle ages began its tradition with Arthur of Britain, the champion of a legendary golden age, the pattern of a just society that should be, but was not; and the legend retained its dignity until it was degraded by the banality of Tennyson. The time of the early English kings remained the starting-point of national history, until ignorant contempt divorced the 'Anglo-Saxons' from their English descendants; and as late as the 17th century it still worked powerfully upon the minds of English revolutionaries, who rightly saw themselves as rebels against a 'Norman yoke', revitalised by Tudor authority, and strove consciously to revive what they held to be their native tradition.

Earlier instinct did not err. The origins of the modern nations of Britain may be swept aside or hidden, derided as remote, irrelevant and unimportant, but their essential story cannot easily be misrepresented. The brief rule, victory and failure of Arthur shaped sixth-century Britain and equipped the English for mastery over decaying native society. It also gave courage to native protest, whose monastic enthusiasm seized upon the Irish and the English, binding together peoples whom kings had sundered, and carrying their joint reforming zeal to Europe, at the moment when Europe needed and welcomed reformers. The endeavours of the early monks bequeathed as much to the future of Europe as the conflict of popes and kings, lords and landowners.

The history of Europe is nowadays the proper study of all mankind, for all nations now accept the technology and the political philosophies of Europe. National histories are a blend of their own past and of European experience. But the study of Europe is still hampered by exclusive national emphasis, that confines most English students to the history of England and of the nearer parts of Europe that directly concerned England, or of its overseas colonies; and is as cramped in most other countries. It has been freed from its earlier limitation to the record of kings and notables by the stresses of 20th-century disturbance, that have focused attention upon the subjects of the kings. It is now passing out of a rigid academic tradition that carved it into artificially separated compartments, labelled 'political', 'constitutional', 'economic', 'social', and the like. It is no longer sufficient for the 'economic historian' to confine himself to a flat description of the environment in which inert masses were imprisoned; for men now demand to know the ideas that have moved mankind to change their environment, and to enquire into the reasons for their success and failure.

The history of Europe, as of Britain, is misrepresented if it begins in the middle, and emphasises only parts of its origin. Its debt to Rome is plain to see. The social institutions and the urban Christian church of the empire withstood the invaders and absorbed them. But the ferment of ideas that the reformers from Ireland and Britain injected into the settled ways of seventh century Europe are less easily perceived, so long as their origin in their homeland remains in darkness. The future of the Germanic and of the western Slavonic nations owed as much to the monks as to bishops, emperors and kings. The faith of the monks was born and bred in Arthurian Britain, in an age that rewarded initiative.

Therein lies the importance of the little short-lived realm that Arthur salvaged from the ruin of Rome. The tales that immortalised his name are more than a curiosity of Celtic legend. Their imagery illuminates an essential truth. In his own day Arthur failed, and left behind him hope unfulfilled. But the measure of any man lies not in his own lifetime, but in what he enables his successors to achieve. The history of the British Isles is funnelled through the critical years of Arthur's power and of its destruction, for thence came the modern nations. The age of Arthur is the foundation of British history; and it lies in the mainstream of European experience.

SUMMARY OF EVENTS

350–400. The Imperial Government, under pressure on the Rhine and Danube, kept the garrison of Britain under strength. Britain prospered, in spite of occasional raids. Christianity prevailed by the end of the century.

400–450. The Rhine frontier broke, 406/407. The emperor Constantine III, a Briton, cleared the barbarians from Britain and Gaul, but was suppressed by the legitimate emperor, Honorius. The Goths took Rome, 410. Honorius told the British to govern and defend themselves, legitimising local emperors. The British repelled foreign enemies, but divided in civil war. Vortigern (c. 425–c. 458) employed Saxons, or English, to defeat the Picts, barbarians beyond the Forth; he neutralised mainland Ireland and reduced Irish colonists in western Britain. The British nobility, led by Ambrosius the elder, rebelled against Vortigern and the Saxons; Vortigern enlisted more Saxons, who rebelled against both parties, c. 441, and destroyed Roman British civilisation. After heavy fighting, the political leaders of the British were assassinated, and much of the surviving nobility emigrated to Gaul, c. 459.

450–500. A national resistance movement of the citizens (*Cymry*) was initiated by Ambrosius Aurelianus the younger, c. 460, and triumphed under Arthur at Badon, c. 495. The English remained in partitioned areas, chiefly in the east. The political forms of the Roman Empire were revived, but its economy had been destroyed.

500–550. The central government disintegrated with the death of Arthur (c. 515). Numerous generals became warlords of regions, Maelgwn of North Wales the most powerful among them, and provoked the resentment of civilians of all classes. A monastic reform movement on a mass scale freed the church from dependence upon the warlords; it spread to Ireland, and also prompted a massive migration to Brittany. Bubonic plague ravaged the mediterranean and also Britain and Ireland, 547–551.

550–600. The second Saxon, or English, revolt permanently mastered most of what is now England, destroying the remnants of the warlords. By 605, Aethelferth of Northumbria and Aethelbert of Kent were between them supreme over all the English. Kent was converted to Roman Christianity, 597. Columba of Iona established Irish monastic Christianity among the Picts, and among the Scot or Irish colonists of Argyle, 563–597.

600–650. The empire and Christianity of Kent collapsed, 616. Northumbrian supremacy, 617–642, was overthrown by Penda of the Mercians, with Welsh allies. The monastic impetus faded in Wales but renewed its vigour among the Irish.

650–800. The Mercian kings held empire over the southern English; the Northumbrian monarchy lost authority after 700. The Northumbrians and Mercians accepted monastic Christianity from the Irish, and the English and the Irish carried it to Europe north of the Alps. Its practices conflicted with those of Rome. Archbishop Theodore, from Tarsus (669–690), presided over the fusion of native monastic and Roman episcopal Christianity among the English; the Irish and the Welsh conformed later. Scandinavian raids began in 789, and sovereignty over the English passed from the Mercian to the West Saxon kings early in the 9th century.

TABLE OF DATES

Capital letters denote Emperors, Popes and major rulers. (W. . West; E . . East).
Italics denote battles. Italic capitals denote Irish Kings.
The span of years shown indicates either the reign or the effective adult life of the individual concerned; birth dates are not given.

THE EMPIRE

350
CONSTANS (W) 337–350
CONSTANTIUS (E) 337–361
MAGNENTIUS (W) 350–353
JULIAN (W) Caesar 355–361
360
JULIAN 361–363
JOVIAN 363–364
VALENTINIAN I (W) 364–375
VALENS (E) 364–378

370
GRATIAN ((W) 375–383
Adrianople 378
VALENTINIAN II (W) 375–393
THEODOSIUS I (E) 379–395
380
MAGNUS MAXIMUS (W) 383–388

390
Offa of Angel c. 390/420?
ARCADIUS (E) 395–408
HONORIUS (W) 395–421

400
THEODOSIUS II (E) 408–450
CONSTANTINE III (W) 407–411
410
Goths take Rome 410

Visigoth federates in Gaul
418

420
Eomer of Angel c. 420/460?
VALENTINIAN III (W) 423–455
Vandals take Africa c. 429

THE CHURCH

Hilary of Poitiers
353–368

Synod of Rimini 359

DAMASUS 366–384
Ambrose of Milan
371–397
Martin of Tours
372–c. 397

Augustine of Hippo
386–430

Victricius in Britain
c. 396
St. Albans, Whithorn ?
founded

Pelagius c. 400–418

Sicilian Briton 411
Fastidius 411
Amator, Auxerre -418
Germanus of Auxerre
418–448

Jerome died 420
CELESTINE 422–432
Germanus, Britain 429

BRITISH ISLES

MUIREDACH 325–355

Paul the Notary 353
EOCHAID 356–365

Barbarian raids 360, 364, 367

CRIMTHANN 365–378
Border dynasties founded c. 3

NIALL 379–405

First Migration to
Brittany ?388

Saxon raid c. 397

NATH – I 405–428

Britain independent
COEL HEN dux ? c. 410/420
AMBROSIUS the Elder
? c. 412/425
Drust (Picts) 414–458

VORTIGERN c. 425–c. 459
LOEGAIRE 428–463
HENGEST and Horsa land c. 4

ABROAD	THE CHURCH	BRITISH ISLES
430 Aëtius supreme in the west c. 433–454	Patrick in Ireland 432–c. 459 SIXTUS III 432–440	Cunedda, and Cornovii, migrations c. 430? *Wallop* c. 437
440 Aëtius consul III 446 CHILDERIC I (Franks) c. 440?–481	LEO I 440–461 Patrick's *Declaration* c. 440/443 Germanus in Britain	First Saxon revolt c. 441/2 *Aylesford, Crayford* c. 445/449
450 MARCIAN (E) 450–457 AVITUS (W) 455–456 Aegidius in Gaul 455–464 LEO I (E) 457–474	Patrick's *Letter* c. 450 Northern Irish sees c. 459	*Richborough* c. 450 Coroticus, Clyde, c. 450 Massacre c. 458. Aelle, South Saxons Second Migration to Brittany c. 459
460 Icel of Angel c. 460/480? Syagrius in Gaul 464–486 ANTHEMIUS (W) 467–472	HILARY 461–468 Faustus at Riez 462–c. 495 Ibar, Enda, Kebi in Rome c. 465	AMBROSIUS AURELIANUS c. 460–c. 475 *AILLEL MOLT* 464–482 *ANGUS* of Munster c. 465–492
470 ZENO (E) 474–491 Odovacer ends western emperors 476 **480** CLOVIS (Franks) 481–511 *Soissons* 486	Sidonius of the Auvergne 470–479 Docco died c. 473 Illtud's school c. 480–c. 510 Brigit c. 480–524	ARTHUR c. 475–c. 515 *Portsmouth* c. 480 Cerdic c. 480–c. 495 Migration of Angel kings c. 480 *LUGAID* 482–505
490 ANASTASIUS 491–518 THEODORIC in Italy 493–526 **500** *Poitiers* 507 Gaul becomes France End of main Elbe cemeteries	Abban and Ibar, Abingdon, c. 498 Benedict of Nursia c. 500–c. 542	Irish attacks on Britain 495/510 *Badon* c. 495. Partition. Demetia recovered c. 500/510 Dal Riada Scots c. 500 Dyfnwal, Clyde, c. 500 *MAC ERCA* 505–532
510 SONS OF CLOVIS 511–561* JUSTIN I 518–527 **520** Beowulf c. 520/550 JUSTINIAN 527–565	Dubricius c. 510–c. 540 Samson c. 525–c. 563	*Camlann*, Arthur killed, c. 515 Vortipor c. 515–c. 540 MAELGWN c. 520–551
530 Africa reconquered 533, Italy 533–544 THEUDEBERT (East Franks) 533–548	Finnian of Clonard c. 530–551 Gildas' book c. 538	Saxon migrations from Britain to Europe c. 530/550 *TUATHAL* 532–548
540 Bubonic plague 543–547 THEUDEBALD (East Franks) 548–555	Kentigern exiled c. 540 Columba, Derry 544 Cadoc c. 545–c. 580 Brendan's voyages 545/560	Eliffer of York c. 540/560 Morcant, Clyde, c. 540/560 Gabran, Dal Riada, 541–560 *DIARMAIT* 548–564 Plague 547–551

ABROAD	THE CHURCH ABROAD	THE CHURCH IN THE BRITISH ISLES
550	Radegund at Poitiers 550–587 PELAGIUS I 555–560	David c. 550–589 Comgall founded Irish Bangor 558
560 CLOTHAIR killed Chramn and CONOMOR 560 BRUNHILD 566–613 JUSTIN II 565–578 Lombards in Italy 568		Daniel at Bangor, Menai c. 560–584 Columba at Iona 563–597 Gildas in Ireland 565
570 TIBERIUS 578–582	Gregory of Tours 573–594 PELAGIUS II 578–590	Gildas died 570 Kentigern, Glasgow, c. 575–c. 603
580 MAURICE 582–602		Aedan of Ferns c. 585–627
590	GREGORY the Great 590–604 Columban in Gaul and Italy 595–615	Augustine Archbishop of Canterbury 597–604
600 PHOCAS 602–610		
610 HERACLIUS 610–641		
620 PEPIN I Mayor 624–639	HONORIUS I 625–640	Edwin baptised 625
630 DAGOBERT I 630–638 Arabs took Damascus 634, Jerusalem 637		Aedan of Lindisfarne 635–651
640 Arabs in Egypt 640, Persia 642, Africa 647 GRIMOALD, Mayor, 642–656	Eligius bishop 640–659	Hilda of Whitby c. 640–680

BRITAIN	IRELAND	THE ENGLISH
550		
RHUN of Gwynedd 551–580?		CYNRIC took Salisbury 552
BRIDEI, Picts, 554–584		AETHELBERT of Kent 555–616
560		
PEREDUR, York, c. 560–580	*AINMERE* 565–569	IDA, Bamburgh, c. 560–c. 570
RIDERCH, Clyde, c. 560–c. 600	*BAETAN* c. 569–588	*Wibbandun* 568; Ceawlin
CONALL, Dal Riada, 560–574		and Cutha beat Aethelbert
570		
URIEN of Reged c. 570–c. 590		*Bedcanford* 571
Arthuret 573		*Dyrham* 577
AEDAN, Dal Riada, 574–609		
580		
MOURIC, Glevissig,	*AED* m. Ainmere	ADDA, etc., Bernicia,
c. 580–c. 615	588–601	c. 570–588
Caer Greu 580. PEREDUR killed		AELLE occupied York?
Tintern c. 584		AETHELRIC 588–593
590		
Lindisfarne c. 590		CEAWLIN killed 593
OWAIN of Reged c. 590–c. 595		AETHELBERT supreme
Catraeth 598?		c. 593–616
		AETHELFERTH 593–617

	NORTHERN ENGLISH	SOUTHERN ENGLISH
600		
Degsastan 603	AETHELFERTH in York 604	
610		
Chester c. 613	EDWIN 617–633	CYNEGILS, West Saxons,
		611–643
620		
		PENDA 626–655
630		
Catwallaun killed Edwin 633	OSWALD	
	634–642	
640		
Penda and Welsh killed	OSWY 642–670	CENWALH, West Saxons,
Oswald 642		643–672

ABROAD	THE CHURCH ABROAD	THE CHURCH IN NORTHERN BRITAIN AND IRELAND
650		
EBROIN, Mayor, 656–681	Fursey died 649	
660		
Arabs took Syracuse 664		Synod of Whitby 664
670		
Arabs besiege Constantinople 673–675	Killian of Wurzburg c. 670–689	Wearmouth founded 674 Caedmon died c. 678
680		
PEPIN II, Mayor, 681–714		Bede at Jarrow c. 681–735 Adomnan, Iona, 686–704
690		
	Willibrord, Frisia, 695–739	
700		
Arabs in Spain 710 CHARLES MARTEL 714–741 *Poitiers* 732 PEPIN III 741–768	Boniface of Mainz killed 755 Alcuin of York and Tours 766–804	
800		
CHARLEMAGNE, 768–814		

*SONS OF CLOVIS
    THEODORIC I,   East Franks, 511–533
    CHLODOMER,   Orleans, 511–524
    CHILDEBERT,   Paris, 511–558
    CLOTHAIR I,   Soissons, 511–561
                Orleans, 524–561
                East Franks, 555–561
                Paris, 558–561

THE CHURCH IN SOUTHERN BRITAIN	THE NORTH	MERCIA AND THE SOUTH
650		
	Oswy killed Penda 655 OSWY supreme 655–658	WULFHERE 658–675
660 Theodore Archbishop of Canterbury 669–690	Plague 664	Second *Badon*; Morcant killed 665
670 Barking, Chertsey founded 675 Aldhelm c. 670–709	EGFERTH 670–685 *Trent* 679	West Saxon underkings 672–c. 682 AETHELRED 675–704
680	ALDFRITH 685–705 Ferchar, Dal Riada, 680–696	CEADWALLA 685–688 INE 688–726
690		WIHTRED, Kent, 691–725
700	Pict and Scot wars Northumbrian civil wars	Coenred 704–709 Ceolred 709–716 AETHELBALD 716–757 OFFA 757–796 First Scandinavian raid 789
800	KENNETH MacAlpine 830–860 united Picts and Scots	EGBERT, West Saxon, 802–839 RHODRI MAWR, Wales, 844–877 ALFRED 871–?900

ABBREVIATIONS
used in the Notes

Italic figures and letters give National Grid Map references:
Two letters and four figures, as *TL 01 23*, refer to Great Britain.
One letter and two figures, as *N 58*, refer to Ireland.
One letter and one figure, as *H 2*, refer to Brittany.
The National Grid for Great Britain is explained on Ordnance Survey maps, in the Automobile Association Handbook, and elsewhere.
The Irish National Grid is shown on Maps 9 and 27, pp. 153 and 373 above.
The Grid devised for Brittany is shown on Map 14, p. 255 above, and explained in the notes thereto.

A single bold capital letter, as **A**, refers to the appropriate section of *Arthurian Sources*, cf. p. xi above, whose contents are

A	Annals	**H**	Honorius' Letter
B	Badon	**I**	Inscriptions
C	Charters	**J**	Jurisprudence, Law
D	Dedications	**K**	King Lists
E	Ecclesiastics	**L**	Localities, Geography
F	Foreign persons and places	**M**	Miscellaneous
G	Genealogies	**N**	Names of Places
G A	Armorican	**O**	Ogam Script
G B	British	**P**	Persons, laymen
G E	English	**Q**	Quotations from texts
G F	Foreign	**R**	Roman institutions
G I	Irish	**S**	Saxon Archaeology
followed by the initial letter(s) of the territory concerned		**T**	Texts discussed

AASS   E. T. Leeds *The Archaeology of the Anglo-Saxon Settlements* Oxford 1913

AB   *Analecta Bollandiana* Brussels 1882–

AC   *Annals of Clonmacnoise* translated C. Mageoghagan (1627) from an original of c. 1408, now lost; ed. D. Murphy, Dublin 1896

ACDS   J. M. MacKinlay *Ancient Church Dedications in Scotland* 2 vols. Edinburgh 1910–1914

ACm   *Annales Cambriae* Rolls 20, 1860; YC 9, 1880, 152; MHB 830; *Nennius* ed. Morris, forthcoming; cf. Welsh Literature, Bruts

ALI   *The Ancient Laws of Ireland* ed. W. M. Hennessy and others, 6 vols. Dublin 1856–1901; cf. p. 445 above

ALW   *The Ancient Laws and Institutes of Wales* ed. Aneirin Owen, 2 vols. London 1841

Ant.   Antiquity 1927–

Arch.Jl.   Archaeological Journal 1845–

ASE   Nils Åberg *The Anglo-Saxons in England* Uppsala 1926; F. M. Stenton *Anglo-Saxon England* Oxford 1943

ABBREVIATIONS

ASH	*Acta Sanctorum Hiberniae* I ed. J. Colgan, Louvain 1645, reprint Dublin 1948
ASP	J. N. L. Myres *Anglo-Saxon Pottery* Oxford 1969
AT	*Annals of Tigernach* (1088) ed. W. Stokes RC 16, 1895, 375–419: 17, 1896, 6–33; 119–263; 337–420: 18, 1897, 9–59; 150–198; 267–303; 374–391
BBA	*Black Book of St. Augustine* ed. G. J. Turner and H. E. Salter, 2 vols., London and Oxford 1915–24
BBCS	Bulletin of the Board of Celtic Studies 1921–
BCS	*Cartularium Saxonicum* W. de G. Birch, 3 vols. London 1885–1893; Index of Persons 1899
BHL	*Bibliotheca Hagiographica Latina* Brussels 1898–1901, reprint 1949; supplement Brussels 1911 (*Subsidia Hagiographica* 12)
CA	Ifor Williams *Canu Aneirin* Cardiff 1961
Caspari	C. P. Caspari *Briefe:* see I Sicilian Briton
CEIS	K. Hughes *The Church in Early Irish Society* London 1966
CPL	L. Bieler *Codices Patriciani Latini* Dublin 1942
CPS	*Chronicles of the Picts and Scots* ed. W. F. Skene, Edinburgh 1867
CS	*Chronicon Scotorum* (1660–1666) ed. W. M. Henessy, Rolls 46, 1866; W. F. Skene *Celtic Scotland* 3 vols. Edinburgh 1876–1880
CSW	E. Davies, ed. *Celtic Studies in Wales* Cardiff 1963
CTh	*Codex Theodosianus* ed. T. Mommsen, Berlin 1905, reprint 1954
DBB	F. W. Maitland *Domesday Book and Beyond* Cambridge 1897, reprint (Fontana) London 1960
DC	*The Ancient Laws and Institutes of Wales* ed. Aneirin Owen, 2 vols. London 1841. Vol. I contains the so-called Demetian Code
DCB	*Dictionary of Christian Biography* ed. W. Smith and H. Wace, 4 vols. London 1877–1887
DEPN	*Dictionary of English Place Names* ed. E. Ekwall, Oxford 1936; ed. 4, 1960
ECMW	*The Early Christian Monuments of Wales* ed. V. E. Nash-Williams, Cardiff 1950
EHR	English Historical Review 1886–
EPNE	*English Place Name Elements* A. H. Smith EPNS 25–26 Cambridge 1956
GC	*The Ancient Laws and Institutes of Wales* ed. Aneirin Owen, 2 vols. London 1841. Vol I contains the so-called Gwentian Code
GM	P. Vinogradoff *The Growth of the Manor* London 1911
HA	Bede *Historia Abbatum* ed. C. Plummer, Oxford 1896, reprint 1966
HE	Bede *Historia Ecclesiastica Gentis Anglorum* ed. C. Plummer, Oxford 1896, reprint 1966 OEV of HE in *Early English Text Society* 95–96, 110–111 London 1890–98
HF	*Historia Francorum* and other works ed. Gregory of Tours
HS	ed. A. W. Haddan and W. Stubbs *Councils and Ecclesiastical Documents relating to Great Britain and Ireland* 3 vols. Oxford 1869–71, reprint 1969
HWL	T. Parry (translated H. I. Bell) *A History of Welsh Literature* Oxford 1962
ITS	*Irish Texts Society* publications, with English translation on facing pages, Dublin 1899–
JBAA	Journal of the British Archaeological Association 1846–
JTS	Journal of Theological Studies 1900–
Kalendars	A. P. Forbes *Kalendars of the Scottish Saints* Edinburgh 1872
KCD	*Codex Diplomaticus Aevi Saxonici* J. H. Kemble, 6 vols. London English Historical Society 1839–1848
Kenny	J. F. Kenny *The Sources for the Early History of Ireland* I, Ecclesiastical (all published), New York 1929, reprint Dublin 1969
LBS	S. Baring-Gould and T. Fisher *The Lives of the British Saints* 4 vols., London 1907–13
LEEK	*The Laws of the Earliest English Kings* ed. F. L. Attenborough, Cambridge 1922, reprint New York 1963
LH	*The Irish Liber Hymnorum* ed. J. H. Bernard and R. Atkinson, 2 vols. London, Henry Bradshaw Society 13, 14, 1898

ABBREVIATIONS

LHEB	K. H. Jackson *Language and History in Early Britain* Edinburgh 1953
Lismore Lives	*Lives of the Saints from the Book of Lismore* ed. W. Stokes, Oxford 1890
LL	*Liber Landavensis* J. G. Evans *The Book of Llan Dav* Oxford 1893
LRE	A. H. M. Jones *The Later Roman Empire* Blackwell, Oxford 1964
LW	*Leges Walliae*
MA	Medieval Archaeology 1957–
Mansi	J. D. Mansi *Sacrorum Conciliorum nova et Amplissima Collectio* 1759; facsimile, Paris and Leipzig 1901
MGH	*Monumenta Germaniae Historica* ed. G. H. Pertz, T. Mommsen and others, Hanover, Berlin, 1826–
NH	*Natural History* ed. Teubner, 1875–1906
NQ	Notes and Queries 1849–
O'Curry	Eugene O'Curry *Lectures on the Manuscript Materials of Ancient Irish History* Dublin 1861
OIT	K. H. Jackson *The Oldest Irish Tradition; a Window on the Iron Age* (Rede lecture) Cambridge 1964
PFE	J. E. A. Jolliffe *Pre-Feudal England* Oxford 1933, reprint 1962
PL	*Patrologia Latina* ed. J. Migne, Paris 1844–
Sal.	*Vitae Sactorum Hiberniae e codice Salmanticensi* ed. C. de Smedt and J. de Backer, Brussels, 1887; ed. W. W. Heist, (*Subsidia Hagiographica* 28), Brussels, 1965. (References are here given to the columns)
SASI	H. M. Chadwick *Studies in Anglo-Saxon Institutions* Cambridge 1905
SCD	F. Arnold Foster *Studies in Church Dedications* 3 vols. London 1899
SCSW	E. G. Bowen *The Settlements of the Celtic Saints in Wales* Cardiff 1954
SEIL	R. Thurneysen and others *Studies in Early Irish Law* Dublin 1936
TCASL	F. Seebohm *Tribal Custom in Anglo-Saxon Law* London 1911
THSCymm	Transactions of the Honourable Society of Cymmrodorion 1892/3–
TRHS	Transactions of the Royal Historical Society 1868–
TSW	F. Seebohm *The Tribal System in Wales* London 1904
TT	*Trias Thaumaturgo* (Patrick, Brigit, Columba) ed. J. Colgan, Louvain 1647
VC	*The Ancient Laws and Institutes of Wales* ed. Aneirin Owen, 2 vols. London 1841. Vol. I contains the so-called Venedotian Code
VSH	*Vitae Sactorum Hiberniae* ed. C. Plummer, Oxford 1910
VT	*The Tripartite Life of St. Patrick* ed. W. Stokes, Rolls 89, 2 vols., 1887 (*Vita Tripartita*)
WHR	Welsh History Review 1960–

NOTES

The notes aim to indicate the main sources relevant to each subject discussed. Space prevents discussion of many of the possible alternative interpretations that could be based upon them. The figures refer to the page and paragraph where the word noted is to be found.

Proper names are themselves references, since they are discussed and indexed in *Arthurian Sources;* whose relevant sources (*see* Abbreviations) are here cited for many of the more important persons, places and subjects. References are to the page and paragraph.

Introduction

xi	BIELER: *Irish Ecclesiastical Record* 1967, 2.
xi	GILDAS, NENNIUS, PATRICK: text and translation, ed. M.Winterbottom; J.Morris; A.B.E. Hood, Phillimore, forthcoming.
xi	ARTHURIAN SOURCES: Phillimore, forthcoming.
xiii	CHADWICK: *Growth of Literature* I, xix.

18 Fifth-Century Church (pp. 335–355)

335.1	CHRISTIAN RELIGION: cf. pp. 12 and 23 above.
335.1	ALBAN: and other personal names, see E. Alban, *Hertfordshire Archaeology* I, 1968, 1.
335.1	AFRICA AND EGYPT: Tertullian *adversus Iudaeos* 7, written before 209; Origen *Homily 4 on Ezekiel, Homily 6 on Luke*.
335.1	ARLES: Mansi 2, 466 (HS I, 7); cf. *Ant.* 35, 1961, 316.
335.1	ORTHODOXY: e.g. Hilary of Poitiers *de Synodis* Prolog. and I, PL 10, 457, 459 (HS I, 9); cf. passages cited HS I, 7–13, from Athanasius and others.
335.1	CONTEMPT: e.g. the British bishops who rejected government subsidies at Rimini, p. 13 above.
335.1	BISHOP OF LONDON: see E Augurius, and p. 14 above.
335.2	CLERGY: e.g. the priest (Calpurnius) Odysseus, great-grandfather of Patrick (see E) about the beginning of the fourth century.
335.2	ARCHAEOLOGICAL EVIDENCE: summarised in JBAA 16, 1953, 1 ff.; 18, 1955, 1, ff. *Christianity in Britain* 37 ff., cf. 51 ff., 87 ff.
335.2	LONDON: see L.
336.1	VICTRICIUS' LETTER: *de Laude Sanctorum* PL 20, 443; a long extract is reprinted in HS 2, xxi.
336.1	MARTIN: cf. p. 26 above.
336.1	POPE INNOCENT: *Ep.* 2 (PL 20, 471).
337.2	HALF A DOZEN ... MONKS: Pelagius, Coelestius, the Sicilian Briton and his fellow authors, Faustus, Constans Caesar (see E); Antiochus and Martyrius (Sicilian Briton *Ep.* 1) were monks in Britain, but might have been native or foreign by birth.
337.2	WANDERING MONKS: Fastidius, *de vita Christiana* 15 (PL 40, 1046), enjoins his widowed correspondent to delight in washing the feet of travelling saints.
337.2	SHRINE OF ALBAN: cf. p. 344 below.
337.2	MARTYRS SHRINES: Gildas 10; *sanctorum martyrum ... corporum sepulturae et passionum loca ... quam plurima.* He names St. Albans and Caerleon; St. Martha's, near Guildford, *TQ 02 48*, is probably another, cf. Arnold-Foster

SCD 2, 559, cf. 509; and EPNS Surrey 244. The place name Merthyr, usually joined with the name of a sixth-century saint, is common in south Wales, in and by the territories where Roman literate civilisation was deep rooted. Some of these shrines may have held imported relics maintained by monks.

337.2   BEDE: HE 1, 26.

337.2   SCHOOLS: see p. 409 and E Coelestius.

337.3   PATRICK: *Ep.*, 2 and 15, cf. E.

337.3   NYNIA: Bede HE 3, 4, cf. E and p. 191 above.

337.3   CHURCH . . . NAME: see D and p. 146 below.

337.4   ROSNAT: see L.

338.1   EXCAVATION: see L Whithorn.

338.3   PELAGIUS: see E, cf. JTS 16, 1965, 26 ff.; his *Commentary* on the Pauline Epistles, PL Sup. 1, 1110 ff.

338.3   JOHN CASSIAN: see F.

338.3   JURA: cf. Greg. Tur. *Vitae Patrum* 1, and BHL Lupicinus, Romanus, 5073–4, 7309.

338.3   MONTALEMBERT: *Les Moines d'Occident* 1, 288 (English edition, 1,514).

338.4   HONORATUS: see DCB.

338.4   FAUSTUS: see E. The suggestion that he was 'Breton' rather than British is anachronistic. Faustus came to Lérins 40 years before the second migration to northern Gaul, a century before the third migration turned Armorica into 'Lesser Britain'.

339.1   AMATOR: see DCB, and p. 349 below.

339.2   AUGUSTINE: and other European ecclesiastics, see DCB, cf. F.

339.2   AUGUSTINE: the texts of the Pelagian controversy are assembled in PL 45, 1679 ff.; 48, 319 ff.; 56, 490 ff.; cf. Mansi 4, 444 ff.; and are discussed in JTS 16, 1965, 51 ff.

340.1   ONE MAN: Sicilian Briton *de Divitiis* 8, 1–3.

340.2   LOOK YOU NOW: *de Divitiis* 6–7.

341.1   CAMEL: *de Divitiis* 18, 1–3.

341.2   LISTEN: *de Divitiis* 17, 3, concluding words.

341.2   MANKIND IS DIVIDED: *de Divitiis* 5 *tria enim ista sunt in quae humanum gens dividitur; divitiae, paupertas, sufficientia.*

341.2   ABOLISH THE RICH: *de Divitiis* 12 *tolle divitem et pauperum non invenies . . . Pauci enim divites pauperum sunt causa multorum.*

341.2   THEOLOGIANS: cf. C.P. Caspari *Briefe*, page v.

341.2   UNIQUE: the nearest parallels to the Sicilian Briton's concepts are expressed by his contemporary John Chrysostom of Antioch, Patriarch of Constantinople 398–404; but Chrysostom's argument is less analytical, simple and direct, his practical conclusion less sharp and positive.

342.2   PROTESTANTISM: cf. e.g., G. de Plinval *Pélage* 405 *combien d'éléments inconsciemment pélagiens ont reparu dans le protestantisme anglo-saxon ou scandinave.*

342.2   WORKS COPIED: listed in Migne PL Supplement 1. Many MSS are known by the name of the monastery from whose library they come; the origin of those known only by the catalogue number of a major central library has not yet been systematically explored.

342.3   PELAGIAN WRITERS: Pelagius, the Sicilian Briton, Fastidius, and the author of *de Virginitate* were British, Coelestius probably Irish; Julianus of Aeclanum was Italian, the author of *de Divina Lege* of unknown origin. The writings of several other continental Pelagians have not been preserved; the writings of Faustus, also British, imply a Pelagian background in youth.

342.3   CITED IN BRITAIN: Gildas 38 cites *de Virginitate* 6 as the work of *quidam nostrum*, 'one of us', of our fellow countrymen, cf. JTS 16, 1965, 36. The tract is one of half a dozen similar works similarly preserved, and it is therefore probable that the whole collection was known to Gildas, and approved by him; though the sentiment is repeated by the Sicilian Briton and others, the exact wording is used only in *de Virginitate*.

343.3   GERMANUS IN BRITAIN: Constantius *vita Germani* 12 ff., excerpted word for word by Bede HE I, 17 ff., cf. p. 62 above. Prosper says that he was sent by Pope Celestine, Constantius that he was sent by a Gallic synod at the request of anti-Pelagians in Britain. Both are plainly right; a Gallic synod could not intervene without the Pope's approval, nor could the Pope wisely intervene without Gallic support. MGH wrongly omits the words cited on p. 344. See E.

345.2   PALLADIUS: see E.

345.2   PATRICK: see E and p. 64 above.

345.3   POPE CELESTINE: Prosper *contra Collatorum* 21 (PL 51, 271).

346.4   PRELATES LEARNED: Patrick *Confessio* 13.

348.2   TWO PATRICKS: see E., and especially T.O'Rahilly *The Two Patricks*; J. Carney *The Problem of Patrick* and SILH 324 ff.; D.Binchy *Studia Hibernica* 2, 1962, 7–173; JTS 17, 1966, 358 ff.; for older views cf. e.g. Todd *Patrick* and Bury *Patrick*.

348.3   INFORMATIVE TEXTS: the *Hymn of Secundinus* LH I, 7 was probably composed in the 5th century, Kenney 260, CPL 16; but, though its author may have known Patrick, it gives little information about him.

348.3   MUIRCHU: see T.

348.3   ANONYMOUS LIFE: Colgan's *vita Secunda* TT 11 ff., cf. E Patrick; the texts and traditions that underlie this Life require study.

348.3   OTHER EARLY ACCOUNTS: Tirechan, 'Muirchu Book II', Probus, the Book of the Angel, etc. collected in Stokes VT and Colgan TT; several texts have been published independently; cf. Kenney 165 ff.; 319 ff.

348.4   VICTORICUS: see E, cf. also JTS 17, 1966, 359.

349.2   AMATOR: see E; Muirchu, and derivative texts, have Patrick ordained by Germanus and consecrated by Amator(ex), a neighbouring bishop; Muirchu's source did not make it plain to him that Amator was Germanus' predecessor, and died in 418; he understood *ordinatio* by two separate bishops to mean two contemporary bishops; since the bishops were successive, the original probably meant that he was ordained deacon by Amator, priest by Germanus.

349.4   FARTHER REGIONS: *Confessio* 51.

350.1   PATRICK ... FORGOTTEN: Kenney p. 324.

350.3   DOCCO: see E.

350.3   ST. KEW: founded long before Samson's visit, c. 530, cf. E Samson.

351.1   BISHOP CONSECRATED: the normal reluctance of popes and patriarchs to permit a multiplicity of bishops and a potentially independent metropolitan is emphasised by the exceptional nature of the privileges granted to Augustine among the English and to Boniface in Germany. Results were sometimes bizarre; until the 20th century, only one bishop was permitted in Abyssinia, and each new bishop was obliged to travel to Egypt for consecration. The mid seventh century plague produced a comparable temporary difficulty in the English church; without sufficient bishops to consecrate new bishops, the episcopate could not have continued in Ireland in the fifth century after Patrick's death.

351.1   NORTHERN SEES: see A index. Few of the sees became permanent.

351.1   CHURCHMEN ... BRITISH: e.g. Mel (Mael), Mocteus, etc., see E index.

351.2   ARMAGH ... DEFERENCE: e.g. the bishop of Armagh is named first in the address of Pope John's letter to the Irish bishops in 640, Bede HE 2, 19.

351.2   ARCHBISHOP: Cogitosus, prologue (TT 518), writing not later than c. 650 (cf. E) calls Conlaed of Kildare (died 517, see E) *archiepiscopus Hiberniansium episcoporum* and describes Kildare as *caput pene omnium Hiberniensium eclesiarum ... cuius parrochia per totam Hiberniensem terram diffusam a mari usque ad mare extensa est* 'head of almost all the Irish churches ... whose diocese extends throughout Ireland from sea to sea'. The claims are no less extravagant than those put forward for Armagh half a century later; but are less remarked because they were not accepted, and not repeated. Some later Leinster clerics (e.g. Maedoc, see E) are entitled 'archbishop of Leinster', but not of Ireland.

351.2   DIOCESAN CLERGY: the sources are surveyed by Kathleen Hughes, CEIS especially pp. 79 ff.

351.3   BRIGIT: see E.

351.3   CONLAED ... CHAPLAIN: Cogitosus, prologue (TT 518) is explicit; Brigit was 'prudently concerned' that the Kildare houses should be governed 'properly in all respects', and because

> without a bishop who could consecrate churches and appoint clergy ... this was not possible, she summoned an illustrious hermit ... to govern the church with her, with the status of bishop, so that her churches should not lack clergy.

Nothing is said of how she got him consecrated, or by whom.

352.2   AILBE, CIARAN, DECLAN, IBAR, ENDA, KEBI: see E.

352.2   EUGENIUS, TIGERNACH: see E.

352.3   FAENCHA: she is likely to have been one of the numerous Irish girls to whom Patrick gave the veil, see E.

352.4   ROSNAT: Whithorn, see L and p. 337 above.

353.1   ANGUS: see A 492.

353.2   POPE: the patriotic tale of the two-day British or Irish pope occurs in several Lives.

353.2   FINNIAN, MACCRICHE, ERLATHEUS: see E.

353.3   ETELIC: see G BM; made uncle of Cadoc and of Paul Aurelian, both born in about 500.

353.3   FINTAN: see E.

355.2   VOYAGES: cf. p. 384 below.

355.2   CORNWALL: cf. p. 130 above.

19 Sixth-Century Monks (pp. 356-388)

356.2   BRIOC: and other names, see E.

357.1   LIFE OF SAMSON: see T. The Life was written before the episcopate of Thuriau, bishop of Dol about 610.

363.2   LIFE OF PAUL AURELIAN: early spellings, e.g. Tigernomaglus (ch. 11); Quonomorius (ch. 8); villa Banhedos (ch. 8).

363.2   WILDERNESS: *ut heremi deserta penetraret, ibique a consortio mundalis vitae sequestratus ... vitam duceret* (ch. 6).

363.3   CHILDEBERT: often called 'Philibert' in the Lives.

364.2   PLOU-...TRE-: Paul Aurelian (*vita* 12) found a still recognisable Roman estate (*fundus*) in the *Plebs Telmedovia*, now Plou-Dalmazeau (Map 14, p. 263, D 2, number 22) which became 'one of his hundred *tribus*' wherein his followers built their *habitacula* (houses); Fracan (*vita Winwaloe* 1, 2) found another estate, near St. Brieuc (Map 14 *N 2*) 'of the right size for a *plebs*', which 'is now named after its finder', to-day Plou-Fragan. Both Lives are 9th-century texts that used 6th-century written sources.

The organisational form of a *plebs* comprising a number of *tribus* containing houses has one precedent. Jerome's account of Pachomius' organisation of the Egyptian monks (PL 23, 69 ff.; 50, 275 ff.; preface 2, and *passim*) explains that 'three or four houses were federated into one *tribus*' with 'thirty or forty houses to one monastery', a *populus* or *plebs Dei*, a people of God; Bangor-on-Dee was also divided into seven *portiones*, equivalent to Jerome's *tribus*, 'none with less than 300 men', who necessarily lived in separate houses (Bede HE 2, 2).

The monastic terminology was riveted upon secular usage. *Plou-* and variants are the normal names of early district centres in Brittany and sometimes in Cornwall; *plwyf* is used for parish in Welsh, but does not occur in place names. *Tre-* is the commonest form of village name in all British lands where monasteries were numerous, Brittany, Cornwall, Wales and the Clyde kingdom (Watson CPNS 358 ff., with some possible extension as a suffix in Pictland), but not in Reged, between the Solway and the Mersey, (EPNE 185; EPNS Cumberland 116), where monasteries were limited to a small region (Map 26, p. 371). *Tref* (*trev* in Brittany) is the normal Welsh for village, equivalent to English *-tun*. *Ty*, house, and, in Brittany, *ker*, fortified enclosure, are also common in the names of farmsteads. Once established, the name forms remained in use, to give Treharris, Treherbert etc. in the 19th century; but very many of the personal names attached to *Tre-* are those of persons known to have lived in the 6th or 7th centuries.

The linguistic origin of *tribus* and *tref* is not known. It may derive from an Indo-European original, that might also underlie Germanic *terp*, *dorf*, *throp*, *thorp*, etc, but no such root is known; it does not occur among the very numerous Celtic place names of the Roman world, and is unlikely to be connected with Gallic *Atrebates*, since, apart from linguistic difficulties, 'those who live at home (or in houses)' is an unlikely name for nation. Irish *treabh*, village, also exceedingly rare in place names (Watson CPNS 357) is likely to derive from *tref*. The short vowel of *tribus* would by oral transmission be expected to give Welsh *trif*, or perhaps *trwyf*; but the term was no longer in normal spoken use in the late Empire; it was adopted by men who read what Jerome wrote; similarly the English read Jerome's *tribus* and pronounced it 'tribe', with a long vowel. The linguistic origin of *plebs*, *plou-*, *plwyf*, and of words for 'house', is clearer.

366.3   DEMETIA ... GLEVISSIG: Teilo is said to have instituted bishops in both kingdoms, in or about the 570s, LL 115; 131. The appointments corresponded with the creation of the separate Glevissig monarchy, cf. pp. 228 and 208.

367.3   DAVID: see E. He was born *anno XXX post discessum Patricii* ⟨*de Menevia*⟩ ACm, at 458. The words *de Menevia*, 'from St. David's', are evidently a gloss added to the original by a copyist who mistook *discessus*, death, for 'departure', and allied it with a tradition that Patrick had sailed for Ireland in 432 from Porth Mawr, by St. David's. The round figure of 30 years after the death of Patrick, entered in most annals at various years in the 490s, gives a date in the 520s, consistent with baptism by Ailbe. He died in 589, A (AI, cf. AT, AC, CS). The corrupt entry or entries of ACm 601 *David Episcopus. Moni Iudaeorum* (perhaps for *Mons Giudiorum*, intending *Urbs Giudi*, Stirling), whatever their meaning or origin, do not evidence a belief in a variant death date at odds with the main Annals tradition. *David Episcopus* might derive from an Irish

Annal, not otherwise preserved, concerning Mobhi of Inch (see **E**), who is sometimes called David in Irish texts.

368.1 PAULINUS: ECMW 139, cf. **E**.

368.2 RULE OF DAVID: Ricemarchus *vita David* 21–30. The words transcribed by Ricemarchus, *suffosoria vangasque invicto brachio terre defigunt* (22), are also cited by Gildas *Ep.* 4 *suffosoria figentes terrae*, and therefore derive from a sixth-century original. Ricemarchus cannot have copied Gildas, for even if he had known his Letters, he could not have identified the unnamed monk whom Gildas abused with his own hero.

368.3 ABSTINENCE . . . : Gildas *Ep.* 2.

368.3 THEY CRITICISE BRETHREN . . . : Gildas *Ep.* 3.

369.1 ABBOT: Gildas *Ep.* 4.

369.2 CASSIODORUS: see **F**.

369.3 ABBOTS: Gildas *Ep.* 5.

370.1 BREFI: see **L**.

370.1 DIFFERENT REGIONS: see especially Bowen SCSW, particularly the maps on pp. 38 and 52.

370.3 PLACES UP THE FOSSE WAY: see **E** David, Samson.

370.3 FOSSE WAY: beyond it, Elphin of Warrington, and of North Frodingham in the East Riding, was Welsh by name.

370.3 IRISH MONKS: see **E** Abban, Columba of Terryglass, cf. pp. 386 ff. below.

370.3 WINWALOE: cf. p. 314.3 above.

372.1 WILFRED: Eddius 17.

374.3 SCATTERED HERMITS . . . BRITISH: e.g. Daniel of Hare Island (*vita Ciaran Clonmacnoise* 25).

374.3 FIRST ORDER: *Catalogus* see **T**.

374.3 MONASTERIES: most were far removed from the seats of kings; the few that lie near to royal centres include Columba's Derry and Kells, and the Leinster houses of Kildare, Glendabough and Ferns.

375.1 TUATHAL: cf. p. 169.2 above.

375.3 SAINTS OF IRELAND CAME: Irish-language Life, Stokes *Lismore Lives* 2640.

376.1 FULL OF KNOWLEDGE: *vita Finniani* 34.

376.1 DAVID, CATHMAEL: Irish-language Life, Stokes *Lismore Lives* 2527 ff.

376.2 WINE: *vita Ciaran* 31.

376.2 AGRICULTURE: cf. pp. 432 below.

377.2 BLESSED IS GOD: *vita Ciaran* 33 cf. p. 169 above.

377.3 CUIL DREMHNI: cf. p. 173 above.

377.4 ADOMNAN: *Columba* 3, 3; I, I.

378.1 WHEN THE NEWS CAME . . . : *vita Columbae* (O'Donnell) 2, 5 (TT 410), cf. ZCP 9, 1913, 268, paragraph 180.

379.3 TRADITION OF GILDAS: *vita Gildas* (Rhuys) 11–12 *Ainmericus rex . . . misit ad beatum Gildam rogans ut . . . veniens ecclesiasticum ordinem in suo regno restauraret* etc.; cf. *vita Gildas* (Caradoc) 5 *Gildas . . . remanens in Hibernia studiam regens et praedicans in civitate Ardmaca.*

379.3 ELDERS OF IRELAND: Colgan TT 463 (50), also printed Reeves *Adomnan* 193, note a.

379.3 COLUMBAN . . . GILTA: MGH *Epp.* 3, 158.

379.3 GILDAS' RULE: *Penitential* 17–18; 22; 27.

381.2 AGRICULTURE . . . ECONOMY: cf. p. 432 below.

381.2 SCIENTIFIC ENQUIRY: e.g. Virgilius, Dicuil, etc. cf. p. 402 below.

381.3 LITERACY: some of Taliesin's poems in Welsh were probably composed as early, but were probably not written down until the 7th century.

381.3 DAGAEUS: *vita* (Sal) 3, cf. 4–6.

381.4 KILDARE CHURCH: Cogitosus *vita Brigit* 35 (TT 523–4).

382.5 CHURCHMEN AND KINGS: e.g. Benedict Biscop; Ine and Ceadwalla, Coenred and Offa, Bede HA 2 ff.; HE 5, 7; 5, 19.

382.5 AETHERIA: CSEL 39, 35 ff., cf. T.

383.1 XENODOCHIA: e.g. the 4th-century British frequented the *Xenodochium in Portu Romano* Jerome *Ep.* 77, last paragraph.

383.1 BONIFACE: *Ep.* 78.

383.1 BRITISH MONK: Greg. Tur. HF 5, 21; 8, 34, cf. E Winnoc, and p. 250 above.

383.2 RADEGUND: see E John of Chinon, Radegundis.

383.2 CARANTOCUS: *vita Columbani* 7, cf. E.

383.2 NORTHERN GAUL: see D and Map 4, p. 89, cf. p. 90 above. Casual observation has remarked about a hundred place names and church dedications extending from western Normandy as far east as St. Pol (de Leon), the proper name of the Dunkirk beaches, and Samson near Namur; systematic enquiry, so far confined to Canon Doble's study of the records of the diocese of Rouen, is likely to discover more. Many of these names are due to the Armorican British, some to migration direct from Britain. On the Belgian littoral, Winnoc's name is still prominent, though it is nowadays most obvious in the names of boarding-houses, restaurants and branded goods. The monks probably often preached where their countrymen had settled previously.

383.2 SPAIN: see E index. Excerpts from the texts are reprinted in HS 2, 99 ff. and discussed by E.A.Thompson in *Christianity in Britain* 201 ff., citing P.David *Galice et Portugal*.

384.1 VOYAGES: *Immrama* cf. Kenney 406 ff. CEIS 233 ff. Some of the Irish-language tales are translated in P.W.Joyce, *Old Celtic Romances*, the *Navigatio Brendani*, in J.F.Webb, *Lives of the Saints*, cf. Selmer *Navigatio Sancti Brendani*.

384.1 BRENDAN AND MALO: see E. The two voyages, *vita I Brendani* 13; 64–66.

384.1 ITA: *vita I Brendani* 71.

384.1 SAILED WESTWARD . . . : *vita I Brendani* 13.

384.2 THIS IS THE LAND . . . : *vita I Brendani* 65.

385.1 BRITAIN . . . HERESY: *vita I Brendani* 87.

385.1 MANUSCRIPTS: date, cf. Plummer VSH I, xxi ff., commenting 'the compiler . . . has earned our gratitude by preserving for us materials which exist nowhere else'; cf. xxxvii and Kenney 410 (ninth-century date).

385.1 ICELAND: see L.

385.2 YOUR KINGDOM . . . : *vita I Brendani* 95.

385.2 FIFTY ROYAL TOWNS . . . : *vita I Brendani* 80, where *oppida regum* probably means the raths of *tuath* kings.

386.1 ABINGDON: *civitatem que dicitur Abbaindun vel Dun Abbain* vita Abbani 14; cf. 13 *civitatem gentilem et deditam ydolis*. The early spellings *Aebbandun, Abbandun, Abbendun,* originally referred to another site, perhaps Boar's Hill, whence the name was removed to the later abbey and town DEPN 1; cf. MA 12, 1968, 26 ff.; see L. Medieval English tradition held that a Roman temple had formerly occupied the site; some 500 Roman coins are reported from Abingdon. The number is exceptionally large for a rural site away from a road; such concentrations are commoner in Roman temple enclosures than on farms.

386.2 COLUMBA OF TERRYGLASS: *vita* (Sal.) 10 cf. E. The direct route from Tours to Ireland passed through no English area at this date. Columba's detour suggests a visit to Abingdon, or possibly to Caistor-by-Norwich or Leicester, the nearest likely centres of royal cremation.

387.2 HOMELESS LAND: Reeves *Adomnan* 274; 266.

20 Seventh-Century Church (pp. 389–405)

389.1   BEDE: HE 3, 4.

389.3   AUGUSTINE: Bede HE 1, 26.

390.1   BRITISH . . . MEETING . . . AUGUSTINE: Bede HE 2, 2, at *Augustinaes Ac*, 'on the borders of the Hwicce and the West Saxons', perhaps Aust, *ST 57 88*, now the English end of the Severn Bridge.

390.2   THIS PRESENT LIFE . . . : Bede HE 2, 13.

391.4   AEDAN: Bede HE 3, 5, cf. **E**.

392.2   WEST SAXON . . . BAPTISM: Bede HE 3, 7; cf. 3, 22 (East Saxons), 3, 21 (Mercians, Peada).

392.2   BARKING AND CHERTSEY: Bede HE 4, 6.

392.2   BURGH CASTLE, BOSHAM: cf. **E** Fursey, Dicuil, Cedd etc.

392.2   BRIXWORTH: see **L**; cf. also Lyminge in Kent.

394.2   LINDISFARNE: Bede HE 3, 26.

394.3   WILFRED . . . ENDOWMENTS: Eddius 17.

394.4   EASTER CONTROVERSY: see p. 399 below.

394.5   WHITBY: Bede HE 3, 25, dated 664 HE 3, 26, after Easter, but early in the year, since Chad left for the south after the synod, but had not heard of the death of Deusdedit of Canterbury (14 July 664) until he reached Kent (HE 3, 28).

395.2   CHAD: Bede HE 3, 28.

395.3   CHAD AND THEODORE: Bede HE 4, 3.

396.2   PICTS, MERCIANS, IRISH: Eddius 19–20, Bede HE 4, 26.

396.3   HEXHAM: Eddius 22.

396.3   WORLDLY GLORY: Eddius 24.

397.1   FOUL WEEDS . . . IRISH: Eddius 47.

397.1   RULE OF BENEDICT: the Rule is named, and chapter 64 cited by Bede *Historia Abbatum* 11, cf. 16. The Rule was probably set down before 550, and made extensive use of an earlier Rule, probably of about 500 or soon after, perhaps drawn up at Lérins or Marseille; the arguments are discussed by David Knowles, *Great Historical Enterprises*, 1963, 137 ff.

397.2   IONA CUSTOM: Bede HE 3, 4.

397.3   LLANDAFF: see **T** Gospel Books, *Liber Landavensis*.

399.2   CONFORMITY WITH ROME: summarised by Kenney 210 ff., Plummer *Bede 2*, 348 ff., etc.; see **E** Aed of Sletty etc.

399.2   KILDARE: cf. p. 351 above.

399.2   MEMORY OF PATRICK: cf. p. 350 above.

400.2   MONASTICISM IN EUROPE: the sources are summarised by Kenney 486 ff., cf. **E** index.

402.3   VIRGILIUS: see **E**.

403.2   ALCUIN: see **E** and pp. 331 ff. above.

403.4   NATIONALITY . . . MONASTICISM: much misunderstanding arises from the indiscriminate and undefined modern terminology of 'Irish' or 'English' missionary movements in Europe, particularly in accounts of the 8th century. Boniface and Virgilius of Salzburg disagreed deeply on matters of moment; but their disagreements had little to do with the accident that one was of English birth, the other Irish. Modern emphasis on their birth often leads to considerable confusion, cf. e.g. note to Map 29; and sometimes tempts historians to exaggerate the importance of their fellow-countrymen and to belittle the impact of the foreigner upon their own history. The initial driving forces behind the monastic movement in Europe, north of the Alps and the Massif Central, were a blend of Irish zeal and English discipline. But after the first pioneering generations these influences, together with those of the environment of each monastery, worked with differing strength on different individuals, English, Irish, French or German, whatever their personal national origin.

21 Letters (pp. 406–428)

406.2   ROMAN EMPIRE: the evidence is surveyed in Jones LRE 991 ff.

406.2   ANKARA: Jerome *Commentary* on the Epistle to the Galatians 2(3) (PL 26, 357).

406.2   SEVERUS: Dialogues 1, 27.

406.2   SIDONIUS: *Ep.* 3, 3, 2, *sermonis Celtici squarma.*

407.2   LONDON ARTISANS: Merrifield *Roman London* plate 101.

407.2   LATIN WORDS: Jackson LHEB 78–80 lists a selection.

407.3   BRITISH LATIN: Jackson LHEB 108 ff.

408.2   AETHERIA: the Rhone, ch. 18, 2. The date is probably early fifth-century, but might be later, as Meister in *Rheinisches Museum* 64, 1909, 337 ff. The Latinity is analysed and discussed by E.Lofstedt, *Peregrinatio Aetheriae.*

408.3   LATIN . . . DIED: the late 6th century Armorican British Latin of the first Life of Samson is as pedestrian as the language of Aetheria, but is still a living idiom; but in the 8th century Nennius is 'laboriously thinking first in Welsh and then translating', LHEB 121, cf. THS Cymm., 1946–7, 55–56.

408.3   MORI MARUSA: Pliny NH 4, 27, citing Philemon.

409.1   MAEGL: SC 577, which has 'the look of contemporary record' LHEB 677.

409.2   IRISH . . . SCHOOLS . . . PRESERVE LATIN: and Greek, see especially K.Meyer, *Learning in Ireland*, where, however, the statement of a 12th-century MS that 'all the learned of the whole empire fled abroad and increased the learning of Ireland' is unfounded (cf. **M** Gallic Migration); cf. LHEB 122 ff.

409.3   EDUCATION: the evidence for Roman education is collected and discussed by H.L.Marrou, *Education in Antiquity*, cf. *St. Augustin*, and is summarised by Jones, LRE 987 ff.

409.3   SICILIAN BRITON: away from school *Ep.* 1, 5; classes *de Divitiis* 12, 5; cf. **E**.

409.3   FLUENT GREEK: *eius responsionem Graeco eloquio prolatam* Augustine *de Gestis Pelagii* 4, cf. 2; and cf. 19 (Orosius).

410.2   WHITHORN: cf. **L** and **E** Maucennus.

410.2   COELESTIUS: cf. **E**; p. 339 above; JTS 16, 1965, 41.

410.2   ILLTUD: cf. **E**. His school is described in the Lives of Samson, written about 600, and of Paul Aurelian (9th century), both of which used written texts of the 6th century.

410.2   SONS OF LAYMEN: e.g. Maelgwn, Gildas, Faelan, Colman of Leinster, (*vita Coemgen* 31), and others.

410.3   OUR THINKING: *vita Pauli Aureliani* 6.

411.1   GIMNASIA: e.g. *vita Kebi* 1.

411.1   COLLEGIUM: *vita Winwaloe* 1, 11.

411.1   CANE: *vita Niniani* 10; *Kentigerni* (Jocelyn) 5; cf. e.g. Ausonius *Protrepticon* 33; Augustine *Confessio* 1, 28; Sidonius *Ep.* 2, 10.

411.1   TEILO: LL 101, cf. 98, *stultorum philosophorum.* These attitudes are noticeably rare in the accounts of other saints.

411.2   TEACHERS . . . GAUL AND BRITAIN: for the modern myth of a migration of Gallic scholars see **M** Gallic Migration, and p. 409 above.

411.2   MOCTEUS: see E.

412.1   DRUSTICC: see E Finnian of Moville.

412.2   CURRICULUM: in Britain, Samson was at school from the age of 5 to 18 or 20; Leonorus from 5 to 15; Kebi from 7; Brioc from 10 or 12 to 24; Malo and Paul Aurelian from 'an early age', Paul to 16. The curriculum seems to have regarded Leonorus' 10 years as normal; Winninus stayed for 'the two *lustra*', the ten year period, and Maudetus 'finished his curriculum in 7 years' and therefore 'did not complete his *decennium*'; cf. E. In Ireland, Brendan of Clonfert entered school at 5, Findchua Bri Gobban (*Lismore Lives* 2834) at 7; in England Bede's education lasted from the age of 7 until his ordination as deacon 12 years later, Willibrord's from 'weaning' till the age of 20.

412.2   PAYMENT: e.g. *vita Samson* (1) 7, cf. (2) 1, 5, *donaria secundum morem*; one cow, *vita Ciaran Clonmacnoise* 15.

412.2   FUNDS: e.g. *vita Columba Terryglass* 5; in the early days of Finnian of Clonard's school his pupils took it in turns to provide the common meal, by labour, by purchase, or *per postulationem ab aliis*, by asking from others, lay neighbours.

412.2   STUDENT MEALS: e.g. *Hisperica Famina* 303 ff., cf. 222 ff.

412.3   AGILBERT: Bede HE 3, 7.

412.3   IRISH EDUCATIONAL SYSTEM: Bede HE 3, 27.

413.2   TECHNOLOGICAL SKILLS: see p. 433 ff. below.

413.3   RUADAN: vita 14, cf. *vita Finnian* of Clonard 24–26, cf. E.

414.1   ALDHELM: *Ep.* 5., cf. 3.

414.2   GREGORY: HF, *Praefatio Prima*.

414.3   LITERATURE: comment is here restricted to matter relevant to the history and impact of the Arthurian period. Space does not permit a balanced survey.

414.3   GILDAS: see M. Winterbottom, *Gildas*, introduction.

415.1   MAELGWN'S BARDS: Gildas 34, 6, cf. p. 219 above.

415.3   VIRGILIUS MARO: see F.

415.3   BONIFACE: *Ep.* 9, written in youth to Nithard, is phrased in extravagant Hisperic. Boniface (Winfrith) was educated at Exeter and at Nursling, near Southampton, but in adult years in Europe wrote normal European Latin; cf. E.

415.3   ALDHELM: see E, and p. 498 below.

415.3   WESTERN LATIN: the main texts are summarised by Kenney, 250 ff.; cf. E Aldhelm, Boniface; F, Virgilius Maro. The word Hisperic is best confined to texts with fantasy vocabulary, as the *Hisperica Famina*, the word Western used for the wider literature, including Aldhelm.

415.3   HISPERIC: named from the *Hisperica Famina*, ed. F.J.H.Jenkinson, Cambridge, 1908, including related texts; cf. M. Winterbottom *Celtica* 8, 196, 126 ff., and Ker *Dark Ages* 31 note 4, etc.

416.3   CUNOBELINUS, BELIN: cf. G BE. The words of Suetonius, *Caligula* 44, *Adminio Cynobellini Britannorum regis filio* are transcribed by Orosius (7, 5, 5) as (*ad*) *Minocynobelinum Britannorum regis filium*; in Arthurian Britain the name was evidently read, with the corruption of a single letter, as *Minocyni Belinum*. The earliest person known to have been named Beli(n) was born about, or just before, the middle of the sixth century, see G BG. The name was readily accepted because it occurred occasionally in Irish and Gallic mythology, though not as the name of a historical person (cf. CGH index p. 519); and 'Minocynus' resembled the Irish sea god Manannan, son of Lir, later adopted into Welsh literature as Manawydan.

416.4   COROTICUS: Muirchu 28, *musicam artem audivit a quodam cantare, quod de solio regali transiret* cf. p. 219 above; the poet 'blasphemed' or 'satirised' the king, foretelling his end. To be effective, he is more likely to have sung in British than in Irish.

416.4   MAELGWN: Gildas 34, 6, cf. p. 415 above.

416.4   NENNIUS: 62, cf. **Q**.

417.1   OLDEST POEMS: see **M** and **T**. Most of the early poems survive in a few major medieval collections. Texts, not always accurately transcribed, were published by W.F.Skene FAB, with translations that outdo all other publications of bad verse in the English language. Most of the main MSS were published in transcript or facsimile by J.G.Evans 70 years ago, and several of the main poems have been edited by Sir Ifor Williams, with notes and introduction in modern Welsh, and by A.O.H.Jarman. Only the *Gododdin* has been accurately but literally translated in full, by Kenneth Jackson, but selections have appeared in most anthologies and histories of Welsh literature, cf. Works Cited, Sources, below.

417.3   DINOGAD: CA 88 (lines 1101 ff.), translated Parry HWL 22.

419.2   MAXIMUS' WIFE: Maximus first came to Britain in 367–368; his son was a child in 383, cf. PLRE I, Victor 14, and is shown on coin portraits of 384 to 388 as a boy of 16 to 18. In 388 Maximus' daughters were apparently still unmarried, Ambrose *Ep.* 40, 32. He may have met and married his wife in Britain; her name is not known; several fourth-century empresses were named Helena.

420.2   ISIDORE: *Etymologiae* 9, 102, *Britones quidam Latine nominatos suspicantur eo quod bruti sunt*; cf. Heiric *vita Germani* 3, 246–247, *Britannia, brutis Barbara quo feritet gens ultro moribus omnis.*

420.2   CUANU: cf. **E**; ' "Britus son of Silvius son of Ascanius . . . Aeneas the father of Ascanius, ancestor of Britan the odious". Thus our noble senior Guanach deduced the genealogy of the British from the Chronicles of the Romans', Irish Nennius (*Lebor Bretnach*) 6, translated into Latin, Zimmer, *Nennius Interpretatus*, MGH AA 13 p. 152. 'Guanach' is a mis-spelling of Cuana (cf. MGH p. 141), who probably died c. 640, cf. **E**.

420.3   LOEGRIUS: cf. e.g. the 14th century pleas to the Pope, printed in Skene CPS, especially pp. 222, 243–247.

420.5   WELSH LITERATURE: surveyed by T.Parry and H.I.Bell: anthologies and translations, in OBWV, by Gwyn Williams, Conran, Bell, Graves, E.D.Jones and others include medieval and modern verse, cf. CSW 103 ff., and Works Cited, I.

421.3   ENGLISH LITERATURE: see especially Works Cited, I.

421.3   AETHELBERT: Attenborough LEEK, cf. Bede HE 2, 5.

421.4   CAEDMON: Bede HE 4, 24. The curious modern notion that he was a 'cowherd', of 'humble' origin, rests on inexact reading of Bede's words, cf. **E** and p. 314 above.

421.4   CAEDMON'S VERSES: cf. Plummer *Bede* 2, 248–258 and subsequent literature; in the 19th century his name was read after verses inscribed on the Ruthwell Cross, in Dumfriesshire; cf. Sweet OET 125, etc.; the reading is doubted.

421.5   ENGLISH . . . LATIN: see especially · Manitius *Lateinischen Literatur* and Laistner *Thought and Letters*.

421.5   BEOWULF, WIDSITH: cf. **T**.

421.5   SAXON CHRONICLE: see **T**.

421.5   MONASTIC . . . RECORDS: Wilfred at Selsey, in the early 680s, was able to look up the day of Oswald's death in the 'books in which the burial of the dead were recorded' (Bede HE 4, 14). Selsey kept an up-to-date Martyrology, and is likely to have matched it with an annalistic record. The probable form is an entry in an Easter Table *Occisio Osuualdi nonis Aug*, under the year 642, transcribed into a copy of a Martyrology under the 5th day of August.

422.2   IRISH LITERATURE: see especially Dillon and Chadwick *Celtic Realms* 239 ff.; Schoepperle, *Tristan*, and Works Cited, I.

422.2   ROMAN WRITERS: especially Posidonius, most fully reported by Diodorus 5, 31; Caesar *de Bello Gallico*, especially 6, 13; Strabo 4, 4, 4; Ammian 15, 9, 8 citing Timagenes, where *euhages* misreads Greek *ouates*. The texts are summarised in N.K.Chadwick *The Druids* xiii ff.; cf. T.Kendrick *The Druids*; cf. A.Ll.Owen *The Famous Druids* 15 ff.; PIRA 60 C, 1959–60; cf. Jackson OIT, especially 39, ff.; etc.

422.3   FILID: the principal text is the Preface to the List of Tales in the Book of Leinster 189 b (24,915 ff.; 4,835), translated O'Curry 583 ff.

422.3   SECULAR SCHOOLS: cf. *Book of Aichill*, preface, cf. O'Curry 512, translated 50–51.

422.4   OGAM: cf. **O**; O'Curry 464 ff., Jackson LHEB 151 ff., where however the description of the staves as 'short', the 4th-century date, and the suggested origin among Irish colonists in Britain do not accommodate all the evidence. The script does not distinguish 'pagans' from 'Christians', Jackson LHEB 176, note 1. Varying sizes of sticks are envisaged in different tales. Some of them were long staffs cut from the trunks of small apple or yew trees (O'Curry 473, 475); others, as Patrick's 'wooden tablets', evidently Christian texts in Ogam characters, looked like swords (Book of Armagh 8 b 2, VT 300–301, with note), while others were much smaller. For the so-called 'Pictish Ogams', see p. 191.1 above.

422.4   CENNFAELAD: cf. **E**, and **G** INE.

423.2   REMOTE PAST: cf. p. 147 above.

423.2   WINDOW ... IRON AGE: Kenneth Jackson OIT.

423.2   ANCIENT STORY: S.H.O'Grady, *Silva Gadaelica*, vol. 1 (text), 2 (translation), contains a considerable collection, principally of tales set in the period of Finn or of the Historical Cycle; P.W.Joyce, *Old Celtic Romances*, translates a number of mythological tales, and some of the late extravagant and tediuos *Imrama* (Voyages), that contrast with the more matter-of-fact Latin versions, as the Irish-language Saints' Lives compare with their Latin originals. The *Tain Bo Cualgne* (Cattle Raid of Cooley), of the Heroic Age, has been several times edited with translation. There are several translations of smaller sections of the literature; K.Meyer and others have translated a number of poems; cf. also M.Dillon and N.K.Chadwick, *The Celtic Realms*, 227 ff., 244 ff., and Kenneth Jackson, *The International Popular Tale*.

423.4   MACFIRBIS: O'Curry 122, reproduced CS, introduction p. xix.

423.4   LITERARY FORMS: cf. e.g. Carney *Medieval Irish Lyrics*.

424.2   MILKING A BULL: Adomnan, 2, 17, in a partially rationalised version.

424.2   FECHIN OF FORE: *vita* 9 (VSH 2, 79) *Res miranda atque novitate inusitata. . . . Hoc enim possibile fuit illi solo qui produxit mel de petra, oleumque de saxo durissimo.*

424.3   SENAN: *vita* 20 (Sal. 748–749), lines 673–711. Translation loses some of the wit of the original, which is reinforced by solemn rhyme and alliteration. The fourth verse here cited, lines 683–684 reads

> *Nam, interruptis precibus,*   *egre ferebat monachus*
> *ablucione parvuli*   *sanctum liquorem pollui*

The tenth verse, lines 697–700 reads

> *Metitur quoque baculo*   *que sit maris altitudo*
> *volens tantum procedere*   *ut premineret pectore*
> *Huic inde, inquam, anxio*   *ista erat intencio*
> *Ut non intraret alcius*   *quam demonstraret baculus*

426.2   ATTRACTA: *vita* 12, Colgan ASH 280, *taediosus factus est tibi Dominus Deus tuus*.
426.2   ADOMNAN: Irish Life, extract printed with translation, Skene CPS 408.
427.2   GEOFFREY: see T.
427.3   GEOFFREY'S ... FANCY: in the 12th century deliberate satire need not involve modern rational detachment. In all ages the human mind is capable of believing what it knows to be untrue; and to creative writers of fiction the characters they invent are easily invested with reality. The sharp classical and modern distinction between fiction and fact was alien to the complex psychology of Geoffrey and his age; neither he nor his readers found difficulty in accepting the reality of his inventions, when they had been written down, published to the world, and established in the consciousness of men. There was no contradiction between a conscious jest and a genuine belief in its truth. Geoffrey's academic contemporaries were open to the charge that they could not see the wood for the trees, but Geoffrey's artificial trees made a real wood, a concept of British history fully in accord with the beliefs and aspirations of his own day.

22   The Economy (pp. 429–444)

429.1   ANCIENT LAWS: see J, and pp. 445, 467 below.
430.2   CURRENCY: see R.
430.3   MORE PEOPLE LIVED ... OR ... DIED: neither the size of the population of Roman Britain nor fluctuations thereof have yet been closely studied. Modern estimates have risen from about half a million in 1937 (Colingwood) to about two million in 1968 (Frere), and there is no sign that the estimates have stopped rising. They have however been limited to generalisations about the whole province, and have been hampered by an assumption that it is commendable to strain the evidence to make the figure as small as possible. Avoidable error in either direction is equally undesirable.

Closer estimates will be possible when the archaeological records of a large number of localities have been examined, and interpreted in the light of what is known of Roman population densities elsewhere, and of the earliest statistical record of Britain, the 11th-century Domesday Book.

At present it is only possible to note that in several parts of the country it is difficult to make the minimum Roman population implied by archaeological record as small as the population listed for the same areas in Domesday Book.

In the counties where the population is enumerated, Domesday Book lists a little under 300,000 adult males; the numbers of unlisted wives, children and other relatives are likely to multiply this figure about three to five times, giving a population in the neighbourhood of a million to a million and a half. To these must be added the population of Wales, of the northern counties excluded from the Survey, and various categories of unlisted persons, ploughmen in many regions, the occupants of houses and land entered as such, without numbers of people, and other categories. A substantial addition is needed to assess the mid 11th-century population. King William's devastation of the north is said to have cost 100,000 lives. The figure is patently a guess and doubtless exaggerated, but the casualties were plainly enormous; in Yorkshire the Survey listed 43 persons in one group of 411 manors, whose earlier population was necessarily much greater. Severe but less concentrated devastation is also reported in the Survey in many other parts of the country.

It is therefore probable that the mid 11th century population of the former Roman province was of the order of two to three million. If the thorough study of recorded Roman sites should suggest that the Roman population was normally somewhat greater, then it may argue an overall population of three to four millions.

The available evidence suggests that there were significant movements of population during the later Empire, but does not yet indicate whether the total population increased or decreased. The disasters of the Arthurian period however clearly reduced overall numbers. The urban and industrial population plainly declined; lands were wasted, and emigration and casualties removed people, though losses were doubtless partially offset by the weakening of imperial taxation, formerly a main factor in keeping down the birth rate, and by the immigration of some tens of thousands of English.

These considerations rest on inference rather than information, but the document termed the 'Tribal Hidage' (see T and p. 492 below), which iists a little over 200,000 hides in the midlands and the south, suggests the possibility that by the later 7th century population had fallen to a level not greatly in excess of the mid 11th century, when allowance is made for Wales, the north and the south-west. The Scandinavian invasions thereafter doubtless reduced native numbers, but added immigrants.

Until the evidence is more exactly studied, it is possible only to record that between the 4th century and the 11th the population is likely to have fluctuated between the outside limits of about 4,000,000 and about 2,000,000.

430.3   AUSONIUS' GRANDSON: 'Paulinus of Pella', cf. Works Cited, I.

431.1   GILDAS: ch. 26, 2; see p. 137 above.

431.3   ANIMAL BONES: L.Alcock (*Dinas Powys* 36) tabulates an analysis of animal bones, together with comparable figures from three sites in the Wessex downland (Woodyates, Rotherley and Woodcuts), and from a number of Irish sites. The proportions are

	Dinas Powys	Wessex	Ireland
Cattle	20%	33–39%	70–97%
Sheep	13%	29–40%	1–15%
Pig	61%	2–13%	1–27%
Horse	under 1%	10–26%	1% or less

V.B.Proudfoot (MA 5, 1961, 106) catalogues the presence or absence of animal bones reported in the excavation of some 45 Irish raths, but not the quantities. Cattle were reported at 20 sites, sheep at 8, pigs at 15, horses at 11. The figures in general match Alcock's; horses seem more numerous, for a number of sites each produced horse bones in small numbers. But among the animals named in the Book of Rights tribute lists, sheep are relatively commoner; the figures total 25,220 cattle, 12,340 sheep, 6,410 pigs, in percentages 57%, 28%, and 15%.

432.1   LLANCARFAN AND LLANDAFF: see T Gospel Books.

432.1   THREE OR FOUR COWS: 25 times out of 30. The five more expensive values are 10, 14, 14, 25 and 70.

432.1   LANDEILO: the Book of Chad, T Gospel Books.

432.1   WESSEX: Laws of Ine 70, 1.

432.1   BOOK OF RIGHTS: tributes summarised on pp. 179 ff. The legend of the *Boruma*, the cattle tribute levied on Leinster (cf. A 134 note), gives a payment of equal numbers of cattle and pigs, some texts adding sheep. Cauldrons are required for the king's brewing, but not barley to supply them, nor brewed beer. The lists include cloaks, flitches and beeves, in much smaller quantities than the animals. The texts are late, long after the expansion of arable farming. Legal texts and incidental stories place the same emphasis on cattle.

432.2   MONASTERIES . . . MANY: their size varied. Initial numbers are often small; Winwaloe and Paul Aurelian (with sufficient slaves) began with 12 monks, Samson with 14 monks and 7 *famuli*, Lunaire and Tudwal with 72 monks. In developed houses, Brioc had 168, Gudwal 180, Petroc and Paternus 80. Lasrian of Leighlin with 1,500 and MoChuta with 867 claim unusually large communities. Brendan's numerous monasteries held 3,000 between them. Maedoc took 150 out to harvest. Cadoc, Illtud and Kentigern (at Llanelwy, St. Asaph) are credited with a division between *clerici* and *operarii illiterati*, analogous to that drawn by Cassiodorus in Italy; Illtud and Cadoc maintained the poor, and Cadoc also maintained widows; Cadoc, king as well as abbot, is also assigned a military force, giving totals of 300 to Illtud, 500 to Cadoc, 965 to Kentigern. The traditions that Mocteus of Louth and Ruadan of Lothra, until constrained, maintained clerics who did no agricultural work implies a similar division. These figures are not excessive, though in the nature of the transmission they are liable to inflation in honour of the founding saint. Bede's figure (HE, 2, 2) of over 2,000 in a single monastery of Bangor-on-Dee is exceptionally large. Their hierarchical organisation is matched by Kentigern's '*illos per turmas et conventus dividens*'. The implication of the evidence is that most houses could be numbered in scores or hundreds; their impact was due to their number rather than their individual size.

432.3   DAVID, CARTHACUS; and others. See E, under the saints named.

433.2   TOOLS: e.g. the schedule of goods to be divided on divorce, p. 445 below; the price list of 250 items (VC 3, 22, etc) is probably copied from a Wessex list, and concerns the English more than the Welsh, cf. **Q, T.**

433.2   WATERMILL: e.g. Carthacus, Ciaran of Clonmacnoise, Eugenius (in Gaul), Fechin and Mo Choemog, Finnian of Moville, Fintan of Dunblesc, Gildas (in Brittany), Ita, Lugid, Gudwal (tidal), Flannan; canalisation, e.g. Fechin, Frigidian (in Italy), Moling. Usually, the nature of the mill is not specified; the donkey mill does not appear; where the power is specified, it is water, occasionally tidal.

433.2   CORN DRYING: Cainnech (Sal.) 35; Ciaran 12, *rota de virgis contexta plena spicis igne supposito*; Finnian (*Lismore* 2629); poem, Mocteus *M.Don.*, *M.Oeng.*, FM 535, also printed Todd *Patrick* 30. Three or four kilns have been excavated in raths (Proudfoot MA 5, 1961, 108 cf. 106), and the corn kiln (*odyn*) is frequently mentioned in Welsh Law (ALW indices).

434.4   ULTAN: the Life is early, written when prayer with arms outstretched was still normal in Ireland.

434.4   NOBLEMAN OF MACHA: *vita Brigit* (Ultan) 61 (TT 534).

435.1   ANOTHER OCCASION: *vita Brigit* (Ultan) 80 (TT 537).

435.2   GERALD: ch. 12 (VSH). 'Gerald' is represented as an Englishman; a number of English followed Colman of Lindisfarne, when he returned to Ireland, to found Mayo, in 664.

435.2   IUGERA: evidently translating Irish *immaire*; cf. a jumbled rehash of the story told in the *vita Gerald*, in the Hymm of Colman, preface, LH 1, 25; 2,12.

435.3   FLANNAN: (of Killaloe) ch. 31 (Sal.).

435.3   ANOTHER TRADITION: *Lebor na hUidre* 128, cited Plummer VSH xcvi 6.

436.3   LAW TRACT: the *Uraicecht Becc*, or 'Small Primer', ALI 5, 1, cf. MacNeill PIRA 36 c, 1923, 255 and *Celtic Ireland* 96 ff., dated by Binchy *Eriu* 18, 1958, 44 ff. to the '8th century or earlier' (p. 48), possibly contemporary with texts of c. 680 (pp. 51–52).

436.4   EXCAVATED RATHS: MA 5, 1961, 94 ff., especially pp. 94, 103 and selected plans p. 100.

436.5   LAW TRACT: ALI 5, 483, cited MacNeill *Celtic Ireland* 167–169.

437.3   STIRRUP: the metal innovation is well dated because it is preserved from numerous dated graves.

437.3   HORSE COLLAR: made of perishable material, and not buried in graves, and therefore less directly evidenced. Various early Slavonic forms are known, but cannot be closely dated; their ultimate origin seems however to be related to that of the stirrup. The evidence is discussed by Lefevre de Noëttes *Attelage*, and others.

437.4   NORICUM: the build of the animal, similar to the medieval Shire horse, is most clearly demonstrated by Roman figurines in Austrian museums, notably at Wels, the Roman Ovilava.

437.4   MONKS ... SLAVS: cf. Map 29, p. 401, and notes thereto.

437.4   SLAVS ... SUNDERED: cf. Map 17, p. 277.

438.2   PICTS: cf. **L**.

438.4   ENGLISH: see **S**.

440.2   CHURCHES OF WOOD: e.g. Cadoc and David in Wales, Goueznou in Brittany, Winniocus at Luxeuil in Burgundy (Jonas *Columban* 1, 15; 1, 17), Enda, Flannan of Killaloe, Mo-Choe and many others in Ireland, Finan of Lindisfarne and Aedan at York in Northumbria. Cianan's stone church at Duleek and Ninian's at Whithorn were both regarded as exceptional, the work of foreign craftsmen.

441.2   WINE: in Britain, cf. e.g. Piro, p. 360 above; in Ireland, Muirchu 18, cf. Stokes *Lismore Lives* 316; *vita Ciarani* clonmacnoise 31, cf. *Lismore* 4402.

441.2   COLUMBA: Adomnan 1, 28. *Sulfurea de caelo flamma* that killed 3,000 sounds like a volcano; perhaps Etna, since Vesuvius is not known to have erupted during Columba's lifetime. Reeves' 'Istria' derives from a late martyrologist's guess, cf. **L** Caput Regionis (Kintyre).

441.2   COLUMBAN: Jonas 23 *navis quae Scottorum commercia vexerat*, cf. *vita Winwaloe* 1, 19 *mercatoribus transmarina negotia ausportantibus ... ad Scotos* (from Brittany).

441.2   PORTH MAWR, PADSTOW: cf. **L**.

441.2   FINNIAN: *vita Finnian Clonard* (Sal.) 4, cf. **E**.

441.3   JOHN THE ALMSGIVER: ch. 9; about AD 600. There is no reason to change the date given in the text.

441.3   VALUE: did not greatly change in many centuries. Over 700 years later, the Book of Ballymote was sold for 140 cows, Kenney 24.

442.1   BOOK OF TEILO: LL xliii, cf. **T** Gospel Books.

442.2   SILVER INGOTS: cf. e.g. H. Willers, *Die roemischen Bronzeeimer von Hemmoor* 291, 'ex offi(cina) Isatis', found at London, Richborough, Coleraine in Ulster, Dierstorf (Minden) in Germany, and elsewhere.

442.4   WEST SAXON LAWS: Ine 25, ... *ceapie, do thaet beforan gewitnessum*, 'if a trader trade up country, he shall do so before witnesses.'

442.4   KENTISH LAW: ... *gebycge*, 'if a Kentishman buy goods in London, he shall have reliable men, or the King's reeve to witness'. The law protects the Kentishman against suit for theft; he must prove by witnesses or oath that he had bought the *feoh* with his own *ceape*, or surrender it. Both words commonly mean property in general, and cattle in particular. Ch. 15, demanding surety for the foreign *ciepeman*, implies that traders felt the need of a local patron, for whose protection they presumably paid. The probable context of ch. 16 is that the Kentishman sold cattle in London and bought foreign imports; ch. 15 and the Wessex law appear to envisage a travelling salesman of humble status and dubious honesty, nearer to the 18th-century 'chapman' than to the 'merchant'. These are the only references to traders in the 7th-century laws.

443.2 BOOK OF RIGHTS: p. 432 above.

443.2 HOARDED WEALTH: p. 236 above.

443.2 PENDA: Hostage, Bede HE 3, 24. Distribution, the *Atbret Iudeu* Nennius 65, cf. p. 302 above.

443.3 ENGLISH MONEY: fines, etc. expressed in money values in the laws, may or may not have been paid in cash; cf. M.

23 Welsh and Irish Society (pp. 445–465)

445.1 LAW: see J. The comprehensive collection of *Welsh Laws*, with translation and glossary, is the *Ancient Laws and Institutes of Wales* (AWL), ed. Aneurin Owen, 1841; vol. 1 contains the texts named Venedotian, Demetian and Gwentian Codes (VC, DC, GC); vol. 2 the 'Anomalous Laws' (AL), or 'Cyvreithiau Cymru', and various versions of the 'Laws of Hywel Da', the 'Leges Wallicae' (p. 749) (LW), 'Leges Howelli Boni' (p. 814) (HD), 'Powys Laws' (p. 881), a second 'Leges Howelli Boni', principally concerned with royal rights (p. 893), and the Statute of Rhuddlan (p. 909). A number of other MSS have been published since, usually without translation (cf. J), but the laws have not been collated; see CSW 73 ff.; WHR 1963 Special Number; T.P.Ellis *Welsh Tribal Law.*

The comparable comprehensive collection of *Irish Laws* is the *Ancient Laws of Ireland* (ALI). The material is enormous. Among later works, R. Thurneysen and others, *Studies in Early Irish Law* (SEIL) is especially useful. The interaction of Irish and of Roman and Church law is clearest in the *Hibernensis*, cf. Kenney 247, of the early 8th century.

445.1 WELL INHABITED LAND: GC 2, 39, 28.

445.1 COHABITATION: VC 2, 1, 30–31; DC 2, 18, 10 etc.

445.1 BRAKE AND BUSH: VC 2, 1, 33 etc.

445.1 COMES OF AGE: e.g. VC 2, 28, 5 ff.; 2, 30, 3; 5.

445.1 GIRLS' PROPERTY: VC 2, 30, 3; the MS variant 'he wishes' contradicts the rest of the passage, and is clearly wrong.

445.2 VIRGIN BRIDE: e.g. VC 2, 1, 27.

445.2 CHILDREN'S UPBRINGING: e.g. VC 2, 28, 5–8.

445.2 IRISH LAW: cf. the texts cited in SEIL 187 ff.

445.3 DIVORCE: the principal sections of the laws are VC 2, 1; DC 2, 18; GC 2, 29; cf. LW 2, 19; HD 2, 23.

446.3 CHARGE OF IMPOTENCE: VC 2, 1, 66 (cf. 67, variant, 'rape'), discreetly translated into Latin rather than English.

446.4 IRISH . . . DIVORCE: a number of the principal texts are surveyed in SEIL 241 ff.

446.4 HIBERNENSIS: 46, 8–10, Isidore *de Officiis* 2, 20, 12; the text describes and rejects grounds for divorce that were acceptable in Wales and Ireland.

446.4 CHURCH LAW: VC 2, 16, 2.

447.3 INHERITANCE: the principal Welsh texts are VC 2, 12; DC 2, 23; GC 2, 31; cf. AL 9, 26–27, LW 2, 11. Daughters' rights differed in north and south; cf. VC 2, 1, 64, DC 2, 23, 7 and scattered references, cf. AWL indices; the main Irish texts are summarised in SEIL 133 ff.

447.3 CENEDL: see p. 461 below.

447.3   FINE: see especially *Senchus Mor* (ALI I p. 261 etc), and MacNeill *Celtic Ireland* 159 ff.

447.4   COMPENSATION: the assumptions of Roman and English law have prompted the notion that a 'blood-feud' must be invented to explain Welsh compensation laws. No evidence supports the assumption, and no word for such a 'feud' exists in Welsh. Germanic law permitted *faida*, legalised enmity, (cf. note 485.2 below) in the exceptional cases when compensation was not paid; in the middle ages, in some Germanic and southern European lands, when customary sanctions broke down, *faida* developed into a chain of violence and counter-violence, that gave rise to the concept of 'blood-feud'. The notion is alien to early Welsh society, and belongs only to a political philosophy which maintains that 'human nature' is mutually destructive unless it is subjected to the authority of an élite.

448.4   RIGDOMNA: cf. MacNeill *Celtic Ireland* 114 ff; the evidence of the Annals and Genealogies argues that practice was more varied and less schematic than MacNeill suggests.

449.4   IRISH SOCIETY: cf. especially the 'Small Primer', p. 436.3 above, and the book of Aichill, cf. **J**.

450.4   DRESS: ALI 2, 146, 10 ff. I am indebted to Professor Binchy for drawing my attention to this passage, which prescribes colours for foster sons, presumably those to which their fathers were entitled. The later texts (e.g. LG 9, 8 (ITS 5,208), cf. Book of Leinster 2035 ff. (ITS 1, 64); FM 3664, cf. 3656; Keating 1, 25 (ITS 2, 123) ascribe their regulations to the mythical Bronze Age kings of the second millennium BC, Eochu Etgudach ('Goodclothes') and Tigernmas; see also the poem LG 96, 2 (ITS, 435).

451.2   SENCHUS FIR nALBAN: CPS 308 ff., see **Q** and p. 180 above.

453.1   PICT INHERITANCE: cf. p. 192 above.

453.2   TRAVELLERS: e.g., among many, Alexander Carmichael, reproduced in Skene CS 3, 378–393, cf. A.N.Palmer, YC 11, 1892, 176 ff., and other accounts.

453.3   CLAN: most of the evidence here discussed is assembled by W.F.Skene in *Celtic Scotland*, especially 3, 303 ff.

454.4   IN BUCHAN: grants inscribed in the Book of Deer.

454.4   MORGAN: see **G** I DRL.

455.1   CAMPBELLS: cf. the pedigree printed Skene CS 3, 458.

455.1   LENNOX: cf. the pedigree printed Skene CS 3, 475; **G** IMW; **L** Dergind. The principal adaptations are to turn the Irish Loch Lein into Leamna (Lennox), Maine Munchain into Maine Leamna, and Dergind, p. 158 above, into 'Gergind', equated with Circin or the Mearns.

455.2   SAVAGE AND RUDE: Fordun *Chron.* 2, p. 38, cited Skene CS 3, 307.

455.2   HIGHLAND CLANNA: Wyntoun *Chron.*, ed. 1879, 3, p. 63; *Scotichronicon* 2, p. 420, etc., cited Skene CS 3, 310 ff.

455.2   18th CENTURY OBSERVER: Gartmore MS (1747), cited Skene CS 3, 318.

455.3   DEGENERATE TO . . . COMMON PEOPLE: cf. Sir John Davies' description, in 1607, of the means whereby *tanists* of 'septs' in Ireland 'did spoil and impoverish the people at their pleasure', cited Seebohm EVC 220. In Ireland, as in Scotland, English administrative notions turned local dynasts into 'chiefs' of 'tribes', or 'clans' or 'septs', and rewarded their loyalty to the conqueror by according them the legal right to exploit their own people. In Ireland succession to the 'chieftaincy' normally passed to any member of the *Derb Fine*, elected by show of hands and termed *tanist*, equivalent to the *rigdomna* of the greater dynasties; but in Scotland succession normally passed from father to son.

457.2   EOIN MACNEILL: 'more than any other' Kenney 81; on the clan, *Celtic Ireland*, 1921, 155-156; cf. p. 152, on Joyce's *Social History*, 'from book to book a thousand talkers and writers have said that the social organisation of ancient Ireland in historical times was on a tribal basis, and they have called it the Clan System. Joyce . . . is unable to find a single ancient authority to support it.' Nor has anyone else discovered such evidence. MacNeill protested that the 'cocksure people' who talked of tribes and clans in 1921 constituted a 'formidable body'; they still do. The recent mushrooming of 'clan societies', the 'discovery' of 'clan chiefs', the issue of 'certificates' and the proliferation of new 'tartans' serves modern commercial and political interests; it has no connection with the early history of Scotland, except that its confusion smears the dignity of genuine tradition and record, and tends to make them suspect associates of the current farce.

457.2   SKENE: cf. note 177.1 above.

457.2   TOO LITTLE HEEDED: e.g., among many instances, T.C.Smout *A History of the Scottish People*, 1560-1830, p. 24; 'Celtic society was clearly tribal, based on a real or fancied kinship between every freeman and the head of his tribe. The tribes apparently occupied fairly distinct areas of the country . . . and possessed differing tribal laws', cf. p. 334 'in the early 10th century . . . the Highlands were tribal, in the exact sense that nineteenth century Africa was tribal.'

       Published in 1969, nearly 50 years after MacNeill wrote, and 100 years after Skene, this preamble to a history of a later period typifies the 'rubbish' that is still 'imposed' upon otherwise well-informed authors, who have not themselves had occasion to study the evidence.

458.2   SLAVE: the modern word derives from Slavs, prisoners taken by Charlemagne and his successors, who were a mobile marketable commodity, as homeborn agricultural *servi*, serfs, were not, and lacked an appropriate descriptive term.

458.3   CAETH: the laws distinguish different kinds of *caeth*, domestic, agricultural, royal; and differentiate the voluntary *caeth*, a dependent stranger who prefers to give himself to the *uchelwr* rather than to settle as a king's *aillt*, from the purchased *caeth* (e.g. AL 6, 1, 72). The voluntary *caeth* appears to have enjoyed a status not greatly different from the English *hlafaeta*, 'loaf eater', (p. 486 below). Close research into the usage of the texts is likely to reveal more subtle shifts of meaning; but in general *servus* tends to mean *caeth* in legal language, whereas colloquial usage often wrote *servus* for *taeog*. The codes include both legal texts and some texts written in colloquial language, as the 'Privileges of Arvon' (VC 2, 2 etc., cf. J) and some of the 'Legal Triads'.

458.4   GILDAS: *Ep.* 3, cf. p. 368 above.

458.4   SAMSON, HERVE, JUSTINIAN: see E.

458.4   WESSEX: Ine 74, 1, cf. p. 485.2 below.

458.5   TATHEUS, MALO, WINWALOE: see E.

459.3   PLEBES . . . TRIBUS: cf. N Tref, and p. 364 above.

459.3   SCHEMATISM: VC 2, 17, 6 ff.; cf. N Tref.

459.3   MAINAUR: Book of Teilo (Chad) folio 216, memorandum 6, printed LL xlvii *mainaur Med Diminih*, cf. BBCS 7, 1935, 369, and, for the date, Jackson LHEB 47. The word, superficially similar to *manerium*, manor, was a gift to Norman lawyers, who so translated it.

459.4   AILLT, ALLTUD: cf. J.

459.4   VALENTINIAN III: Novella 31, CTh 2, pp. 129-132. It is theoretically possible that up to the late 450s the British government was able to accept and enforce imperial constitutions if it wished, or that Valentinian renewed older laws already in force before 410, and that the Welsh law re-enacts the Roman, but it is more probable that similar causes inspired similar legislation.

460.2   TIR CYVRIV: also called *tir kyllydus*, tax or rent-paying land, cf. especially VC 2, 12, 6 etc. Both king and lord might possess *tir cyvriv*, and on behalf of its *tref* allocate the *tref* land.

460.3   CYLLID: its main constituent was *dawnbwyd*, food render.

460.3   GWESTVA: payable by free *uchelwr*, VC 2, 17, 14–15, but not due from *tir cyvriv*, AL 5, 1, 28; 14, 32, 4 etc. It began as the entertainment of the king's household while on progress; it became a tribute of food, later a tax in money; when commuted to a money payment, *gwestva* was termed *tunc*, cf. 221.2 above.

460.3   CYLCH: cf. ALW indices, 'Progress'.

460.3   PROGRESS: cf. texts cited in *Angles and Britons* 156–157.

460.3   DISPENSING JUSTICE: *vita Gwynlliw* 16 gives a lively account of a dean riding hard through a night of wind and rain to be in time for the hearing of a case at a royal feast in Gwent.

460.3   PAYMENT: exacted by e.g. Maelgwn *vita Cadoci* 69; by 'Arthur', as a compensation fine, *vita* Cadoci 22.

460.3   ANCIENT BREED: white cattle with red ears, in Britain, VC 1, 2, 2, cf. DC 1, 2, 6 and *vita Cadoci* 22 (red in front, white behind), exacted as the kings *saraad*, compensation fine; white with red ears imported into Ireland from Britain, Cormac's *Glossary* 72, *Fir*; white-headed cows in Ireland, CPS 120 encountered in Brittany by Herbot (cf. E); cf. S. Baring-Gould, *A Book of Brittany* 277 (white cows). The breed perhaps survives in modern park cattle, notably the Chillingham herd in Northumberland (*Eriu* 14, 1946, unnumbered page placed after the first of two pages numbered 169, citing several references in early Irish literature and one from 13th-century Flanders, cf. Whitehead *Cattle*, and BBCS 23, 1969, 195 on wild white cattle in the 'Caledonian Forest'). Some of these notices suggest European white cattle, possibly descended from the aurochs, but white or white-headed cattle with red ears in Wales and Ireland may derive from loose references to Herefords.

460.3   FIRE PREVENTION: VC 3, 3, 13 ff. etc.

461.1   TRE'R CEIRI: RCHM Caernarvonshire.

461.1   DINAS POWYS: cf. p. 431 above.

461.2   CANTREF: the principal texts are assembled and discussed in Lloyd HW 1,300 ff. The *cantref* were later subdivided into *cwmwd* (commotes), to which the assembly was transferred.

461.3   CENEDL; cf. ALW indices, 'Kindred', 'Chief of Kindred', 'Caput Gentis', etc. The *cenedl* is frequently named in the codes, but most of the rulings about the *Pencenedl* are in AL.

461.4   LUIDT: Book of Teilo (Chad), folios 141 (memorandum 2) *luidt* and 18 (memorandum 3) *luith*, printed with facsimile LL xliii, xlv; for the date, cf. Jackson LHEB 43–46.

462.1   TEUYTH: *vita Wenefred* 5 *Teuyth . . . interpellans ut sibi fatteret quod de suo patrimonio deliberaret. Ille (Cadfan) refert 'O vir wenerande, nequaquam mihi vel tibi sortitur. Tamen sequestrare rus a provincie communione ne sibi sit inutile vel mee necessitati. Sed harum quamcumque villarum trium elegeris ad divinum officium tibi libere annuo, si placatus fueris, mihique reliquas relinque.* The place was perhaps Whitford, near Holywell in Flint, *SD 14 78*, the only church in Tegeingl known to have been dedicated to Beuno, cf. Bowen SCSW 83, with figs. 22, 23; cf. Map 24, p. 359 above.

462.4 SURVEYS: large extracts are printed in F. Seebohm, *Tribal System in Wales*, appendices, and discussed pp. 1 ff.

464.1 LLANCARFAN: the grants appended to the Life of Cadoc, cf. **T** Gospel Books. The grants cited are 65; 62; 55; 60; 68. In another, 59, a nobleman 'commended' an estate to his son, with a rent charge to the church.

464.1 LLANDAFF: **T** Gospel Books. Llandaff gives much detail of prices, rentals, extents, that concern its claims. In the one grant that the two have in common (LL 180 = *vita Cadoc* 67) Llandaff reproduces the reasons for the grant more fully, but leaves out many of the details of who made what gift to whom.

464.5 BOOK OF ARMAGH: folios 16 r to 18 v, also printed AB 2, 1883, 213 ff., and VT 334 ff., commonly known as the *Additamenta to Tirechan* 1–16. Sections 8 to 16 are in Irish. The scribe, Ferdomnach, writing in 807, apologised for not translating into Latin passages that he found 'badly written in Irish; not because I am unable to write Latin, but because these accounts are barely intelligible in their original Irish', *finiunt haec pauca per scotticam imperfecte scripta; non quod ego non potuissem romana condere lingua, sed quod vix in sua scoti[c]a hae fabulae agnosci possunt*. Irish that was scarcely intelligible by c. 800 is unlikely to have been much less than a century old; the two datable grants (Cummen, 11; Aed of Sletty, 16) are both late 7th century, and the text transcribed by Ferdomnach was therefore nearly contemporary with the original grants.

464.5 CUMMEN: *add. Tirechan* 11 (VT 340). The genealogies place the chief, Eladach, about 680, (**G** IACF 650 Mael Odur); Colman (of Lindisfarne? **E**) was established at Inis Boffin from 665 to 675.

465.2 FETH: *Add. Tirecham* (VT 338); Drumlease **G** *83* in Callraige, Hogan 366, 152.

465.3 FOIRTCHERN: Add. *Tirechan* 4 (VT 336).

465.3 BINEAN: Add. *Tirechan*, 7. (VT 337); the scribe wrote *d[eu]s* for *dedit*; a later hand added *cui dedit* without erasing *d[eu]s*.

24 English Society (pp. 466–505)

467.2 LAWS: conveniently collected by Attenborough LEEK, based on ALE and the *Gesetze* of Schmid and Liebermann; extensively discussed by Seebohm TCASL, cf. EVC, TSW, and others: see **J**.

467.2 CHARTERS: the principal collections are BCS and KCD. The charters are comprehensively catalogued by Sawyer, and many are summarised by Finberg ECMW etc., and by Hart; see **C**, and p. 328 above.

467.2 CHARTERS ... ALTERATIONS: among the commonest changes are the conflation of the witnesses to the original grant and to subsequent confirmations, that creates a superficial appearance of chronological contradiction and ensnares the incautious critic; and the alteration of rights and properties to suit the interest of the copier, with the insertion of words, and of the names of people and titles, places and regions, that belong to the copier's time, but were unknown at the time of the grant. The use of, for example, *Anglia* dates a copy to the 11th century or later, but frequently derives from an original that used a cumbrous old-fashioned term, as 'all the provinces of the English'.

467.2 FORGED ... GENUINE: the provisional system devised by Finberg, of marking texts by stars, whose number indicates the degree of alteration, is a considerable advance upon the crude categories employed in earlier inexact modern conventions of classification; but is no substitute for precise analysis of what is added to each text.

467.3 GRAVES ... SOCIAL DIFFERENCE: cf. p. 281 above.

468.2 PLACE NAMES: EPNS, DEPN, EPNE; notes to maps 30 to 36; see **N**.

468.3   ELEMENTS: EPNE (cf. additions and corrections in JEPN I), from which the meanings here given are cited.

468.3   STUDY OF . . . -ING: J.M.Dodgson MA 10, 1966, 1 ff., and *Beitrage zur Namenforschung* (Heidelberg), NF, 2, 1967, 221 ff. and 325 ff.; 3, 1968, 141 ff., on whose work maps 30 and parts of maps 33 and 34 are based. Other maps are adapted from EPNS volumes, and from unpublished material kindly made available.

470.2   ARTOIS: see p. 287 above.

470.4   TUN: EPNE 2, 188 ff. The word already meant a village in the 7th century, *Hlothere* 5. The suggestion in EPNE 2, 190 (5) that many or most began as 'single farms' and later grew into villages is unlikely and unwarranted, and contradicts the archaeological evidence. Later usage, translating *tun* as Latin *villa*, *ham* as *civitas*, contrasts an estate with a community, and does not concern size. See N. Relatively few -*tun* names are likely to be earlier than the 7th century.

470.4   TUN . . . SECONDARY COLONISATION: EPNE 2, 191 (9).

472.2   -BOTL: especially EPNE 1, 43–44. Its distribution in Europe is limited and localised; A.Bach, *Deutsche Namenkunde*, II 2 map 44, p. 333, para 610 ff., where the Carolingian date suggested is not probable; see Map 17, p. 277.

472.2   -WORTH, -COTE: EPNE 2, 273 ff., especially 274 (3); 1, 108 ff.

472.2   -INGTUN: EPNE 1, 291 ff., especially 295 (5); *Teottingtun* (Teddington) distinguishes 'Teotta's village' from *Teottingatun*, the 'village of Teotta's people'. It is often impossible to tell the forms apart; but when they can be distinguished, -*ingatun* rarely forms as much as one-fifth of the total, and it is therefore probable that -*ingtun* is normally the form of the great majority; but both forms imply lordship, and also secondary colonisation.

      It is however not easy to discover names in any form of -*ingtun* attested before the middle of the 8th century. Their rarity is partly explained by the nature of the record; most such places were too small to figure in the works of Bede, Eddius, or other early writers; and charters commonly grant either royal land or small portions of estates, rather than centres of individual lordship. In some instances however, the name of a settlement is recorded substantially earlier than its -*tun*. *Tun*, though it was the general word for a village in the 7th century, is itself rare in place names of the late 7th and early 8th centuries. Closer study may therefore suggest that 7th century settlements founded by an individual lord with his dependents were at first known by his name, followed by -*inga lond* or the like, but did not acquire their administrative centre and suffix -*tun* until some generations later. Records of -*cote* also begin late.

474.3   KENT: the custom of Kent is lucidly described by Joliffe PFE, emphasising (p. 3) that 'the manors of Kent are more like those of Wales than of Oxford and Berkshire'. The suggestion that Frankish influence on Kentish ornament indicates that the Jutes of Kent and their customs came from the Rhineland (Leeds AASS 126 ff., developed by Joliffe 102 ff.) was made when dates were less understood; Frankish ornament was favoured by the grand-daughters of the first settlers, many of whom came from Jutland (Myres ASP 96, map 7; p. 289 above; see S). Third generation ornament has nothing to do with the nationality of the first comers; the nationality of the first settlers is not determined by the fashions that their granddaughters favoured.

474.3   NINE LATHES: excluding Sutton, outside the early borders of Kent.

474.3   WELKECHILDELAND: BBA I, 229, cited Joliffe PFE 27, note 3.

474.3   NINE RAPES: including Ytene, Meonwara and Wight, now in Hampshire.

476.1   WORTHS ... PENNINES: Heworth, a suburb of York, stands alone in the North Riding; Ravensworth near Richmond is a variant of Ravensford.

476.1   BOTL STRONGHOLDS: Newbottle, etc., by definition secondary, are omitted from Map 35.

476.1   WIDE RANGE OF NAMES: the few that have been examined closely show their potential value; for example, -*wicham* and -*wictun*, derived from Latin *vicus*, are almost entirely confined to the areas of 6th century burials, and are most plentiful where 5th and early 6th century cemeteries are commonest, cf. MA 11, 1967, 87, map. p. 88.

480.1   INTENDS TO DEPART: Ine 64–66.

480.1   CULTIVATED: *gesette* means cultivated and tilled, usually by dependent cultivators, as Seebohm EVC 128, 136 ff., Vinogradoff GM 128, Aston TRHS series 5, 8, 1958, 65; rather than 'sown', as Maitland DBB 238 note 1, Liebermann *Gesetze* (on Ine 64) and others.

480.1   NOBLEMAN: Ine 63.

480.1   UNAUTHORISED EMIGRATION: Ine 39.

480.2   CEORL'S WORTH: Ine 40, 42. Detached words from Ine 42 have been used to suggest the strip cultivation of a later age; in context, they cannot relate thereto, see **Q** and **T**.

482.1   HEBERDEN: BCS 144.

482.1   THURINGIA: *Translatio S. Alexandri* 1.

483.3   SCOTS: cf. p. 451 above.

483.3   WELSH LAW: cf. p. 448 above.

483.3   HIDE: cf. p. 487.2 below.

483.3   ONE TAXPAYER ... ONE HIDE: cf. e.g. the equation in BCS 144, cf. note 487.2 (HIDE) and p. 499 below.

484.1   ALFRED'S LAWS: 42, 7.

484.3   MANY LAWS: e.g. Alfred 37; Edward 11, 7; Aethelstan 11 2; 8; 22, 1; III 4; IV 3; V Preface 1 and 2; 1.

485.2   WEST SAXON ... WELSHMEN: Ine 74, 1. The law contrasts with *Lex Saxonum* 2, 5, which exposes the *litus* to *faida* without alternative.

485.2   RELATIVES ... RARELY: e.g. if a killer escaped abroad, the relatives paid half the *leod* (*wergild*), Aethelbert 23; in Wessex, if no paternal kinsmen were discoverable, the maternal relatives paid one third, Alfred 30.

485.2   FAEHDE: the word is the linguistic ancestor of modern 'feud', cf. note 447.4 above, but does not share its meaning of a chain of violence, see Du Cange, *Faida*. Among the Lombards, whose laws are nearest to the English, *faida* is glossed *vindicta mortis*, the simple avenging of death; Ine's *unfaedhe* (e.g. 28, 35, 74) concerns justifiable homicide, and Alfred's equivalent (e.g. 30, 42) is *orwige*.

485.2   RANSOM: it extended beyond physical violence; relatives might ransom a penal slave, Ine 24, 1.

485.3   LORD: see LEEK index.

485.3   NOBLEMAN'S LORD: Ine 50.

485.3   GYLD: see LEEK index, 'Associates', first named in Ine 74, 2. In Alfred 30–31 *gegildan* and relatives pay one third each; the *heafodgemacene* and perhaps the *gedes* of Wihtred 19; 21; 23 may be a Kentish equivalent. Under West Saxon supremacy, from the 9th century, West Saxon legal terminology tended to oust Kentish and other regional terms.

485.3   TOWNS: the urban *frythegyld*, public order guild, of noble and commoner (*eorlisce ge ceorlisce*), Aethelstan VI (*Iudicia Civitatis Lundoniae*, Preamble 1, 1; 6, 3), preceded separate trade guilds.

485.4   GERMANIC CODES: see J.

486.2   SAXON LAW: *Lex Saxonum* 44 *qui defunctus non filios sed filias reliquerat, ad eas omnis hereditas pertineat.*

486.2   ANGLIAN LAW: *Lex Anglorum et Werinorum* 27 *ad filiam pecunia et mancipia, terra vero ad proximum paternae generationis;* cf. Bede HA II *quomodo terreni parentes, quem primum partu fuderint, eum principium liberorum suorum cognoscere, et caeteris in partienda sua hereditate praeferendum ducere solent,* with reference to Northumbrian Angles.

486.2   WEST SAXON ... MOTHER'S KIN: e.g. Alfred 8; 30.

486.3   FRIGMAN: Aethelbert 4, and regularly thereafter.

486.3   LAET: see p. 313.

486.3   LOAF-EATER: *ceorlaes hlafaeta,* valued at only 6s, Aethelbert 25.

486.4   WERGILD: the essential information, contained in the laws of Ine of Wessex and Aethelbert of Kent, both 7th century, is

WELSH OF WESSEX (Ine)		LAET OF KENT (Aethelbert)
theow	50s or 60s (*23, 3*)	
landless man	60s (*32*)	40s third class (*26*)
half-hide man	80s (*32*)	60s second class (*26*)
tax-payer's son	100s (*23, 3*)	—
tax-payer (*gafolgelda*)	120s (*23, 3*) ⎫	
one-hide man	120s (*32*) ⎬	80s first class (*26*)
horswealh	200s (*14*)	—
five-hide man	600s (*24, 2*)	—

ENGLISH OF WESSEX (Ine)

ordinary *weigild*		*fierdwite* fine (51)		compensation for burgbryc (45)	
a man (normal)	200s (*34, 1*) ⎫	*cierlisc*	30s	—	
aet twyhundum	200s (*70*) ⎬				
aet syxhundum	600s (*70*)	*gesithcundmon unlandagende*	60s	—	
aet twelfhundum	1200s (*70*) ⎫	*gesithcundmon*		*gesithcundmon*	
Cinges geneat	1200s (*19*) ⎬	*landagende*	120s	*landhaebbende*	30s*
(King's companion)					
—		—		king's thane	60s
—		—		ealdormon	80s
—		—		King and Bishop	120s

* 35s, MS.

ENGLISH OF KENT

Medume leodgeld (ordinary wergild)	100s (Aethelbert 21; Hlothere 3)
eorlcundman	300s (Hlothere 1)

Kentish law does not mention a distinct class of landed noble or royal companion. By the 9th century, the *ceorl*'s violated boundary fence (*edorbryce*) was compensated with 5s; the *syxhyndmon* had a *burg*, whose breach was met by 15s; the *twelfhyndmon*'s compensation was still 30s, but the bishop's and the *ealdormon*'s had fallen to 60s, the archbishop's to 90s; the king still received 120s, (Alfred 40). The basic distinction of *ceorl* and *eorl* lasted well into the middle ages, cf. *Consuetudo West Sexe* 70, 1 *twyhindi, id est villani . . . twelfhindi, id est taini* Liebermann *Gesetze* 1, 462 cf. 458.

Fragments of Mercian and Northumbrian law, preserved in the *Gesetze*, show similar classes and values.

This evidence is discussed at length by Liebermann *Gesetze*, Seebohm TCASL, Maitland DBB, Chadwick OEN and SASI, and others.

487.2   HIDE: Bede regularly wrote 'the land of so many families' (e.g. *terra LXXXVII familiarum*, HE 4, 13), or 'possessions of families', or 'of land', or 'of property' (e.g. *possesiones X familiarum, XII possessiones praediorum, XII possessiunculis terrarum*, all in HE 3, 24), described as 'by English measure' (e.g. *mensura iuxta aestimationem Anglorum* HE 2, 9; *quasi familiarum V, iuxta aestimationem Anglorum* HE 3, 4). Bede gives overall figures of 5 families for Iona HE 3, 4; 960 for Anglesey and 300 for Man HE 2, 9; 7,000 for Sussex HE 4, 13; 1,200 for Wight HE 4, 16; 600 for Thanet HE 1, 25; and 5,000 and 7,000 for South and North Mercia HE 3, 24; as well as for numerous individual estates. The figures for Sussex and Mercia agree with those of the 'Tribal Hidage' (p. 493 below), and that for Thanet is proportionate to the total for Kent (15,000); but the assessment of Wight, 600 in the Tribal Hidage, was doubled, evidently after Ceadwalla's conquest, in or about 686. The hide and the individual family remained normally identical into the mid 8th century, since oaths in Ine's law were normally reckoned as of 30, 60 or 120 hides (e.g. 52-54; cf 14; 19; 46), but in Northumbria as of 30, 60 or 120 cultivators (*tributarii* and *manentes*) Dialogue of Egbert (Archbishop of York, c. 750) 1, Oaths are discussed by Chadwick SASI 134 ff.

487.2   TRIBUTARII . . . HIDES: in 725 the Heberden Charter of Nunna of Sussex (p. 499) granted twenty *tributarii* in the Latin text, but twenty hides in the English endorsement, which is probably contemporary.

487.3   UNCIA . . . IUGUM: cf. pp. 459 and 5 above.

487.3   RUSTIC DEIRANS: the nobleman Imma pretended to be a *rusticus* of the supply train, but his Mercian captors observed *ex vultu et habitu et sermonibus eius non erat de paupere vulgo sed de nobilibus* and sold him to a Frisian slaver of London, who allowed him parole to find his ransom, Bede HE 4, 22.

489.1   BENEDICT BISCOP: Bede HA 1.

489.2   BEDE . . . EGBERT: *Epistula ad Egbertum* 10 ff.

491.2   ATTAIN . . . RANK: the texts are discussed by Chadwick SASI 80 ff.

491.4   FOLC GEMOT: Alfred 22; 34; 38, 1. BCS 201.

491.4   REEVE: steward or bailiff, equivalent to the classical Latin *procurator*; the king's reeves, like the emperor's *procuratores*, were officers of importance; the later shire-reeve, or sheriff, was translated *vice-comes*, 'deputy earl', in medieval Latin, whence the modern title 'viscount'.

491.4   EALDORMAN: elder, or senior. The title was restricted to royal princes and great nobles; the *ealdorman* of a region was commonly its greatest magnate, sometimes equivalent to an underking.

492.1   HARROW: BCS 201, *ab omnium fiscalium redituum operum onerumque seu etiam*
492.1   *popularium conciliorum vindictis.*
492.1   INE . . . HUNDRED: Ine 54, *on thaere Hyndenne.*

BARROWS: e.g. Loveden, Lincolnshire; Broadwater, Redbourn (Standard Hill) Hertfordshire; Effingham (Standard Hill), Surrey; and many others, see **S.**

492.1   THORSBERG: cf. e.g. the description in *Ant.* 26, 1952, 14.

492.2   LONDONERS: Aethelstan VI 3.

492.3   TRIBAL HIDAGE: BCS 297; Rolls 2 ii 296; see JBAA 40, 1884, 30 and n.s. 35, 1929, 273; EHR 4, 1889, 335; 27, 1912, 625; 40, 1925, 497; NQ 10th series 9, 1908, 384 and 192, 1947, 398 and 423; *Traditio* 5, 1947, 192; TRHS n.s. 14, 1900, 189, etc. See **T**.

493.1   SURREY: see p. 322 above. Surrey and East Kent formed a distinct territory in the 5th and 6th centuries, until annexed by Aethelbert, in or soon after 584, when the East Saxons acquired London and its territory north of the Thames, the future Middlesex, under Aethelbert's suzerainty. On his death, during Redwald's brief supremacy in the 620s, king Taeppa (see p. 323 above), known only from his tomb, appears to have ruled a substantial kingdom north of the Thames, which may have wrested London from the East Saxons for a few years. The name Surrey, southern region, doubtless balanced by a northern region across the Thames, may have been then brought into use. Thereafter the London region was for a while disputed between the West and East Saxons and Kent.

   The enduring boundaries were drawn after Wulfhere's conquest, when Surrey was established as a distinct kingdom, whose ruler the copyist of a charter described as *Fritheuualdus provinciae Surrianorum subregulus Wlfarii Mercianorum regis* (BCS 34). Its northern boundary was sealed by the grant of almost all the Thames bank from Chertsey to Bermondsey to monasteries, and the London region on the opposite bank then or soon after became the *provincia* of Middlesex, though no *subregulus* is there attested. The Tribal Hidage lists the separate names of the small peoples who were organised into these two *provinciae*, in spellings that later copyists grossly corrupted, which have not yet been examined by philologists; but it did not know the names or existence of the future Surrey and Middlesex, and it is therefore probable that the original text was drawn up before Wulfhere's reorganisation created them.

493.2   DOMESDAY ... PERSONS: adult males are numbered. Since some men were unwed brothers, the number of families was necessarily a little smaller, perhaps nearer to 200,000.

493.3   HUNDREDS ... MET MONTHLY: cf., e.g. Edgar I 1; Edward II 8.

494.2   SHIRES: the word means a 'sheared' portion of a whole, and is rendered in Latin by *comitatus*, in English 'county', the territory of a *comes*, used to translate English 'earl'. The shires and counties had differing origins. The earliest were the five, or six, constituent kingdoms of Wessex (pp. 324–325 above), some of which were termed shires while still ruled by kings. Outside Wessex, the imperial arrogance of Offa abolished the monarchies of the old kingdoms of the south-east, to the distress of Alcuin (p. 331 above), and restricted their rulers to the humbler style of *dux* or *comes*. In the 9th century, Egbert and his sons for a while themselves exercised the title of king of East Anglia or Kent, but the title 'king' lapsed in the course of the Scandinavian wars. East Anglia reverted to its two original 5th and 6th century constituents, the North and South Folk. The old south-eastern kingdoms retained their identity as counties, and as such were included under the generalised heading of 'shires', but, since they were not 'sheared' portions of a whole the suffix 'shire' was not and is not appended to the former kingdoms or *provinciae* of Sussex, Kent or Surrey, Middlesex or Essex, Norfolk or Suffolk.

   In the east midlands, the tenth century Danes organised the Hundreds, in their language *wapentakes*, military districts, into army areas grouped round fortresses or boroughs. The West Saxon kings of the English applied their own word shire to these regions, and extended it to the west midlands, English Mercia. North of the Trent, the former Mercian territory south of the

Ribble remained part of Cheshire until the 12th century, while the Pennines, north of Danish Derbyshire, and all the English northwest, were grouped with the Danish kingdom of York in the huge county of Yorkshire. The old name of Northumbria or Northumberland was restricted to the former Bernicia, and the military border bishopric of Durham became a separate county. Cumberland retained its old name, 'the Welsh land', on its annexation by the English in 1092; Lancashire and Westmorland are creations of the 12th century.

The king's officer, or reeve, in each shire or county was termed shire-reeve, or sheriff, in principle not hereditary. The English term *eorl*, 'earl', originally the general word for nobleman, was influenced by its Scandinavian equivalent *jarl*, used for the head of an army or army district, a midland shire, and was commonly used of hereditary rulers. In the 11th century it was chiefly used of the rulers of former kingdoms, Mercia or Wessex, but from the 12th century onward earls, in Latin *comites*, were increasingly appointed to individual counties, and in time *dux*, duke, came into use as the title of a superior earl, at first for royal princes.

496.3   OSRIC: see **G** EMH.

497.1   BATH: BCS 43, dated 6 November 676.

497.1   GLOUCESTER: BCS 60; Finberg ECWM 158. *Oba* (huba), meaning *numerus mancipiorum, praedium*; and *sule* (sola), a measure, see Du Cange.

497.1   VICARIUM: Cartulary of Landevennec para. 45, cf. 46, 17 etc. The word renders the ecclesiastical and colloquial *plebs, plou-* etc.

498.3   ALDHELM: see pp. 415 and 496 above and **E**.

498.3   PAGHAM: BCS 50, see John *Land Tenure* 8 and Finberg *Lucerna* 149.

499.1   NUNNA: BCS 144, see p. 482 above. *This is seo Landboc the Nunna cyng gebocade Eadberhte b' into Hugabeorgum xx hida.*

499.1   AETHELRED'S GRANT REVOKED: Evesham Chronicle, cited Finberg ECWM 170.

499.1   TOKI: KCD 805

499.2   CHURCH RIGHT: wording varies, e.g. *ecclesiastica ratio atque regula; monastica ratio* BCS 157; *ecclesiastica* (sic) *ius* BCS 182; *ius episcopalis sedis* BCS 76, etc.

499.2   GRAVER SCANDAL: Bede *Ep. ad Egbertum* 12.

499.2   WITHINGTON: BCS 156.

500.3   KIN RESTRICTION REMOVED: e.g. BCS 77.

500.3   BOOKED TO HIMSELF: BCS 451 *Aethelwulf . . . ruris partem . . . mihi in hereditatem propriam describere iusi; id est me ad habendum . . . et iterum qualicumque prout me placabilis sit aeternaliter relinquendum* 26 December 847.

500.3   INE: BCS 142.

500.3   BEORTRIC: BCS 258.

500.3   KENTISH KING: BCS 496

500.4   ALDHELM: e.g. BCS 108, cf. 109 etc., *Ego Ini . . . rex, cum consilio et decreto . . . Aldhelmi . . . privilegii dignitatem monasteriis confero, ut . . . absque tributum fiscalium negotiorum . . . Deo soli serviant*, without reservation of the public services.

501.1   PUBLIC SERVICES: see p. 492 above.

501.1   LOANLAND: e.g. Alfred *Soliloquies of Augustine*, preface; a man normally cultivates land loaned by his lord until he is granted 'bookland and perpetual possession'.

501.1   ENTAIL: Alfred 41.

501.2   EALDORMAN: Aelfred dux, BCS 558.

501.2   ILLEGITIMATE: so Maitland DBB 246, Stenton ASE 307. The objections of Chadwick SASI 171, note 1, are rightly rejected by John *Land Tenure* 16, note 2.

501.2   FOLK LAND: and Bookland. The problems are discussed, from the point of view of the later middle ages, by Maitland DBB 244 ff.; Pollock and Maitland, *History of English Law* 1, 37 ff.; Vinogradoff EHR 8, 1, ff.; GM 142 ff., 244 ff.; John *Land Tenure* 1 ff.; and others.

501.2   REEVE: Edward I, Preface.

501.2   LONDON: *Libertas Londoniensis* 6.

INDEX

Italic figures refer to the notes.
An asterisk (*) indicates a note on the name or word concerned.
The letters f (*filius*) and m (*mac* or *map*) mean 'son of'; f. means 'following'.
Modern conventions on the spelling of names vary, and are often arbitrary; thus, Aethelbert or Ethelbert are nowadays equally familiar, Athelbert unfamiliar, but Athelstan prevails over Ethelstan or Aethelstan. The most recognisable form is normally used. Irish names are normally given in plain English spelling.